Children's Rights and Power

Children in Charge series
Editor: Mary John

This series concentrates on the theme of children's rights, reflecting the increasing knowledge in the area. The perspectives of empowerment and of 'voice' run through the series, and the United Nations' Convention on the Rights of the Child is used as a benchmark. The editor, Mary John, is a developmental psychologist, an emeritus professor at the University of Exeter, and honorary adviser to the Childhood and Youth Policy Unit at the University of West Sydney. She has worked in the field of disability rehabilitation and independent living and has researched with minority rights groups.

Children's Rights in Education
Edited by Stuart Hart, Cynthia Price Cohen, Martha Farrell Erickson and Målfrid Flekkøy
ISBN 1 85302 977 7
Children in Charge 11

Young Children's Rights
Exploring Beliefs, Principles and Practice
Priscilla Alderson
ISBN 1 85302 880 0
Children in Charge 10

Traveller Children
A Voice for Themselves
Cathy Kiddle
ISBN 1 85302 684 0
Children in Charge 8

Educational Citizenship and Independent Learning
Rhys Griffith
ISBN 1 85302 611 5
Children in Charge 6

Children as Citizens
Education for Participation
Edited by Cathie Holden and Nick Clough
ISBN 1 85302 566 6
Children in Charge 5

A Charge Against Society
The Child's Right to Protection
Edited by Mary John
ISBN 1 85302 411 2
Children in Charge 3

CHILDREN IN CHARGE 9

Children's Rights and Power
Charging Up for a New Century

Mary John

Jessica Kingsley Publishers
London and New York

First published in the United Kingdom in 2003
by Jessica Kingsley Publishers Ltd
116 Pentonville Road
London N1 9JB, England
and
29 West 35th Street, 10th fl.
New York, NY 10001-2299,USA

www.jkp.com

Library of Congress Cataloging in Publication Data
A CIP catalog record for this book is available from the Library of Congress

British Library Cataloguing in Publication Data
A CIP catalogue record for this book is available from the British Library

ISBN 1 85302 659 X paperback
ISBN 1 85302 658 1 hardback

Printed and Bound in Great Britain by
Athenaeum Press, Gateshead, Tyne and Wear

For Cerys
Warmly welcome little torch bearer
for the next generation of the family

Contents

Acknowledgements

I am grateful to the University of Exeter Research Fund for supporting the data collection for this book and to the University of Veracruz, Mexico and the University of Western Sydney, MacArthur, Australia, for research support. I thank Goran Therborn and Sage Publications for permission to reproduce the table in Chapter 5.

Children have clearly been a major influence on my perspective. To my sons, Dan and Adam, and children I have been close to – Ivan, Pippa, Nicky, Emma, Trudie, Oliver, Frances, Doug, Caroline, Eva, Diane and Neil – my grateful thanks for their patience with this slow learner. Students always provide a rich diet for the nourishment of academics. Gourmet morsels were shared with me by Barbara Antolik, David Panter, Patricia Rock, Rhys Griffith, Angela Horton, Brian Cooney, Michael Grey, Margaret Rolph, Rhonda Lovell and Pat Hill and countless others who suffered my questioning and shared their enlightenment with me.

Colleagues, in the rare moments we have been able to wrest for ourselves, have shared beguiling ideas about children, the world, about change, about power and empowerment. In particular I thank Adrienne Levin, Vic Finkelstein, Peggotty and Andrew Graham, Martin Hughes, Mike Golby, Edith Jayne, Gael Parfitt, Susan Churchill, Nick Givens, Wendy Titman, Sarah McCrum, David and Lynette Gribble, Scott Forbes, Marianne Hester, Gillian Hanscombe and Ian Gordon. Lesley Kerman, Graham Rich and Steve Hughes have thrown shafts of light in dark corners with the brilliance of their own thinking, for which I am grateful. Braveheart, as ever, the accomplished 'helmsman', navigated me through the voyage with feats of technical and imaginative daring. To him and his craft, and for a whole season of racing single-handed while his crew met a deadline rather than the finishing line, my heartfelt thanks.

The mental journey has been taken with these friends and mentors as my light luggage of essentials. A very real journey was undertaken in collecting further materials for the book. The international support network is too huge to identify in detail but I would like to thank a few crucial people by name. In the Barefoot College in Rajasthan, Srinivasan shared a lifetime of educational experience with me, and in Japan, Frances Hirayama opened my eyes to education in a rapidly changing culture. Mary Leue saw to it that I really learnt about democratic education in the United States and that I learnt the only way to learn – by being there at the Free School in Albany: to all the community there my thanks. George and Glenys Gunkel helped me further assimilate the North American experience before moving on to Mexico where Aracelli Brizzio de la Hoz and the 'tribo de la Hoz' made further explorations of the issue of child labour possible and illuminating if deeply depressing. In Australia all my documentation, preliminary manuscript and photographs were stolen but I was amply resourced in my stay there and since by Jan Mason, Judy Cashmore and Duane Spanswick. As you will see in the model I propose in this book, how we react to risk and challenge is an important part of how we ourselves become powerful – so maybe I should also acknowledge the importance to me of a latter-day light-fingered resident of Botany Bay!

I am grateful to Reshma Agrawal who has performed the impossible with good humour, diligence and great professionalism in micro-editing my manuscript and to Angela Garry and Will Preston for technical support. To Jessica Kingsley personally I owe much. Helen Parry and Amy Lankester-Owen at JKP have been most supportive. To them and a publishing house which now amply demonstrates qualities of endurance and indomitability by over fifteen years as an independent publisher – my sincere gratitude.

Preface

This book has been in the process of being written, or rather lived, for over half a century. It started in the head of a child abandoned, bewildered, wounded, drugged, hallucinating and desperately solitary in a hospital bed. This child faced the same problems that have beset children in many places, at many times – problems of recognition of her needs, of establishing identity, agency, of managing relationships wisely and richly, of exercising power and of finding a voice that is heard, of being someone who counts, who has a future as a citizen and a participant in the world of which she was born a part. These are the challenges which, often against apparently impossible odds, are experienced in their most acute form in childhood but remain lifelong struggles.

This child was taught that a feature of good literary style is to expunge the 'I'. In doing so, she realises that much of what it is important about agency, power and autonomy is precisely that it is uniquely personal. Moreover, feminist research and activities have underlined how important autobiography is in capturing, archiving and legitimating experience. Hence she must, having lived to tell the tale, write in her own voice as an 'I'.

Like many, I have been seeking to voice my concerns for well over half a century – the self-same search which has, I believe, united this one-time child with the world's children and energised my work. All children have rights, but first have to have some sense of personal powers to exercise those rights, yet almost everywhere they are rendered powerless. Their efforts are constantly routed into searches for love, for happiness, for recognition. The struggle has occasionally found a voice, and at times been so overwhelmed with non-recognition that it has been silenced.

In 1992, shortly after the ratification of the United Nations (UN) Convention on the Rights of the Child in the UK, I hosted in Exeter a 'World Conference on Children's Rights: a Question of Empowerment', to look at the state of international progress in research and practice in

11

this very newly emerging area so that we could profit from it and build upon it. This conference was largely planned in conjunction with a team of young people who also acted as the evaluators for the conference. It also gave birth to the Children in Charge Series with Jessica Kingsley Publishers, the first three volumes of which present very largely the proceedings of that groundbreaking conference (John 1996a, 1996b, 1997b). A lot has happened since then and now this field is burgeoning, so it seemed that, ten years on, this was an appropriate time to take stock again. The field has been largely neglected by psychologists, for reasons I suggest in the book, but colonised by lawyers and sociologists.

The United Nations had also decided that it was time to review what progress had been made over the last ten years. For three days in September 2001, therefore, it had been planning that the eyes of the world would be on children, focusing on what it is really like growing up in the twenty-first century. It had been hoped that the United Nations General Assembly Special Session on Children between 19 and 21 September would be one of the highest profile summits ever to address children's issues. During the summit, world leaders were to look at what has been achieved for children over the last ten years and set out plans for their future wellbeing and development. After all, 40 per cent of the world's population are now children, the highest proportion it has ever been. What did these leaders actually look at when the time came?

They looked at the devastation terrorists had wreaked on a small proportion of the world's population. Traumatic and tragic though that suffering was, attention was diverted to a war on terrorism and resources allocated to this great task. Children were again put to one side to be considered some time in 2002. The priorities were clear. This deflection of attention and the rerouting of resources probably delay yet again the urgent need to focus on the state of the world's children. It may even exacerbate their state. Did the Summit in May 2002 give children the place they deserve in the world's priorities?

Against this tragic backdrop we have to remind ourselves that tomorrow is not necessarily available for children. In working with children, as I shall argue, it is the present we must respond to and honour.

...the understanding which we want is an understanding of the insistent present. The only use of knowledge of the past is to equip us for the present. No more deadly harm can be done to young minds than by depreciation of the present. The present contains all there is. It is holy ground; for it is the past, and the future. (Whitehead 1932, pp.3–4)

This book, while started over half a century ago, is not about the past but about the insistent present.

PART I

Powerful People

CHAPTER ONE

'As If'

Multiple Representations
of the Person

Changing economic realities coupled with children's access
to information about the adult world have drastically changed
childhood. The traditional childhood genie is out of the bottle and is unable to return. (Steinberg and Kincheloe 1997,
p.3)

INTRODUCTION

So wrote Steinberg and Kincheloe in addressing what they regarded as a
contemporary crisis in their thoroughgoing analysis of the corporate
construction of childhood. Is there indeed a contemporary crisis *in
childhood* or can one argue that the acknowledgement of children as
powerful individuals has precipitated a crisis in power relations in the
contemporary world? Access to information is indeed important. An
epigram attributed to Francis Bacon declares 'knowledge is power'. Is
information enough to change the world of children? What parts do
economic and political changes play? Steinberg and Kincheloe write *as
if* the childhood genie was in fact at one time *in* the bottle. Was the child
and childhood ever this bottled up or did we simply act as if that were
the case? For many years Philip Aries, the French historian, had
convinced us in his *Centuries of Childhood* (1979) that in the medieval
mind, at least, infants simply did not count. He argued that until the
sixteenth century children were regarded as small and inadequate adults
and had no separate culture of their own. In medieval society the idea of
childhood, he claimed, simply did not exist. Conversely, Nicholas Orme
(2001) has assembled much visual and written evidence, most of it
admittedly from English sources, to demonstrate that the Middle Ages
could be more enlightened in its treatment of children than we have

been led to believe. Orme's book illustrates over and over again that in medieval England there was attentiveness to children, to their separate status and stubborn individuality, their names and birth dates, their rights and needs. Ideas of the clean break, with history marking a time when children and childhood did not exist, are challenged and what is emphasised is continuity.

Old myths and illusions die hard, including precious notions of what children are really like. In a powerful opening to Blake Morrison's non-fiction book *As If* (1997), which is primarily about the murder in 1993 of a two-year-old child in the United Kingdom by two ten-year-old boys, Morrison refers to the Children's Crusade in the thirteenth century. He describes this legend of the Crusade, then goes on to doubt the innocence, charm and courage of that whole adventure – '"as if" children would ever have behaved like that'. He turns to documents that provide the revisionist version, which turns out to be an epic of suffering, massacre, death, misery and disillusion involving not innocents but big 'children' with evil propensities. This is the version, he argues, that is easier to believe at this point in our collective history. He goes on:

> The Crusade, in this version, has lost its magic – is short on hope and conviction. Disenchantment: something that happened to me at a certain age, in my teens; is something that happened to the Age, too. The state seems widespread now, in the 1990s. You don't have to grow up to feel cynical. You don't even have to be a teenager. *As if,* my children say, as I used to say at their age, but the phrase doesn't mean what it did. We'll be sitting around the television together, *The Nine O'clock News* on with its cries of pain from other countries (Bosnia, Somalia, Rwanda), and every two minutes or so my son (who's twelve) will be there with his four letters, his two blunt words, coming down like a brick against anything that is wishful or implausible. Hopes are high that a peace agreement can be reached next week. *As if.* American scientists believe a new drug may provide a significant breakthrough in the treatment of cancer. *As if.* The England manager today named the squad which he is confident will bring home the next World Cup. *As if.* The trope used to be enlarging, wondrous, a means of seeing beyond our noses, the prison house of fact. *As if.* It was the sound the swing made as it scythed us upward through the air, the whisper of dreams and lovely

promises. Much virtue in *as if*. Now, in kids' mouths, it means the opposite. Earthbound scepticism and diminution: tell me about it, dream on, get real. Not hope but extinction of hope. *As if*, not a candle to light me to bed, but a chopper to chop off our heads.[1] (Morrison 1997, p.13)[2]

Hence now 'as if' challenges some representations of reality with the scorn of the young – 'Who are you kidding?', implying not me! My book about children's rights and power at the start of a new century is written around the counterpoint of the old meaning of 'as if'. It takes as its focus not children's needs and deficits, but embraces their hopes and aspirations, their dreams, their visions and their untrammelled imaginings – *as if* these things mattered. Doing so will treat children and represent them as if they are people, powerful people, not as people in the making.

PERSONHOOD

When and how does personhood begin? If we are to take the *experiences* of children seriously – a new interest which, as we will consider later, has provided a watershed within the discipline of psychology – we might try to answer this question by thinking about the child's first experiences as a person. Some aspects of contemporary life have thrown into question the extent to which even now we respect children as people – take, for example, early in 2002 in Northern Ireland the abuse and threats faced by young Catholic schoolgirls going to school across a Protestant area. The trial of the ten-year-old boys accused of the murder of the two-year-old James Bulger raised questions about our attentiveness to children as people in the late twentieth century. In the tenth century, King Athelstan for instance set the age of criminal responsibility at 12 and then later raised it to 15 on the basis that he felt it was wrong to use the full rigour of the law against children. By the seventeenth century the age of criminal responsibility was 14, which is four years higher than it is now. Just as young offenders were not always flogged, so also were disabled children not always shunned. Moreover Orme (2001) illustrates cases of hunchbacks and conjoined twins who were dealt with compassionately as people.

The issue of what constitutes personhood became particularly sharp for me at the point at which it seemed to be completely obliterated by hospital practices and prejudices of the time. I was admitted to hospital as an emergency at the age of seven, seriously ill with suspected polio. As was common practice at that time my long hair was shorn, since it was believed that hair sapped one's strength. This constituted a serious assault on my identity as up to that point everyone had always remarked on what beautiful blond hair I had and that I looked like an angel/Hollywood film star and so on. I can remember to this day the size of the scissors that chopped it off – all without a word of explanation to me. Like a novitiate in a convent I was also stripped of my clothes and dressed in a hospital gown. I was removed from an iron lung, rushed to theatre for an operation for peritonitis in the middle of the night, developed septicaemia and was given hallucinogenic sulphonamides. My parents were not allowed to visit because, long before Robertson's films on children in hospital made everyone think again about this practice (Robertson, J. 1953; Robertson, J. and Robertson, J. 1967–72), it was believed that a visit from them or any visitor would upset me and delay my recovery. Nobody explained to me what was happening or the background to the decisions that had been made. I was deprived of parents, siblings and, in effect, peers as the other children in the ward were all very ill and bed-bound. I hoped forlornly for a magical rescue over the hospital wall. I did have two objects that had been sent to me as presents, which marked for me my tiny hold on a personal identity. One afternoon while I was asleep the ward was rearranged and my locker moved and those objects were never found again. I was left with only the ceiling at which to gaze and rearrange my mental furniture as I ceased to be a person in anybody else's eyes. No hospital schools, no reading practice, no conversation and a confusion of languages that was the legacy of a childhood as a partially bilingual child. The isolation went on even after leaving hospital; complications to the wound meant that I could not return to school for another year and did not master reading until I was almost ten. School reports during that time typically said, 'Mary is a dreamer...' Perhaps that was the one skill I had developed, along with the ability to tolerate my own company and thoughts for long periods of time – an important quality for a female academic! The seeds of my interest in personhood had been firmly sown.

My book develops ideas about endurance, resilience, courage and fearlessness as these are personal powers which ensure that, whether one is young or old, one continues to count, to be a force to be reckoned with and not ignored, obliterated or put 'back in the bottle'. In a world which is changing so rapidly that we cannot possibly predict what we have to prepare our children for, what they will have to face and survive, research on resilience is particularly important. The development of a flexible person rather than formulaic thinker must surely be what we now have to concentrate on in our child-rearing.

A primary aim in socialisation is to protect children while respecting their rights and personhood. We are now more than ever aware that it is not possible to protect them from all the troubles that life might bring. The development of resilience is therefore an important focus since, in a changing hurtful world, this is probably one of the few ways we can work towards a responsible and realistic way of protecting children while respecting them as autonomous people. Edith Grotberg describes the International Resilience Project, which analysed ways of strengthening the human spirit (Grotberg 1995). She has written a guide which turns a set of concepts derived from the project into practical tools that can be used in a variety of contexts in work with young children. Grotberg defined resilience as a 'universal capacity which allows a person, group or community to prevent, minimise or overcome the damaging effects of adversity' (1995, p.5). She identifies, on the basis of data collected from 589 children from around the world, that every country in the study was drawing on a common set of resilience factors to promote resilience in their children – that there was in some sense a common vocabulary of resilience. The three common resilience factors were 'I have', 'I can' and 'I am'. While there was some evidence of cultural variation it was not possible to analyse this in any detail, as the number of respondents per country was too small.

One of these three common factors, '*I have*', relates to the social capital the child has, which identifies a variety of supportive people and clear guiding relationships that the child can 'call on' mentally or in actuality, giving this child a sense of support, explicit or implicit, in facing up to a crisis. Sadly, for me, given hospital practices of the time I could not, in any practical sense, call on my social capital when I appeared to have been abandoned. Recent work in *Reaching Young Europe* by Befrienders International (an organisation which works to prevent suicide worldwide), on teaching children how to cope with difficulties so that they should be better able to handle problems and crises in adolescent and adult life, similarly places considerable emphasis on other people. It demonstrates the importance of talking to other people when we feel sad or angry and indeed how important it is to listen to other people when they feel such emotions. In fact it affirms the child's ability to give and use support (Befrienders International 2001).

The second factor in the International Resilience Project relates to children's perception of their own competence – what they feel that they can do. '*I can*' forms an important element in how they face challenges, danger and distress. Similarly the *Reaching Young Europe* materials are not prescriptive but encourage children to explore and think for themselves. While children's sense of their place in a personal social supportive world and their view of their own competence colours their sense of self, the '*I am*' elements of resilience are self-reflexive and important in the child's view of his/her place in what we later call, with reference to Giddens (1991, p.75), 'the reflexive project of the self'. The International Resilience Project suggested what might be key elements in a child's ability to deal with whatever life might bring. The child's sense of self in the here and now, the meaning he/she attaches to the events to be faced and how well equipped he/she is to deal with them position the child in the social world as an agent of his/her own protection. I survived by having some sense of 'I am' – however depleted that became – and by continuing to have the capacity to think – to daydream no less! Grotberg's three elements, it could be argued, are the individual's armoury of personal powers which, while built up through an individual's personal history, are very much in his/her experience of the present and how to deal with it now and in that sense are ahistoric. In a discussion, which follows in Chapter 2, of the genetic fallacy and developmentalism, this emphasis on present experience points to the contribution that it is possible for psychologists to make to this burgeoning field of children's rights which has so far been largely colonised by lawyers and sociologists.

Many have suggested that personhood begins at the moment of conception. I would suggest, for reasons which I hope will become clear, that the child is a person from the moment that child becomes an agent in the social world, which starts when such a child begins to influence the behaviour of others. It is my contention that children's rights as embodied in the UN Convention on the Rights of the Child are fundamentally about being acknowledged, treated and represented as a person and presenting themselves to themselves reflexively as a person in all domains that matter. It is when this is unacknowledged, not understood or not claimed that the child is rendered powerless, often dehumanised and marginalised. Power and representation are therefore, in my argument, closely linked and are fundamental to any appreciation and exercising of rights. This forms the specific focus of the first two chapters of this book and the themes around which the rest of the book is organised.

Putting this view in its historical context, the 1970s and early 1980s marked an interest among sections of the research community in the United Kingdom in the child as a person in his/her own right. Maybe it is a reflection on me as a child of my own time that I start this examination by going back to a 'golden age' of personhood in developmental psychology – an age lost and rediscovered recently as the twentieth century drew to its close. A number of studies emerged then, which collectively marked a change and a coming together in the thinking of many influential developmental psychologists. In the early 1970s Martin Richards and his colleagues in Cambridge drew attention to this in a collection of essays, published as *The Integration of a Child into a Social World* (Richards 1974), which was a new emphasis. The child here is not merely entering the world but has his/her own identity and his/her own name – is '*a*' child not '*the*' child and the task is not simply entry but accommodation, negotiation and integration of *a person*. At about the same time as this publication was jolting the psychological community into thinking further about the nature of a child's individual powers and presence – an emphasis which had been prefigured by Newson's early essays on infant understanding (Newson 1974, 1977, 1978) and Trevarthen's research and writings (Trevarthen 1975, 1977, 1979, 1982) – work was also gathering momentum in establishing the effects the infant had upon its caregiver and the nature of the reciprocity between the two. A central focus was how the concept of intentional action was created by the synchronicity of the infant and their caregiver's shared choreography.

> It is important that we now focus attention on the infant as a source of the formation, regulation and indeed even the malevolent distortion of the caregiver's behaviour…as a result we have begun to see in quite explicit terms that the infant – even at birth – is no passive recipient of stimulation from those around him, ready to be moulded like clay on a potter's wheel. (Lewis and Rosenblum 1974, p.ix)

In 1984 John Shotter, a contributor to Martin Richards' book just cited and himself a distinguished thinker in psychology, produced a reflection on the research activity of the previous decade, trying to address, more generally, what it was to become an autonomous, responsible person. *Social Accountability and Selfhood* was a book which he characterised as a progressive stage in the 'ecology of everyday life' (Shotter 1984, p.ix), a stage which has been augmented by his major writings over the twenty or so years that have followed (Shotter 1993a, 1993b, 1998). He challenged all naively empirical theories of psychology, stressing that accountability is the basis of social life and in this, of course, intention in the social context is all-important. Here is the crux, as he sees it, of the difficulties in the ways in which children are represented in the social world, which is the nature of accountability – 'as if' they were comprehensible people! At the time Shotter was writing he was trying to identify 'a space' in which to conduct a new kind of psychological research about what it is to be a human being. In summarising his quest he said that he saw the goal of the new psychology of the late 1980s as being to increase people's personal powers of responsible action, not by increasing people's domination over others but by mastering their own possible ways of living. He does try to identify some of the criteria in distinguishing people from things, taking the concept of intentionality as crucial. He sees the conceptual framework and terms in which we interact with our children as playing an important part in determining the form of their psychological development.

> But I have not been able to detail the actual criteria relevant to all such practical situations, for the criteria to be a person in one situation is not to satisfy them in general, and in any case the criteria are not general but negotiable – we have to intend personhood continually and discover empirically in each practical situation how to fulfil it. And this is not a natural scientific but a moral task – a choice that is ever present for us. (Shotter 1984, p.72)

The extent to which this choice is exercised or denied – that is, the choice to treat the child as a person so that he/she may be such – forms the substance of my book as this choice implies sharing power. Moreover, how others judge such attempts at personhood and the chasm that often exists between a child's intentions and the interpretation of the adult comes under my scrutiny. Shotter goes on to stress the reflexivity of this process.

> To qualify as an autonomous person, not reliant like a child upon others to complete and give meaning to one's acts, having them decree *what* it is one is doing, one must develop the ability to be able at some point in one's acting to stop and to deliberate, and, as a result make clear to oneself (and/or to others) one's reasons for one's actions. (Shotter 1984, p.73)

One might question in the light of research with children whether they are so reliant on the interpretations of others or whether this is how we, as adults, wish to keep them in an appropriate place in the hierarchy.

Shotter comments that developmental research in the 1970s and early 1980s was marked by a progress away from a peculiarly 'closed' individualistic image of young human beings. An image of the child with a Cartesian starting point was increasingly repudiated, opening up the infant to contextual influences. Vygotsky (1978, p.57) suggested that 'all intra-personal processes are first interpersonal ones'. Therefore, in Shotter's argument, social accountability is a crucial part of selfhood. At about the same time as Shotter was taking stock of a decade of work on 'selfhood', his great colleague and interlocutor Rom Harre was writing about 'Personal Being', also documenting from a slightly different angle a preoccupation of the 1970s with the emergence of the person (Harre 1983). Harre groups modes of individuality in three ways: first he sees personal being as a 'formal unity', emphasising in this analysis consciousness; personal being is then addressed as a 'practical unity', particularly focusing on agency (that is, the ability to act on one's own behalf); finally personal being is seen as an 'empirical unity', using autobiography as the form of enquiry. All of these ways of looking at personhood will be focused on jointly and severally in the material in this book – material which will demonstrate how these preoccupations of over 20 years ago have re-emerged to inform current debates and the ways in which they prefigured the psychology of development on the world stage.

UN CONVENTION ON THE RIGHTS OF THE CHILD

At about the same time as personhood was a hot topic in the UK developmental research community, activities were afoot in the international political arena which were to have profound consequences for children and the recognition of them as people. The original draft of the UN Convention on the Rights of the Child was submitted by Poland to the UN Commission on Human Rights in 1978 in preparation for the International Year of the Child in 1979. It would be nice to think that this was Poland's acknowledgement of one of the most distinguished early writers about children's rights (Korczak 1923; translated 1992), an educator who was known and respected throughout Europe. Janusc Korczak, despite having been offered his freedom by the Nazis on the basis of his renown, went with the children he had taught in the Warsaw Ghetto to Treblinka, never deserting them, sharing their fate and perishing there together with them. Research and the shared wisdom of the writings of practitioners rarely informs or shapes social policy (Tizard 1990) and if it does so it is not immediate or direct. At best, certain activities in the long term create the zeitgeist which subtly infiltrates the mind of the policy maker. Sometimes the climate of thinking can be turned to political advantage. Examining Poland's initiative as a possible legacy of Korczak's work and in the context of an international research community starting to focus on the personhood of the child, it seems clear that the mainsprings of this action were political rather than research-based or philanthropic. Alston (1994) provides a fascinating account of the politics that lay behind the drafting of the Convention itself. The Polish submission he regarded as:

> ...a quintessentially political gesture...the Polish government was probably motivated more by a desire to seize at least some of the human rights initiatives of Jimmy Carter. The rights of the child seemed to be the ideal topic for this purpose, not only because of a long association between Poland and the promotion of the concept at an international level, but more importantly because it was assumed that such a convention could justifiably be confined to the economic, social and cultural rights to which Communist countries wanted to accord priority. (Alston 1994, p.6)

Alston (1994) points out that this whole debate was initially overshadowed, if not silenced, by an ideologically dominated East–West dispute as to whether civil and political rights should be accorded priority over social, economic and cultural rights or vice versa. The UN had always insisted that these were of equal importance. The development of an independent stance by Third World nations – who might well have argued that many of the rights, or indeed the very notion of human rights, were Eurocentric – was deflected by pressure to side with either the East or the West. One of the results of the Cold War was, therefore, the reopening of the cultural relativism debate – that is, the situation of children and their entitlements can only be understood and assessed within their own national context. The Cold War did affect in significant ways the drafting and adoption of the Convention. Initially the West played down the significance of Poland's initiative and tried to drag out the process of drafting for as long as possible.

A NEW PERSON

In France, during the period that both Harre and Shotter were reflecting on personhood and while Poland was pressing for a Convention on the Rights of the Child, Frederick Leboyer, an obstetrician, was challenging everyone on the basis of his innovative practices to think from quite another angle about the very first entry of the infant into the world itself. He wrote about the 'violence' of birth as traditionally experienced and managed (Leboyer 1977). As part of his argument he presented a view of the neonate as a person, a view, which at that time was quite revolutionary.

> When children come into the world, the first thing they do is cry. And everyone relaxes.
>
> 'Just listen to that', the mother exclaims happily, astonished that something so small can make so much noise. Traditionally, this crying means that the reflexes are normal, that the machine worked.
>
> But are we machines?
>
> Aren't cries always an expression of pain?
>
> Could it not be that birth is as painful for the child as giving birth once was for the mother?
>
> And if it is, does anyone care?
>
> I'm afraid, judging by how little consideration we give to a baby, apparently not.
>
> We have a sadly deep-rooted prejudice against believing that this 'thing' can feel, hear or see.

So how could it feel pain?

It shrieks, it howls, and that is that.

In short, it is an object.

But what if it were already a *person*? (Leboyer 1977, pp.4–5)

In addressing the counter-arguments that the baby cannot 'tell' us anything Leboyer cites the example of accidentally swallowing something boiling hot and the way in which, quite without words, a person from virtually any culture will be able to make himself/herself fully understood, without a single word, as to what has happened/is happening to him/her. He goes on to point out that there is one thing which the newborn baby does not lack and that is the ability to express itself.

The tragic expression, those tight shut eyes, those puzzled eyebrows...

That howling mouth, that burrowing desperate head.

Those outstretched hands beseeching; then withdrawn, raised to the head in a classic gesture of despair.

Those furiously kicking feet, those knees drawn up to protect the tender bulging stomach.

The whole creature is one jumping, twitching mass.

Far from speaking, every inch of its body is crying out: 'Don't touch me!'

And at the same time pleading: 'Don't leave me! Help me!'...

So can we say that a new-born baby doesn't speak?

No. It is we who do not listen.

(Leboyer 1977, p.7)

This last is a wonderful line and throughout this book I will be returning to children's voices, however young, and the many ways in which, in a world characterised by rapid explosion of communication of various forms, we are still largely deaf to what they have to say and teach us about the world as they see and experience it. We are deafened by dissonance. Is this inability to listen related to a reluctance to relinquish our view of what children are and, in doing so, to relinquish our own power? Lasri (1994), in an article 'On the Non-existence of the Present in the Adult World', argues that it is not just a matter of not listening but also of not seeing. His article opens with an example of two women looking at a three-month-old baby, wondering what colour eyes he has, agreeing that it is impossible to know. Writing in Israel, he goes on:

> ...while there is an attempt to deal with motion and time, our culture is characterized by a denial of time. When this relationship is translated into the world of the child, it seems that the child does not exist because of being only in process (he is changing), and because of being temporary, private and unable to be directed. The colour of the baby's eyes is an 'illusory' colour because it hides behind the permanent colour of the adult's eyes and only this permanent colour is of value to the existing truth. In the world of culture, childhood is seen as a long corridor that ends in adulthood. What happens in that corridor is important only if it has an influence on the world of the adult... (Lasri 1994, p.4)

Not only listening and seeing but also voicing have been issues in recognising the child as a person. Approaches to voice and voicing the concerns of the 'silenced', prefigured by Lincoln's work in the USA (Lincoln 1993), have aimed to facilitate the child to take an active part in sharing his/her experiences and have posed challenges for rethinking power relations implicit in some research paradigms.

I would like to stop for a moment longer to think about the interplay between research, practice and political decision-making – a link which, as I have said, is always tenuous and rarely synchronous. Nevertheless the climate in France was one that was not insensitive to Leboyer's emphasis on personhood, although possibly not extending it back to quite such early days in the way he argued for. France had long considered itself the champion of children's rights, following on from its position on human rights; the political will was made clear by the President on 10 June 1989, announcing at a conference sponsored by the National Association of Family Associations (UNAF):

> It is my hope that France will be one of the first signatories [of the Convention] and that the implementing legislation will be passed quickly. It is often difficult to adapt internal law, which represents all our traditions and ways of thinking, to a new international law. Nevertheless, we must do so. It is imperative that we reconsider the legal status of the child.

> Children must be respected in their own right. Whoever loves freedom, whoever dreams of it, whoever wishes to see it spread throughout the entire planet knows well that such a phenomenon begins with a clear conception that the child is a person who must not be deformed and submitted to what other individuals or collective bodies would like to impose on him or her. (Rubellin-Devichi 1994)

Fine words but was France, or any other country prepared for what sort of person a child might be? It seems not as, in August 2002, draconian measures were introduced in France to deal with teenagers abusive of adult authority – measures which could include a jail sentence.

CHILDREN'S UNDERSTANDING OF 'PERSONHOOD'

The now-classic study by Dunn and Kendrick during the late 1970s on the effects of the birth of a younger sibling on an older sibling (Dunn and Kendrick 1982) gave some insight, on the basis of direct observation, into the extent to which very young children were indeed people – people with feelings and sensitivities. This early work has now been considerably extended by longitudinal studies in the UK (Dunn 1988; Dunn, Slomkowski and Beardsall 1994) and in the USA (Dunn 1995). It provides stunning evidence of very young children's abilities to 'listen' to and hear others in important ways – ways which, according to the work in the *Reaching Young Europe* project, are likely to contribute to their coping skills in later life. Dunn's work demonstrated how naturally sophisticated young children are in their social understanding, interpreting another's feelings with astonishing insight. The early work also gave some important clues to the understanding and categorisation that children, even those as young as two years old, had of self. This research, while at the time of a pilot nature, was groundbreaking in that it provided a preliminary but awesome view of how very young children saw themselves and their understanding of other people. It provided us with some knowledge of these children's own sense of personal power when very young. This insight was augmented by work going on at a similar time with four-year-olds (Tizard and Hughes 1984) and by the later studies by Dunn herself in Pennsylvania (1995). The Tizard and Hughes studies threw a striking and, at that time, very new light on the nature of four-year-olds' intellectual curiosity and powers of logical thought. This study also demonstrated the potential significance of family conversations for children's cognitive growth. On issues which intrigued them, the children showed energy and persistence in their conversations with their mothers.

> It is sometimes supposed that children of this age have special childish interests, mainly to do with mothers, babies, dolls, teddies and animals. The conversations in our study suggest that, on the contrary, all human experience was grist to their intellectual mill. (Tizard and Hughes 1984, p.128)

Amusingly the children's vigorous enquiries extended from work, birth, growing up and death to 'such diverse topics as the shape of roofs and chairs, the nature of Father Christmas, and whether the Queen wears curlers in bed' (p.8). One of the many significant things about this research was the way it demonstrated the child's agency, in Harre's 'practical unity' terms of personal being. The children were extremely active in engaging in conversations which achieved greater clarity over issues they did not understand and demonstrated, in the conversation with their mothers, considerable powers of logical argument. There were notable differences in their conversations at home compared with those at school. By the time they were four years old they engaged in discussions about people's feelings which were often vivid and they enthusiastically followed the topic of why people behave as they do. It was clear that they were quite sophisticated in their social understanding of 'personhood', fascinated in fact by people operating in the social world. This picture of the child's relative social maturity at four generated much subsequent research into what experiences and developments in the preschool years led up to this. Dunn and her colleagues' work in succeeding years on the child's understanding of others further underscored the importance of conversations between children and other family members as contexts for learning; this learning included learning about themselves. This work reveals children to be engaging in causal discourse about inner states well before the age of four. As this picture was drawn from settings where two people are talking, it is difficult to draw more general inferences.

> But it is beyond question that the evidence from the studies of pretend, deception, argument in disputes as well as causal talk about inner states confirm the general picture: that *when studied within the familiar and emotional world of the family* the early signs of a developing understanding of inner states and their

links to action are evident in the third and fourth year. (Dunn
1996, p.83)

All this early work makes it all the more paradoxical and enigmatic that
children's experiences have been so neglected by many psychologists,
effectively becoming the psychologists' blind spot in the late 1990s.
This had dire consequences for the position of the discipline (as will be
discussed in the next chapter) and, as will become very clear throughout
the book, has seriously disadvantaged abused and troubled children in
claiming their rights and having their rights respected.

The realities of how children see and understand themselves, how
they are actually seen by others as people or as 'unpeople' as is argued in
Chapter 3, and how they are treated and the position they occupy in society provide important counterpoints in the examination of rights and
power. While even very young children might interrogate adults about
feelings, meanings and intentions, there are other sources of information about the world they inhabit, and the sense they make of it to themselves in reading their culture is peculiarly their own.

CHILDREN 'THE NEW DANGEROUS CLASSES'

Articles in the popular press in the UK often seem to indicate all too
clearly that children are to be repressed rather than understood. About
the same time as the research on children's understandings of feelings,
causes, etc., was bearing fruit in published form, Ingleby (1985) made
dramatic warnings about an infiltration of the socialisation process itself
in the interests of the control of the formation of the child's psyche. He
made the provocative claim that children have become the new 'dangerous classes' and questioned on whose behalf parents and other adults
engaged in the socialisation process were acting, and whose interests did
their activities actually serve? To a substantial degree, he believed, the
socialisation of the child had been taken over by the state and its agencies. There was, he claimed, 'a growing army of professionals operating
in the psychological sphere' (Ingleby 1985, p.79). Previous obsessions
with medically-based psychiatry had given way to a collection of agencies, including: educational; clinical and social psychology; social work;
and various parts of the legal system (which then, under the guise of
new legislative instruments such as the Children Act of 1989, tried to
work out how this army could be most effectively co-ordinated).

Interestingly it is partly the protection of the rights of the family from this sort of infiltration that has prevented the USA from ratifying the UN Convention on the Rights of the Child (UNCRC) – the only country in the world, other than Somalia to so desist.

Ingleby (1985, p.79) dubbed as the 'psy complex' those whose aims were to apply psychological technology with varying degrees of expertise and success to social problems. He suggested that the state, mediating the psy complex, was infiltrating the very heart of family dynamics. Professionals maintain power through the parent by educating the parent about the professional's world view and turning parents into what Ingleby referred to as 'proto professionals'. The psy complex homes in on the child's primary induction into the culture by trying to guide the construction not only of the child's behaviour but also the child's developing thinking and awareness.

Ingleby believed that the professionals were themselves duped into thinking that the ends were benevolent and the means of achieving them rational – but were they? The argument went on to suggest that these professionals were trying to produce ways of living and thinking consistent with the social order. They were exercising a form of social control in the production of individuals who would not threaten government hegemony. The focus was not only through an increasingly selective state educational system in the UK but on the inner dynamics of the family. Here a particular form of state ideological orthodoxy is seen as the basis for social hegemony. Ingleby suggested how the psy complex achieves its effects. Children, by their very presence, present a challenge to the social order. He argued that the provision of care for children has increasingly become a matter of socialising people in prescribed ways that were far removed from personal freedom. It had therefore become 'difficult to think of "help" and even protection as separable from "control"'.

> What, then, are the values promoted by the 'psy complex'? This is an enormous question, but I shall single out one emerging priority: to guide the construction of the child's psyche itself... No longer can the formation of the infant self be left to the unknowing parents; there is too much danger that this crucial and sensitive process will go awry, resulting in a 'failure of socialisation'. It seems almost as if children were threatening to refuse to join the human race. Whereas in the

late nineteenth century the danger to social order was seen as
coming from criminals, mental defectives and vagabonds, the
'dangerous classes' now seem to be babies. (Ingleby 1985,
p.103)

This seemed to recognise the personhood of the child in a particularly
powerful and threatening form. He went on to stress the huge contradiction on which the psy complex was founded, in sanctifying family while
at the same time infiltrating those relations and subjecting them to its
management. The result of this paradox was that many of the agents of
the psy complex were confused, with all the resulting dilemmas and
contradictions relating to care and control, libertarianism, welfare, appropriate intervention, etc. Ingleby suggested that the only way forward
was to demystify these forces. Even 12 years after Ingleby had written, it
seems that these forces have not been clearly demystified. Headlines in a
national newspaper in the UK in 1997 announced 'Blair promises all
parents the right to smack their children' (*Independent on Saturday* 1997)
in a bid to court right-wing newspapers and pro-family groups. This
right has been challenged under Article 3 of the Human Rights Convention which protects individuals against degrading treatment. The
government's discussion paper on smacking was alarming and, one
would have thought, a grotesque anachronism. Lyon (2000), a lawyer
looking at this issue, points out in her report that contrary to the government's belief that public opinion will not support wholesale reform in
providing children with protection, the government's own data actually
demonstrates public support for significant reform. The report stresses
that all forms of physical punishment of children should be made un-
lawful. Although Ingleby, in discussing how children were represented,
did not explicitly refer to 'power' (the twin theme of this book), power
relations and imbalances are implicit in everything he said. Analysis of
recent policy in the UK suggests that Children Acts and educational reform exhibit a strengthening of the socialising power over children. The
theme of power will be fully explored in Chapter 2. Let us stay with the
representation of children as 'evil' and in need of control a little longer.
Children maybe are not so much a dangerous class but, as the following
discussion reveals, a misunderstood and misrepresented group.

CHILDREN BEHAVING 'AS IF' THEY WERE PEOPLE

Adults' definitions of reality infiltrate the child's consciousness in a variety of ways in conversations, in their treatment of the child in the socialisation process, through the media and through the child's own observations of adult behaviour in the day-to-day world. David Jackson provides a chilling account of the lives of two ten-year-old boys in the United Kingdom who abducted and murdered a two-year-old infant, James Bulger, in 1992 (Jackson 1995). 'Evil freaks of nature' was the phrase used by the judiciary to explain the boys' actions. Jackson hypothesises about how these young boys tried to fit themselves into what they perceived to be the adult version of the world, emphasising a previously unexamined aspect of the crime – its gendered nature. He gives examples of other violent masculinised crimes committed by young boys in recent times, which indicate that these young boys are not freaks but a horrifying and extreme case of an increasingly common phenomenon. In the making of boys and men and masculinity we are urged to look at the gendered views of reality (Jackson 1995, p.9). In considering power this is important as although children (like disabled people, another minority rights group) are frequently referred to in a gender-neutral way, the adult world and indeed *their* world is not so neutral.

Jackson looks at the complex interweaving of social, cultural and psychic structures in their life at home and at school. He also considered how the boys themselves experienced the world through the media and video games, and he suggests that 'these idealised, fantasy images of masculinity have the power to shape young boys' unconscious desires, dreams and fantasies' (Jackson 1995, p.23). This analysis of their lives at home and at school reveals what they might have been learning from a world in which constant regulation and surveillance, particularly at school, along with academic failure made them feel powerless and bossed around. At home they were at the bottom of the pecking order. What they did learn from their environment, including the fantasy video material, was that adult power had a gendered aspect 'in a world where adult men were expected to exercise commanding authority over women and children' (p.9). Jackson suggests that the images of idealised masculinity that they saw around them and that were provided by the media had a 'thrilling appeal' – they had to bully or be bullied.

It was the daily social practices of being brought up in an ag-
gressive male-dominated family, bullying and being bullied,
having to face the pressures of the male peer group, learning
to dump their pain and hurt onto other people, building fantasy heroes like Rambo and learning to emotionally detach
yourself as a boy from the reality of other people's lives that
socially produced two boys who killed James Bulger. We need
to face up to the ways we have concealed the gendering process...the awkward fact is that our culture and society have
produced two boys who have killed in order to become masculine. (Hill 1996, p.14)

Suzanne Moore (*Guardian* 1996) observed that the boys could not make
their victim stay down, which may have compounded their feelings as
failing boys, causing an escalating rage which led their assaults on to the
brutal murder. They were trying to kill the baby in themselves: '...the
hatred of their own vulnerability, their own babyishness, became so
strong that it is punished, killed off through the body of another'
(Moore, *Guardian*, 26 November 1993).

Children are rarely seen within adult definitions of 'reality' as male
or female – sadly they are often not seen at all. The Bulger murder did
have an enormous impact on the world of the adult and on the police,
with the media, psychiatrists and both main political parties intent on
demonising the children without examining the whole context of what
they did. While we have examined a plausible hypothesis put forward
by Jackson for this, at the time the judge described the boys as 'Evil
freaks of nature' and this immediately caught the imagination of the
popular press, being reflected in alarming headlines which posited dark
forces in these children *themselves*. The trial itself raised questions about
criminal responsibility and the juvenile justice system in the UK (Morrison 1997). This and the media panic continue through all the processes
that have ensued at the beginning of this century to ensure the early release of these boys – now young men – before they enter the adult penal
system. In Norway the rehabilitation work would have taken place
within their own communities. In the UK they are being offered new
identities and guarantees of protected anonymity for life. They are certainly not seen even now as the tragic victims of a culture in chaos...
As if!

Adults' representations of children, their control of them, power over them and the demonisation of them raises questions as to what deep fears about children are triggered by such tragedies. The Bulger murder was not the first death at the hands of a child murderer to arouse such violent reaction. The tragic story of the early life of Mary Bell, her later treatment at the hands of the UK judicial system and by the media, and the way in which this terribly abused child continued to be abused by 'the system' and was later made vulnerable and exposed was documented by her biographer who had hoped to make her plight understood (Sereny 1995). What sort of backlash, threatening the power of adults to control children, gives rise to the hysteria that accompanied cases such as the two I have cited?

CHILDREN AS WITCHES

Power over children is exercised by arousing, in the popular consciousness, fears about the dangers they allegedly represent. Such representations of danger were, as we noted, presented some time ago by Ingleby. It seems that the only group of human beings that can be legitimately discriminated against in the UK after all the equal opportunity and political correctness campaigns is children. Children remain the only members of society whom, despite the ratification of the UN Convention, it is legal to physically chastise. Rosalind Miles says, for instance, that 'From both sides of the Atlantic, evidence seems to be mounting that children are more and more deviant, more delinquent, more out of hand. If they grow up confused and ignorant, destructive and self-destructive, then the society that produces them must be so too' (Miles 1994, synopsis). This concern has continued to grow such that one could take the argument even further and see children as the 'witches' of the twentieth century. If the functions 'witches' used to serve in power relations in a rapidly changing society are examined, this does not seem such an astonishing suggestion − in fact it is far more tenable than it might first appear.

At the beginning of the 1970s, just as in psychology infants and children were beginning to be recognised as people, the anthropologist Mary Douglas in reviewing the work on witchcraft was stating, 'Where social interaction is intense and ill-defined, there we might expect to find witchcraft beliefs' (Douglas 1970, p.xxxv), and observes that there is an increase in the witch phenomenon in communities undergoing social breakdown. 'Witchcraft has no fixed dogma, no single logic; it is utilized in many different kinds of situations as a means of explaining misfortune and expressing social tension' (Brain 1970, p.177). As children become recognised as people, as powerful witnesses to life's goings-on, social interaction becomes less well-defined and tensions do arise.

In Europe and Massachusetts in the sixteenth and seventeenth centuries, child accusers were used for 'crying out' witches. 'Young girls became officials of witch courts where their supposedly unbiased confessions and accusations were accepted as fact. Innumerable people were sent to their death because of the wanton mischief of unruly children' (Brain 1970, p.161). Brain examined the psychology of child witchcraft in the Bangwa, Cameroon, where children were frequently accused. He concludes that in Europe and in Bangwa children have been used by professional witch-hunters for political ends. More recently in the Democratic Republic of Congo, the effects of conflict and the country's socio-economic crisis have seriously damaged the wellbeing of the most vulnerable sections of the population. Serious malnutrition is rife and 20 per cent of the population does not reach the age of five. Save the Children in Kinshasa explains the increase in the number of children rejected from the family as 'child witches' or 'sorcerers'. 'The capacities of Congolese families and communities to assure basic care and protection for children seems to be breaking down' (Reuters 2002). Work has been undertaken to send the children back to their parents, giving aid for food, clothing and education. It was found that most children accused of sorcery are not welcome at home. All 28 girls aged between 4 and 12 years in a home for street children have been so accused. There are anxieties that the economic and political stabilisation causing acute poverty will not be addressed before the current generation of street children come of age. 'They are a menace now,' an American diplomat said, 'and they will get worse' (Reuters 2002). The use of witchcraft beliefs where relationships are ill-defined related to 'a homeostatic model of society in which witchcraft beliefs help to maintain the system, the natural way to account for witchcraft accusations getting out of control was by reference to a general breakdown of society' (Douglas 1970, p.xix). In some societies it seems witchcraft beliefs lie beneath the surface ready to be triggered off by friction and social unrest.

Recent research in the UK with survivors of ritual and satanic abuse seems to reveal how children have been indoctrinated in various harrowing ways into believing they are evil and the embodiment of Satan or the devil and in this way they are controlled and their silence ensured. Their very sense of self and personhood is groomed and shaped by the horrific practices of which they are the victims or witnesses. This whole area has become a contested issue in many quarters including academia as moral panics or 'false memories', which I examine in Chapter 5. The work adds to an understanding of gendered violence, perhaps illustrating the complicity in or (as the perpetrators of these practices) the increase in violence of young women that has been predicted (Wilkinson and Mulgan 1995). The assault on the nature of the child's personhood and identity within the family in transmitting a culture of abuse is deeply entwined within everyday domestic life for many children in this new century.

AS IF THE WORLD'S CHILDREN MATTERED

Thomas Hammarberg was one of the ten experts elected on the basis of individual capacities to the Committee on the Rights of the Child set up in 1991 to monitor the implementation of the Convention on the Rights of the Child in the countries that had ratified it. He speaks, therefore, from a position of considerable insight when pleading for a political awakening leading to increased political attention to children and young people, which he felt was necessary if their actual circumstances are to change.

> Children have always been, and still are, the victims of hypocrisy. Politicians often pay lip service to the well-being of children, many of them are eager to be seen as child-friendly. But in real terms when economy and other interests come into the picture, children tend to be let down. (Hammarberg 1993, p.296)

Returning to the process of the drafting of the UN Convention on the Rights of the Child to illustrate this point, Alston (1994) described how the West dragged its feet in responding to Poland's proposal. It became apparent by the mid 1980s, however, that the draft Convention was gathering a substantial level of support such that it seemed likely that it would be adopted. The response of the Reagan administration was to press for the inclusion of the sort of civil and political rights that it accused Communist countries of trying to deny or minimise. This manoeuvre was designed to make the document lose support from its original sponsor, Poland, and her allies. A number of chance factors played a significant part, in Alston's view, which meant that this ploy did not work. By 1986 the Cold War was ending and UNICEF (United Nations International Children's Emergency Fund) had begun to be active in the drafting process, also encouraging the involvement and active participation of developing countries. This meant that not only was the platform of support extended but also the acceptability of the Convention by those countries was ensured. The end of Reagan's presidency in 1989 at the stage of the final drafting seemed to remove any further delays and obstacles. Former Communist countries were anxious to demonstrate their new commitments to comprehensive and international human rights norms. The result of this history, it was believed, was that the Convention is claimed to be more sensitive to different approaches and perspectives than most of the human rights treaties which preceded it. There have been attacks on it by various cultural relativists claiming that it presents very Western industrialised nations' views of children's lives. One of the outspoken critics has been Judith Ennew (1995) who suggests that it was no coincidence that the Convention on the Rights of the Child was drafted during the same decade as an unprecedented increase in interest in 'street children', and both sprang from the heightened interest in children associated with the United Nations International Year of the Child in 1979. She suggests that:

> In the juxtaposition of the Convention and the image of the street child the entire discourse of children's rights stands revealed. The Convention, in the drafting process, the resulting text and in its implementation, takes as its starting point Western, modern childhood, which has been 'globalised' first through colonialism and then through the imperialism of international aid (Boyden 1990; Detrick 1992; Fyfe 1989).
> (Ennew 1995, p.202)

She goes on to explain that the child thought about in the Convention is a domestic child, a child who lives inside – inside society, inside a family, inside a private dwelling – which in her view means that street children become society's ultimate outlaws. She argues, just as children are increasingly seen as prey to all sorts of influences and dangers outside the private world of the family, so they are banished from the streets. Modern streets become places of danger for the child rather than places to socialise and explore. Boyden says that these streets at night, particularly in Northern Europe and North America, are seen as morally dangerous, especially for children (Boyden 1990). The result in Ennew's view is that 'children who join police, prostitutes and adult vagrants on this arena at night are not only outside society but also outside childhood' (Ennew 1995 in Franklin 1995 p.202). The result has been that as the Convention on the Rights of the Child was drafted with a particular type of childhood in mind, children outside this model are treated as marginal. While certain Articles do indeed target children such as street children for particular attention, as regards child labour and sexual exploitation for example, labelling and targeting can be seen as a marginalising process which could have lifelong effects. Ennew pleads that any special consideration given to them should take account of their individuality, not the category of social needs to which they have been assigned.

This reinforces my ongoing argument throughout the book, which is that children's rights are about their entitlement to be treated as people regardless of age, circumstance or context.

In September 2001 there was to have been a meeting with heads of state, government leaders, non-governmental organisations, children's advocates and young people themselves to examine the extent to which children have been taken seriously as people since the World Summit on Children in September 1990. At that top-level meeting, 180 participating countries signed a final declaration and Plan of Action and following that Summit 155 countries drew up national programmes to ensure the survival, protection and development of children. There have been some successes and it is claimed that more was done for children during the last ten years than in any other period in history. Nevertheless day-to-day life for many children remains the same and few of the promises of a decade ago have been kept. Briefly, 600 million children are in families living on less than US$1 a day. Almost 160 million children under five are malnourished and more than 10 million children die each year from preventable diseases. An estimated 300,000 children – some as young as seven – are fighting in conflicts around the world and 250 million children under the age of 15 are forced to work to survive, often in exploitative conditions.

At the beginning of a new century, are children – 40 per cent of the world's population, the largest proportion it has ever been – being treated as if they were people?

SETTING OUT

In this initial chapter, I have been at pains to stress that for the child to be considered as a powerful member of society, that child has first to be re-cognised as a person. In setting out a rationale for this, I looked at the way that psychologists in the 1970s were demonstrating in their re-searches the way that the interaction between caretaker and infant was choreographed on the basis of beliefs 'as if' that infant was a person ca-pable of intentional action. By such a stance the infant's behaviour be-came comprehensible in terms of purposeful behaviour. It was as if it were a negotiation between equals. Not everybody saw the neonate this way and it was necessary for Leboyer to emphasise that the newborn was already a person. Interestingly Fukuyama, looking at the possibility of cloned infants, provides the counterpoint by asking what if these cloned infants are not people but worse still not even human (Fukuyama 2002)!

I have argued for the newly arrived child's status as a person right from the beginning, and outlined how the United Nations Convention on the Rights of the Child has tried to demonstrate that the child is a person, an individual with rights in a democratic society. Given that a rather ethnocentric view of the child is embodied in this Convention and there is a tendency in many instances to see these rights as bestowed by liberal-thinking adults, it is arguable whether the UNCRC was really predicated upon the child as citizen or as vulnerable dependant. While the child's 'best interest' is the guiding principle, who is the judge and final arbiter of that (John 1997b)? The UNCRC seems to relate to the lifestyle and needs of a Western[3] indoor child. Ironically statistics seem to indicate that this child is most at risk of abuse or violence in just that setting, namely the home and by a family member, where children are assumed to be 'safe' while 'out of range' of the protection of the social services – behind their own front door.

Admitting that the infant and developing child is a person has pre-sented problems. Much of society has failed to be convinced that this is a person but rather a person in the making, and adults, sometimes rein-forced by professional expertise and direction, are sure that they play a crucial part in that making. Moreover questions arise about the nature of this 'raw' material: how malleable is it; what if we cannot shape it into social conformity and obedience? Therefore in arguing for the status of the child as 'a person' the question arises as to what sort of person and what role does that little person occupy relative to us. By what process do children read the text of their culture, which presents such confusing messages, to gather some clues as to what is expected of them so that they can 'pass' as proto-adults in the adult world? Here we can encounter another problem. With the blurring of firm clear 'roles' in society, such as those of parent, child, mother, husband, wife etc., comes the need for the negotiation of one's place in that society, the creation of one's own niche that has meaning for the individual. Giddens (1992), writing about adult relationships but in a way that is worth considering here in relation to parent–child relationships, says:

> ...the radicalising possibilities of the transformation of intimacy are very real. Some have claimed that intimacy can be oppressive, and clearly this may be so if it is regarded as a demand for constant emotional closeness. Seen as a transactional negotiation of personal ties by equals, it appears in a completely different light. Intimacy implies a wholesale democratising of the interpersonal domain, in a manner fully compatible with democracy in the public sphere. (p.3)

If we can reconstrue intersubjectivity in its modern form as being about emotional democracies between equals in a social context in which clearly defined roles and their hierarchies have now disappeared, there is a need to look at the place of children as people and as citizens in a new century in an entirely different way. This homes in on them as people negotiating relationships, adjusting expectations, enduring emotional disappointments and being resilient to all aspects of this negotiative process. This reciprocal activity is the ideal state.

The acknowledgement of the possibility that the child's realities are radically different from our own can create a state of ambiguity and unrest that has sometimes been resolved by recourse to various superstitions and beliefs which relate to dilemmas about how to control this unknown, unpredictable and even feared member of our society. By defining this baffling entity as a dangerous, evil or witchlike person, the adults have then placed the child in a role of their own creation. This excuses the adults from any effort to listen to or understand the child's realities, or to negotiate such understanding, and legitimises any controlling mechanism the adults choose to adopt. By labelling child murderers as 'evil freaks of nature' the adults are giving themselves permission to treat those children vindictively, unrestrainedly and mercilessly as 'non-people'. Labelling recreates the power divide.

While in some ways acknowledging the differences between child perceptions of the world and those of the adult, hence the perceived need for control and firm discipline, nevertheless policies and strategies have been adopted which are developed as if children throughout the world were all the same, that they go through universal developmental stages and that cultural context and experience is an irrelevance.

This book sets out to examine the person of the child in more detail, in a variety of cultural contexts and settings, taking as far as possible the experiences of children as expressed by them as the starting point of the enquiry.

Endnote

1.   This is the last line of an English nursery rhyme 'Oranges and Lemons' which allegedly has its roots deep in an English history of beheadings.

2.   Extract from Blake Morrison's 'As If' (1997) is reproduced with permission from Granta Books.

3.   'Western' and 'Northern' relate to children from industrialised developed countries. Authors tend to use these terms interchangeably, thus avoiding the possibly perjorative use of 'developed/developing', 'third world' etc.

CHAPTER TWO

The Fourth 'P'

The Issue of Power

INTRODUCTION

Having studied the counterpoint between how children see and understand themselves as persons with how they are regarded by others, how they are treated and the position they occupy in society, I now move forward to the issue of power.

The Children in Charge Series, of which this volume forms a part, has examined in various ways the implications of the United Nations Convention on the Rights of the Child for practice and research. The Convention is often discussed and analysed in terms of the 'three Ps' – the three major foci of the Convention – Participation, Protection and Provision. These three formed the organising framework for the first three volumes in the Series. Children's autonomy underlines what I call the fourth 'P'. This 'P' in fact runs through all the previous three volumes and now comes into focus in this book. It is, in my view, the big 'P' – Power. Power is rarely considered when writing about children's rights – a rare exception to this being Priscilla Alderson's work with Save the Children on young children's rights (Alderson 2000). A consideration of power is central to an understanding not only of the three traditional 'Ps' but also of the position of global children in this new century.

Judith Ennew's assertions that street children, in relation to the Convention, were outside childhood itself relates to power (Ennew 1995). These street children were perceived as being outside adult control. In their lives they had agency, autonomy and recognition amid their peers. In fact they had something children rarely have, namely power. An inclusive view of children has to address the issue of power. The way in which street children operate illustrates the enterprise and initiative children can show in especially difficult conditions – conditions faced by increasing numbers of the world's children – and makes us think again about what children are capable of. Street children do not enjoy rights of protection and provision, which makes them seem 'unnatural children' (Ennew 1995, p.210). As people, however, they work for themselves, care for and respect each other and do not in fact ask society to rescue them. The way they operate challenges the hegemony of Northern and Western childhood. Their autonomy underlines the fourth 'P'. Such children may need special thought in relation to notions of children's rights as written by the UN Convention. Judith Ennew (1995, pp.210–213) suggests what these might be; the following list contains some of her suggestions.

- The right not to be labelled.
- The right to be correctly described, researched and counted.
- The right to work, and do so in fair conditions and for fair wages.
- The right to have their own support systems respected.
- The right to appropriate and relevant services.
- The right to control their own sexuality.
- The right to be protected from secondary exploitation.
- The right to be protected from harm inflicted by 'caring' social agencies.

The acknowledgment and respecting of such rights involves accepting the power and autonomy of children. Instead they have been known to be shot, murdered, killed in order to rid the streets of this threatening 'refuse' (Amnesty International 1995). These are all rights that would be argued for by minority rights groups, disabled people, women, ethnic minorities, adults as well as children – rights which respect their personhood, individuality, their special circumstances and their self-determination. Honouring street children in this way requires a rethink of childhood and a need to see the world with their eyes and get inside their views on life. The 'fourth P' is not about satisfying needs for protection or provision but rather about realising aspirations – aspirations which can only be, unlike 'needs', self-defined.

THE NATURE OF POWER

Democracy involves the sharing and negotiation of world views and indeed, at times, the transformation of the nature of power itself. Power has been defined in a whole spectrum of ways. For the position taken in this book, I have used, as the guiding compass, Dorothy Rowe's belief that, 'In the final analysis, power is the right to have your definition of reality prevail over other people's definition of reality' (Rowe 1989, p.16) or, more simply, 'Power is the right to define how others should define' (Rowe 1991, p.159). This neatly captures the usual power relationships between adults and children. It is the adult's view of the world which is most often the framework for understanding, which forms the basis of formal and informal induction into the world and guides the institutions of education themselves. It is inescapably linked with control, both latent and manifest.

Rowe suggests that the trappings of power often obscure who actually has the right to define (Rowe 1991, p.159ff.). Other people can impose their constructions on us, forcibly making us abandon our own, as we will see in the case of abducted child soldiers. Constructions can be imposed on us in an apparently kindly way, making us feel valued, supported and grateful, relinquishing our own realities in the face of such apparent benevolence readily – a technique used effectively in wooing child consumers. Smail points out how subtle and insidious this can be: 'Television is a much more powerful means of ensuring uniformity of belief than was the Inquisition' (Smail 1987, p.87). Rowe comments that childhood fantasies are all about power – using magical powers to make the world into what one wants it to be. Lorna Sage, in one of the best autobiographies to capture the painful business of childhood, touches on the familiar 'foundling fantasy' as a magical way of distancing herself from her parents (Sage 2001). For some children magical escapes from a painful real world, through play and fantasy, make that world tolerable, giving them a sense of power and authority. Children are not the only people who have fantasies to deal with issues of power and control. Some adult fantasies succeed in protecting adults from awful truths. A contemporary review of Lorna Sage's account of growing up exposes this.

> Nothing else I have read destroys so successfully the fantasy
> of the family as a safe place to be or describes so well the way
> in which rage, grief, frustrated desire are passed down the
> family line like a curse, leaving offspring to live out the inher-
> ited, unresolved lives of their forebears. (Wilson, 2000)

Not only family histories but also labelling and descriptions play a part in stigmatising children – very often unfairly. The street children felt that this label often led to unjust and sometimes abusive discrimination against certain children. Sometimes this label 'street child' was incorrect as it implied they had no families, were abandoned and were drug addicts, prostitutes or criminals – all negative connotations. The characteristics frequently assigned to them, the children felt, cast them in a bad light and were often simply untrue. Ingleby has already suggested in relation to 'indoor' children that the 'psy' professionals take a role in labelling and defining (Ingleby 1985). They often define parents' tasks and objectives for them, albeit under the guise of benign concern. Rowe peels things back even further in suggesting that 'in families the people who appear to have power to define may not actually have this power. There are a great many families where the parents, while apparently acting like independent adults, are actually still children accepting without question their parents' definitions of reality…' (Rowe 1991, p.138ff.). Lorna Sage's autobiography places the energy of the 'adult' parents more in escaping their parents' definitions of reality but nevertheless not independent of that history. Adults' definitions of reality infiltrate the child's consciousness in a variety of ways – through the socialisation process, through the media and through the child's own observations of adult behaviour in the day-to-day world.

In order to learn about power, children need to be given opportunities to exercise it. Teaching children how to *become* citizens is misdirected, as Rhys Griffith has emphasised (Griffith 1996), if they are not treated like citizens as part of the educational process.

> Power and rights are not generally popular words. Adults
> prefer to talk about their care and authority or the need for
> firm control, rather than their power over children. Child
> power is a still less popular term. This happens when power is
> seen as something to be divided rather than shared, like the
> slices of a cake when the more power one person has, the less
> everyone else has.

> When adults believe they must set all the rules which the
> children must obey, the adults worry that if they let children
> have a little power they will want more and more, a process it
> is better not to start. This is especially so, if it is believed that
> children should not have any power, with fearful visions of
> powerless but responsible adults, and irresponsible but
> powerful children. (Alderson 2000, p.110)

Lukes suggested that the least effective kind of power is when adults believe that they must set all the rules that children must follow and have
anxieties about any form of power sharing with children, since they fear
that if they give a little, children will want more (Lukes 1974). A second
more forceful form of power, Lukes suggests, is where such clarity is not
possible; people are offered misleading choices as their attention is quite
deliberately not drawn to all the options and relevant information is restricted. This form of power is based on deceit and dishonesty. The
strongest form of power is that in which there appears to be no choice,
such that people not only must but also want to behave in certain ways,
demonstrating that they have thoroughly internalised their own oppression. This is the desired outcome in brainwashing. In this book we
will be taking a view of power which involves this sort of internalisation
in defining power as 'the right to define how others should define'
(Rowe 1991, p.159). It is an often mute acceptance of adult realities that
I examine further in working through the book towards the converse,
namely an architecture of empowerment in which realities are understood and if necessary renegotiated. Robert Chambers, introducing a recent collection of papers on children's participation, has this to say
about the importance of such a transformation of power: 'There is perhaps no more powerful way of transforming human society than changing how the adults of today relate to children, the adults of tomorrow'
(Johnson et al. 1998, p.xvii). I am looking in this book at power as it is
manifested in such relationships.

I have argued elsewhere that conventional educational practices in
the UK do little to develop the child's self-realisation and ability to negotiate his/her own conceptions of reality, thereby excluding the child
from any sense of power (John 1995). This echoed Roger Hart's view
that 'Many western nations think of themselves as having achieved democracy fully, though they teach the principles of democracy in a pe-
dantic way in classrooms which are themselves models of autocracy'

(Hart 1992, p.5). For me, self-realisation and personal autonomy are fundamental educational rights which underpin the power of the child as citizen. In the UK for quite some time children have been 'denied the learning experiences which are fundamental to the development of a sense of personal autonomy and in that way are being denied their rights to education in its most significant and fundamental form' (John 1995, p.122). Many young people have exercised their autonomy in the face of such control by truanting or behaving in such a way at school that they are excluded. While the development of empowerment goes well beyond the child's experiences in school, the school itself mirrors a model of power which is controlling and to many young people quite aversive.

A distinction can be made, which has some resonances with Lukes' approach, between 'invested' power and 'divested' power (John and Griffith, 1994). Rhys Griffith argues that:

> An invested power system is hierarchical, linear and competitive. All traditional institutions conform to this model: from the armed forces, to commerce and industry, to economic trading and banking, to education, to the process of Parliamentary government itself. It is a system that rewards individual success, the rewards being social prestige and economic status. (Griffith 1996, p.214)

He points to the membership processes of invested power being steeped in ritual, initiation ceremonies, dress codes, terms of address, all of which can be seen in various forms within the educational system. Language also plays a part in invested power, 'a language that obscures processes, that sanitises, that depersonalises... Children are referred to as the point-of-delivery consumer in the educational process. It is the language of suave intimidation impelled by a determination to protect its power' (Griffith 1996, pp.214–15). He sees the stakeholders of invested power in the UK as including the Conservative government (as it was then), the right-wing establishment and the upper and white middle classes.

Divested power is seen on the other hand as being the form of power that fits most closely with personal empowerment, as realities are open for negotiation rather than fixed. 'Divested power is characterised by being corporate and distributive in that it diffuses and gives to the periphery with an organic, regenerative and dynamic view of society that regards change and celebrates diversity' (Griffith 1996, p.215). This sort of power is based on an ethical rather than an economic democracy, is non-hierarchical, based on participation in citizenship in an open society enthusiastically embraced as changing, adapting, growing and transforming. Such power is manifest in a society which has an infinite number of interdependent, interactive collaborative and co-operative communities. The transformation of power seen in this model involves a change not in the balance of power, but rather the nature of it from invested power to divested power. This transformation, rather than the transfer of power frees the stakeholders of invested power as much as everyone else. The most notable example of this sort of transformation of power was provided by Nelson Mandela becoming President in South Africa. He wanted not merely a transfer of the invested power from the National Party, but a transformation of that power so that no socio-political faction, including the white minority, would feel dispossessed. 'A great gift of Africa to humankind has been to make manifest the healing powers of magnanimity. Like Mahatma Gandhi earlier, so Nelson Mandela today towers as an inspiration' (Chambers 1997, p.235). Robert Chambers takes up this theme in looking at strategies and tactics for change.

> Personal change is a minefield, the subject of much evangelism, mythology, popular writing, and psychological and managerial lore. It is value-laden. It concerns what sort of people we are and become: closed or open, fearful or secure, callous or caring, hating or tolerant, violent or peacemaking. It raises the question: whose values count? Do we, the relatively powerful have an obligation to enable the lowers to express their values, to question and doubt our own, and to discuss them with others who differ? (Chambers 1997, pp.232–3)

Experiences from Participatory Rural Appraisal (PRA), widely used by non-governmental organisations (NGOs) in developing countries, have, he suggests, indicated practical thrusts to strategies and tactics for change, to which he has added his own: 'Transform through children' (p.233). He believes that family relationships of adults and children are hugely formative.

Those who are violent and intolerant as adults are often those against whom violence was done when they were young and defenceless: Hitler, Stalin and Ceausescu all endured gross violent abuses as children (Miller 1991). It is odd that the treatment of children by their parents is not a matter of massive global public concern, analysis, critical learning and sharing; that organisations like UNICEF and PLAN International, so committed to children do not make it more of a priority. (Chambers 1997, p.233)

These children are the victims of an invested power system. Transforming power involves confronting issues of power and differs from activities associated with altruism or generosity, Chambers suggests, as in such cases the hierarchy remains with the 'first' still first and the 'uppers' still uppers. The framework of power has not been changed by isolated activities. Putting the last first is an altogether more radical activity in that it involves a significant step down by the uppers, which we may see here as adults, disempowering themselves to empower others, such as children. The crux of the issue, and possibly the resistance to it, is that 'the uppers' have to give up something and make themselves vulnerable, i.e. the powerful have to let go and 'lose' something. Taking divested power approach, this does not involve loss of power so much as a renegotiation of the nature of it so that everybody's view counts. Chambers sees that people differ in the ease or difficulty with which they can achieve such a transformation. Some who have been brought up under very authoritarian regimes, who stand to attention and expect the same from others, 'who are given to lecturing and wagging the finger, find participation hard' (p.232). Chambers puts the case for divestment of power as gain. The disempowerment I have described in the interests of reciprocal understanding and power sharing embodies the 'fourth P' as I have chosen to use it here and is a step along the road to the indomitability I wish to see as a characteristic celebrated in all children.

POWERLESSNESS

One could argue that being totally ignored is the ultimate in powerlessness; it means one does not count, that one's existence is immaterial – it is as if you were not just a 'lower' but not even a person. This can be done at a collective as well as an individual level. Some writers suggest that in such circumstances 'ego-adaptive' responses are collectively developed, which are not particularly adaptive for society as a whole. 'The illusion of power is maintained not just by simplification but by unawareness and silence' (Rowe 1991, p.166). Interestingly enough, the timeless essay on 'The Power of the Powerless' by Vaclav Havel makes clear that it was attempts to control the freedom of the young that started to move the avalanche of change in a whole society at a particular point in history (Havel 1986). Before the peaceful revolution in the then Czechoslovakia that transformed him into president, Havel was the country's most important playwright and dissident, 'the laureate of the samizdat'. He suggests, using all his literary skills persuasively, that 'an examination of the potential of the "powerless" – can only begin with an examination of the nature of power in the circumstances in which these powerless people operate' (Havel 1986, p.36). He talks of the need there was in what he dubs a 'post totalitarian regime' (not using this term to indicate that it was over but rather using it to describe a particular form of it) to live within a lie in order to make life possible. He points out the great crisis of identity that it brought about. He says something that is as true today as it was then.

> A person who has been seduced by the consumer value system, whose identity is dissolved in an amalgam of the accoutrements of mass civilisation, and who has no roots in the order of being, no sense of responsibility for anything higher than his or her own personal survival, is a *demoralised* person. (Havel 1986, p.62)

The resonances with many children's lives are painfully clear. He went on to point out that the system, as it was being experienced then in Czechoslovakia, depended on such demoralisation and indeed deepened it and was a projection of it into society. There are painful echoes in many places in the developing world, and indeed in the developed world, of this sort of demoralisation and of the emphasis on *personal* survival in the rentier and stakeholder societies said to characterise much of the modern developed world (Hutton 1995, 1999). It is among the young that this fragmentation is experienced most keenly and lived out most dramatically. There are arguably shades of the 'anomie' detected by Durkheim many years ago (Durkheim 1952). Young people and children, as we see in Chapter 3, are often regarded as 'unpeople', powerless, anonymous – or maybe too 'dangerous' and threatening to be admitted to consciousness as *people*.

In 1990, the journalist John Pilger, evaluating the changes in Europe, referred to the time when he interviewed many of the Charter 77 people not long after the organisation had been driven underground. He was impressed by their courage in seeking democratic forms of their own. 'They knew that, just as socialism had been subverted in their own country, so democracy had been devalued and often degraded in the West.' He was reminded: 'The American sage, Walter Lippman, cited by Noam Chomsky, called this "manufacture of consent" and warned that such "false consensus" could render a free society passive and obedient' (Pilger 1990). Comparisons between the 'free' West and totalitarian regimes had bred a sort of complacency that was further jolted when the banned Czech writer Zdener Urbanak told Pilger: 'You in the West have a problem. You are unsure when you are being lied to, when you are being tricked. We do not suffer from this and unlike you, we have acquired the skill of reading between the lines' (Pilger 1990).

Havel goes on to recount how the climate leading to the appearance of Charter 77, which first brought about the crack in the system leading to its collapse, was provided not, as one would expect, by an immediate political event as such but by the oppression of *young people*. For many, the trial of 'The Plastic People of the Universe', a young rock group, represented the final straw of having to put up with the regime, the end of scepticism and apathy about various forms of resistance, the end of having to live 'within a lie'.

> Many groups of differing tendencies which until then had remained isolated from each other, reluctant to co-operate, or which were committed to forms of action that made co-operation difficult, were suddenly struck by the powerful realisation that freedom is indivisible… The freedom to play rock music was understood as a human freedom and thus as essentially the same as freedom to engage in philosophical and political reflection, the freedom to write, the freedom to express and defend various social and political interests of society. People were inspired to feel a genuine sense of solidarity with the young musicians and they came to realise that not standing up for the freedom of others, regardless of how remote their means of creativity or their attitude to life, meant surrendering one's own freedom. (Havel 1986, p.64)

The protection of individuality, of the freedom to be young and to have good times provided a rallying point for *all* ideas of freedom. The young people were acknowledged as people – like everyone else and not to be ignored. One can contrast that with the curfew on young people recently mooted in our 'democratic' society by the Blair government. What does this signify to us about how young people are viewed in the UK at the present time? Have young people been excluded from political significance? Why do they even acknowledge that themselves by showing very little interest in conventional politics? Why do their oppressions no longer signify to the rest of us a *general* curtailment of freedom? Why do we, in the UK, claim to want to clear the cardboard cities off the streets, the sleepers from the night-time doorways and the itinerant young beggars from their pitches, yet have so little understanding of the powerlessness of the young? It may be that minority rights groups are good at rabble-rousing but not at inclusion – the inclusion of the young in their perspective on oppression. One suspects the NGO campaigns relate more to preserving their own authority and advocacy than to the interests of those they presume to represent.

It seems in the UK, having no-one left to legitimately persecute (as women, ethnic minorities, disabled people and religious groups all have state protection), oppression finds another outlet in the treatment of the most vulnerable and least protected of all – children. This is now further evidenced in the discovery, on a fairly regular basis, of abusive paedophile rings on a wide international scale. Children are still the only members of UK society that it is acceptable to hit. Recent proposals to make Scotland the first place in the UK where it would be illegal to hit children under the age of three were dropped on the grounds that it would be unenforceable. Sweden has had an effective ban since 1979 and ten countries in Europe also have bans so such an excuse is not plausible.

The oppressions and powerlessness that young people experience can become so internalised that a young person can start to actually believe himself/herself to be worthless and meaningless. In recognition of this, various educators have adapted teaching techniques to avoid such an outcome (Griffith 1996, 1998). Freire insisted that the oppressed should engage in concrete reflection on their situation (Freire 1970, p.41). This was not to be by the shoulder-shrugging of the 'as if' referred to in Chapter 1, but rather by entering collectively into a liberating dialogue, which provides a possibility for the transformation of action and in so doing transforms the nature of power itself. Augusto Boal, following this line of thinking in working with villagers in Brazil, developed the 'Theater of the Oppressed' and by this means provided these villagers living in a brutal military regime with a way of reflecting on their situation and effecting social change (Boal 1974, 1992). Similar work has been done in engaging with the counter-culture around issues of oppression, including children's rights, by La Mancha Theatre Company in Chile – a photograph from one of their productions forms the cover of this book. Thinking about children and young people as a minority rights group – 'the oppressed' – and the means by which society can ensure that the voices of young people are heard and contribute to social change are examined throughout this book, as is the question of why are children and young people so excluded for it to be realistic to regard them as 'oppressed' by the societies they live in.

RECOGNISING DIRECT EXPERIENCE

The insights and experiences of other minority rights groups are helpful in looking at children's oppression and at ways of involving them in decision making that affects their lives. Minority rights groups see that the first step towards recognition is to gain acknowledgement that one's experiences are not just personal but are characteristic of the marginalised *group* to which one belongs. It is this move from personal experience to a group identity, an understanding of a common lot, that is possibly the first stage in bringing about change. Unlike other minority rights groups this is probably difficult for children as a group, yet identifying this commonality of experience is crucial. Constantina Safilios-Rothschild, in a seminal piece about the situation of disabled people (a situation which, in these respects, has changed little in the last 30 years), has the following observations to make.

> There is an acknowledged paucity of direct information concerning the feelings, wishes and self-definitions of underprivileged minority groups. Yet, without gathering sufficient direct information from their target populations, professionals assume the authority to decide the fate of underprivileged persons... In the case of the disabled, just as it is true for other underprivileged groups, different professionals connected with rehabilitation define the self-concepts, goals, and inner

motivations of disabled people and determine their 'real' wishes and potential. They often do so either without asking the individuals about their problems, preferred solutions, and alternatives or by openly disregarding all information received from the disabled persons themselves about desirable goals and solutions. (Safilios-Rothschild 1970, pp.141–152 and pp.216–249)

Many children indicate quite clearly that they feel oppressed – the cardinal characteristic of which is that they are ignored, treated as if they were not there by the passive aggression of not being recognised as a person, not counted, being meaningless and being overlooked. In Chapter 1, 'children's rights' were defined as being treated as a person in all domains that matter. The major axes on which rights are examined in this volume are personhood and power. Children and young people are excluded by disregard and failure to value their personhood and the nature and meaning of their lived experiences. Sensitivity to the meanings that children give to their own lives and their own distinct aspirations is important. It is commonly the case that they have their needs and requirements defined by educators, professionals, policy makers, etc., in ways similar to disabled people. In providing services for disabled people, often the takeover of a person's life is justified by implicit assumptions of deficits or biological inferiority lying behind what the professional defines as the person's needs. In the case of children, particularly the very young, the same deficit approach, translating needs into deficits, has coloured the perception of children as not yet competent to make appropriate decisions about their lives or indeed process their experiences meaningfully. In 1995 Jerome Bruner visited Reggio Emilia in Italy to see its world-famous preschools. He said that he was immediately struck by the way the activities there honoured and cultivated the richness of young children's imaginations and empowered their sense of what is possible. This work in Italy has now been shared with many outside the country, thanks to visits and its touring exhibition. In all of that work the children themselves defined their own realities.

> The first thing I sensed in these pre-schools was respect for human beings – whether they were children, teachers, parents, or the community at large. The most profound way in which respect between human beings shows itself is by taking to heart, taking seriously the meanings that each of us

> seeks to create from our experience of the world: the world of things and of people alike. The truest courtesy in human interaction, and in pedagogy (which after all is just an extension of such interaction) is to help others discover what their experiences mean in their minds and hearts. And then help them find richer, fuller, more communicable meanings. (Bruner 1996, p.115)

The importance of recognising direct experience and the need to guard against children being encouraged to map onto stereotypes rather than value their own view of the world seem obvious but, as yet, have not informed practice as extensively as they should have done.

Experience: the psychologists' 'blind spot'

The recognition of personal experience does not necessarily provide the ready currency of psychological study. Far from it – yet, if psychology is to offer some possibility of social change, how is this to be achieved if experience is not to be admitted as legitimate data?

> After all it is not for academics to decide what the problems of working-class people, of women, of black people, of children might be. Rather it is for the academic to find out about and respond to the issues as experienced by such groups themselves (Parker and Spears 1996; Stanley 1990). If our assumptions and our pedagogy allow no space for the expression of the only data that might clue us in to our collective sickness of soul, the repressive tolerance that masquerades as freedom of speech wins out and there can be no reconstruction of psychology as a practice of emancipation. (Bradley 1998, p.69)

In an engaging essay in a collection on *Reconstructing the Psychological Subject* (Bayer and Shotter 1998), Ben Bradley looks at the complex background to this point by making a case that it has been the denial of mind within the intellectual discipline of psychology that has threatened to rob it of any potential utility. In 1969, George A. Miller had raised all our hopes in his much quoted and, as it turned out, over-optimistic theme of his Presidential Address to the American Psychological Association entitled 'Psychology as a Means of Promoting Human Welfare' (Miller 1969). Ingleby has already sown seeds of doubt in our minds about whether the discipline is indeed benevolent.

Bradley exposes the difficulties we would be placed in if we were to deny the relevance of experience altogether. He points out that while behaviourism has given way to the development of psychology as a 'science' in the growth of cognitive psychology and artificial intelligence, this has contributed to the emergence, in his view, of a new orthodoxy. This orthodoxy, he suggests, has further marginalised experience and mental life, this time by the computer modelling of processes that give rise to the capacities that are supposed to frame human behaviour.

Even those coming from a different perspective and putting forward notions of social constructivism also, according to Bradley, exclude mind. He argues that it is this denial of mind that preserves psychology in its present form and prevents it having its full social utility. It could be argued that this has meant that few psychologists have been so active in the field of children's rights as to understand thoroughly the issues one has to address in order to recognise the importance of children's own experiences of the world. He suggests that such is the adherence of traditional psychology to the status quo that students in a typical degree course in psychology are '...unlikely to learn anything that obliges them to think seriously about poverty, alienation, domestic violence, war, starvation or ecological destruction' (Bradley 1998, p.70), all of which profoundly affect children in the global context.

Bradley puts forward three grounds for such a shocking state of affairs. He first describes the dominant hold within developmental psychology of what is known by philosophers as the 'genetic fallacy'. This anchors present life in individual past histories – that is, in what has *already happened* rather than in the meaning and significance of the present and what is still to be.

> Human development is not some change that needs to be collectively struggled for in the here and now. It is something idealised that has always already been fixed by history, in the dim evolutionary conjecture, at the masqued ball of eggs with sperm, in a blooming, buzzing confusion of statements about 'the child'. (Bradley 1998, p.70)

Second, and directly related to this epistemological framework, is the cult of the 'expert'. This emphasises that psychological knowledge must be grounded in procedures which distance the knower from the subject matter under investigation. The search for objectivity has also traditionally dictated that knowledge must be value free. 'We are increasingly reminded that science is a form of transcendence involving a flight from the uncertainties prompted by cultural difference' (Bradley 1998, p.70). The extent to which such a position is tenable in relation to the science of mental life is highly questionable. In no other science does the subject matter under investigation share so many of the same characteristics as those of the investigator. Bradley claims that psychologists have worked hard at maintaining a distance between themselves and the objects of enquiry – so much so that the discipline is widely regarded as a natural science by those outside the discipline and by many within it. He asserts that it is necessary to understand how this separation of psychologists from their subject matter came about before one can consider ways of changing the discipline. He then gives a cogent account of how this came about (pp.71–84) in which the issue of time in developmental explanation is important and which I will examine shortly.

Returning to the reasons he posits for psychology's indifference to social problems, his third suggestion is the commonly held idea that it is possible for psychology to be lived, taught and researched without reference to the dynamics of personal experience. This he claims is true for the teacher, student or the subject even though in much of the work the nature of personal experience must form a central part of private self-understanding. George Devereux some time ago attempted a reconstruction of the behavioural sciences, which acknowledges this element as central (Devereux 1968). He used the psychoanalytic concept of counter-transference. His position is to see that the anxieties, discomfort, fantasies and feelings aroused in the researcher by their research with other people, far from being discounted or denied, should form the pivot of their understanding of the nature of psychology.

In a now-classic critique of traditional psychology that laid down the foundations of critical and feminist psychology, psychologists were entreated to rethink the fundamental assumptions that operate across psychology. In the first edition of *Changing the Subject: Psychology, Social Regulattion and Subjectivity* (Henriques, Holloway, Urwin, *et al.* 1984) the goal was the understanding of subjectivity, which recognises the complex effects of power on the formation of an individual's sense of identity and agency. The authors, picking up on the central dynamics of the work that had been done in intersubjectivity and reciprocity in the previous decade, appealed to psychologists to abandon individual–society

dualisms and the reductionisms affiliated to such schisms and to acknowledge various forms of subjectivities.

Returning to Bradley's argument, it provides some insight into why,
in the past, there has been a near absence of psychologists in work on
children's rights. Such work must be fed and informed by the
subjectivities and experiences of this last minority rights group to be
seen as an 'oppressed' group. Children's experiences have to be valued
'as if' they mattered. Therefore the power of a discipline which might
reasonably have been expected to have ameliorated children's lot has
rarely been brought to bear on the situation of the young and the nature
of their lives as experienced and made meaningful by them. He points
out that it has taken decades of struggles by feminists to persuade developmental psychologists that children widely suffer oppression and
abuse.

> What is the subject-position psychologists traditionally adopt
> that has allowed them to conduct countless pieces of research
> on children, and to spend countless hours assessing and
> therapeutizing the old and the young, without finding out
> about incest or the prevalence of domestic violence in con-
> temporary society, now described as an 'epidemic' by the
> American Medical Association (Gilligan 1994)? (Bradley
> 1998, p.88)

THE 'GENETIC FALLACY': AN OBSTACLE TO UNDERSTANDING OPPRESSION

The successes of evolutionary explanation in biology are claimed by
Bradley to have encouraged developmental psychologists to overlook
what is commonly believed in psychology, which is that we must live
forwards but understand backwards, and led them to commit a version
of what is called the 'genetic fallacy' by philosophers. This fallacy is explained as allowing the question 'How come?' to pre-empt the question
'What?'. This is interesting in any consideration of the nature of power
and, as part of that, oppression. It presupposes that the power of knowledge can be explained away, obliterated or justified by a descriptive account of its history. In scientific terms this would be illustrated by the
way in which scientists might explain how they came to a particular
conclusion and indeed the force of it by describing in precise detail the
procedures they used to arrive at such a view. On a similar basis a

particular argument might be called into question by a social constructivist on account of its historical pedigree. Gergen (1985) has argued this in analysis of the social constructionist movement in psychology citing the arguments Lavine (1962) put forward some 20 years earlier.

The importance of the genetic fallacy to our concerns in this book about children and power is that the fallacy inclines people to forget that the absolute primary and immediate significance, value and meaning of an event has no necessary connection with its causal explanation or its historical origins. How it is being experienced now, how it is being understood, how it is being interpreted reflexively to oneself, what its implications are and the importance attached to that event in relation to the future are what really matter. Bradley continues to develop his analysis of the genetic fallacy by looking at the particular form that it has taken in psychology, which, simply stated, has been that the analysis of an experience's chronology and its origin takes the place of the analysis of the experience itself. This, claims Bradley, is erroneous, as one cannot judge the developmental significance of something until it is in its grown form. This immediately leads us into difficulties when we are dealing with children as frequently their experiences are not accepted as meaningful and significant *even to them*; since they are seen as 'not yet' adults, their world is seen as provisional only and there seems to be no need to take it too seriously. There is low value attached to the child's epistemologies because of their transience. As a result of this approach, what gets lost are the many challenges which have to be addressed in understanding the present in its own right. Bradley contrasts the genetic conception of developmental time with a view which emphasises the way one can see that the meaning of the present depends on what is *yet* to happen.

The meaning that is given to the past arises from the dynamics of the present and even our understanding of today is coloured by our aspirations, hopes, forebodings or whatever of the future. This influences how we value and perceive the past as, if we are deeply discontent with the present, we are likely to have a dim view of the past and want things in the future to change considerably.

THE PSYCHOLOGIST AS AN ALLY IN LIBERATION FROM OPPRESSION

Children's rights are often seen within a developmental framework made up of discrete stages and competencies. Priscilla Alderson explains the scourge of developmentalism in children's rights, explaining how thinking in this way has often led to younger children being excluded from the rights discussions (Alderson 2000). Children's present experiences must be recognised and the child's development understood within the immediate complex interplay of cultural discourses, emotional democracies and the fundamentals of reciprocal respects and tolerances. This context is required for rights to manifest themselves in citizenship behaviours.

Bradley's exposition alerts us to the fact that there are two ways of talking about psychological change, both ways having clear traditions within that discipline. One form is to see personal change as something happening to an individual according to a predetermined plan, an unfolding of an already prescribed developmental sequence. The alternative view, which in some senses has formed the motivation for my book, is of change as something which might be striven for collectively in the present with a view to transforming the future. Changing the relationships between children and adults in the present transforms power relationships between them as the adults they later become and with children in the future.

It has been largely the case, states Bradley, that developmental psychology has been dominated by a view of change, as it applies to individuals, that is fixed in the past. He argues in contrast for a view of psychology as an 'emancipatory discipline that fosters collective development arising out of an analysis of the often oppressive dynamics of the present' (Bradley 1998, p.88) and he goes on to ponder further the reasons why psychologists have been so deaf and insensitive, in his view, to the way people feel and are treated. His arguments are especially important to any consideration of children's rights and the power that children have in their daily lives, the extent to which their views are taken seriously and their own ability to bring about changes on the basis of their position in society.

There are signs that the discipline is starting to reform itself in setting out the conditions for a radical approach to the psychology of human development. Central in this was the formation in 1994 of a new body 'Psychology, Politics, Resistance' (Reicher 1996; Reicher and Parker 1993). This had the aim of persuading both individual psychologists and organisations to adopt active opposition to exploitation and oppression as a central aspect of their work and, in particular, to emphasise such considerations in the education of all psychologists. It follows, says Bradley, that if we organise a space to hear the voices of the oppressed in psychology the matter cannot simply be left there. The logical consequence of hearing the voices of the silenced is that the psychologist then has to confront the task of taking up the social and political implications of the oppressions they learn about in such work. This means hearing the experiences of children, truly understanding the world from their point of view, then campaigning for the necessary social changes that will make those children's lives more bearable and fulfilling. The fact that so few psychologists have been involved – other than in a developmental way – in the social and political contingent activities of working in the field of children's rights within the paradigm, which Bradley outlines, has had something to do with a reluctance to handle the meanings of experience to children themselves, which is a prerequisite for such an approach. It is a matter of the change of focus and perspective. 'That which we call "development" when looked at from the birth end of life becomes senescence when looked at from its close' (Medawar 1957).

NEW PARADIGMS OF EMPOWERMENT

There have been three major influences on my own research in children's rights which have fed into my thinking about new paradigms of empowerment in various ways. I say 'thinking' because, if the truth be told, there are no real well-established paradigms that can be reliably used in children's rights enquiry and development. The challenge for the psychologist in this new century is to find ways of incorporating children's experiences in studies, to engage them as co-researchers and to enter their worlds which will mean a rethinking of the discipline, as in this area it hovers between a science of relationships and relationships themselves almost as a new art form. I would argue, therefore, that I cannot be definitive about new paradigms but can only explain the route I have taken to arrive at the position I hold.

One of the influences goes back to the early 1960s when I was trained in what might be termed the 'Newson School' of developmental research with John and Elizabeth Newson. They first alerted me to the power of the infant in the effects it had upon its caregiver in the elaborate dance of intersubjectivity. (Newson, 1977) They also demonstrated to me that suspicion of 'official' versions of events was wise and that the real experts were the subjects themselves. They did this by interviewing, in ingenious ways, mothers themselves about their child-rearing practices, asking them directly about their experiences and their views (Newson and Newson, 1963, 1968, 1976). This yielded a different picture from that gathered by health visitors and other representatives of officialdom. Valuing direct experience of the world, investigating how individuals make it meaningful to themselves and the influences there are on these interpretative activities shaped my later approach to research and work with minority rights groups. While much of the Newsons' work was empirical, John Shotter, working in the same 'stable', further amplified the theoretical framework. His work underwent a considerable change in the late 1960s to form his 'new psychology', characterised as 'radical humanism' (Henriques *et al.* 1998). He was critical, as were many of his contemporaries, of an attempt to build a psychology upon methods and concepts from the social sciences (Bayer and Shotter 1998). Shotter's influences in providing a basis for the understanding of the social construction of individuals included G.H. Mead's (1934) theory of the social construction of self through the internalisation of the understanding of human behaviour and Vygotsky's (1962) views on the formation of human consciousness.

The belief that this approach was limited was expounded in the previously quoted groundbreaking book – *Changing the Subject* by Henriques *et al.* (1984) – which spoke to me as one of the converted. The limitations to Shotter's approach as the basis for understanding the social construction of individuals were primarily methodological rather than theoretical. They felt that Shotter's approach had been a substantial influence in and informed by empirical studies of mother–child communication (Newson 1977, 1978; Schaffer 1977). This in itself, while valuable, has its dangers in translating 'social' into 'intersubjectivity'. The methodological problem, it is argued, lies in the implied dichotomy between the individual and the social – questions being asked about what the infant is like before it becomes social (Henriques *et al.* 1984). Moreover the 'social' is construed as entirely personal. Trevarthen (1975, 1979), an early influence on my thinking as I indicated in

Chapter 1, unlike Shotter, views intersubjectivity as a biological capacity inherent in infants, which the supportive mother elicits. Later Trevarthen reframed this innate intersubjectivity with innate 'motives' (1982).

It is the concept of a uniquely pre-given subject and individual–social dualism which have acted as obstacles to theorising subjectivity, which starts with the recognition of individual experience that I welcomed in the appearance of *Changing the Subject* (Henriques *et al.* 1984). It addresses problems we were all struggling with then. They picked up on the theme of power, making it quite explicit how, in order to understand subjectivity (which we must if we are to value direct experience in the way I have just argued is essential), the complex effects of power for subject formation have to be registered. This recognition 'thus enables historically subordinated groups to challenge the authority of the discourses that legitimate oppressive practices' (Henriques *et al.* 1984, p.3). This book provided a review of traditional psychology that had informed critical and feminist psychology. It pleaded with psychologists to question their assumptions which shaped much of psychology and to abandon individual–society dualisms and the associated reductionisms. The book received great acclaim and marked a landmark in the field influencing, by its punning title, a rethinking of the nature of the human subject of research enquiries. The child was constructed not just in intersubjectivities but also within the broader base of power relations within a wide social context. This took us beyond individual interactions to the culture and the politics of the child's social context. In *The Political Life of Children*, Robert Coles (1986) argues that a nation's politics become a child's everyday psychology. Walkerdine, in the *Changing the Subject* collection, argues that one of the major problems with the notion of developmental psychology as implicated in a pedagogy of liberation is in the way the terms of the argument are posed.

> What I aim to demonstrate is that the very lynchpin of developmental psychology 'the developing child', is an object premised on the location of certain capacities within 'the child' and therefore within the domains of psychology... Because of the way that the object of a developmental psychology is formulated, it is impossible to produce the radical theory which would fulfil the hopes of the discipline. (Walkerdine 1984, p.154)

Walkerdine went on to host a number of exploratory seminars leading to a series of publications on radical psychology. Psychologists are not the only culprits in inappropriate ways of construing the child. After an investigation in Cleveland in the UK into the handling of allegations of wide-scale child abuse, fixed ideas held by professionals as to what was in the child's 'best interests' disregarded the views and wishes of the children themselves. It is interesting that it should have been the judge leading the inquiry who warned professionals – social workers, doctors etc. – that children should not be treated as 'objects of concern' (Butler -Sloss 1988). Some sociologists have continued to complain about work with children, failing to take account of what they regard as meaningful and significant experiences, their role being merely as 'objects of study' (James and Prout 1990; Mayall 1994a). In psychology, investigations have frequently been on children rather than with them. Malcolm Hill (1996, p.129) remarks, 'Observational studies have produced many fascinating insights, but often the voices and views of children are surprisingly muted even in accounts of social development (for example, McGurk 1992)'. While there has been an emphasis on recognising children's active role and their own insight in making their worlds meaningful and comprehensible to themselves (Woodhead, Light and Carr 1991), nevertheless children's views tend to be seen rather as milestones on the developmental journey rather than a recognition of their life in the present.

Therefore, in searching around trying to find new paradigms of empowerment, it is important to look beyond psychology and indeed, as I have done already, question some of the assumptions of psychologists. A possible route was proposed by a paper by Yvonne Lincoln – on voice. The approach she outlined involved facilitating marginalised groups in voicing their concerns – not speaking for them, but working towards the release of their own views on matters on which they had direct experience. Lincoln's work had been one of the ways in which the issues raised in the first edition of *Changing the Subject* (Henriques *et al.* 1984), while not explicitly accountable to that body of writing, picked up on the climate in the research community. She explored new ways of construing the subject in enquiries and of representing that subject. In an attempt to consolidate the accumulating work in qualitative research, Denzin and Lincoln (1994) edited a collection of papers to provide a *Handbook of Qualitative Research*, which was to become the sacred book for many researchers from a whole variety of disciplines trying to get close to authentic representations of individuals in the social and political world they inhabited.

In their introduction to this handbook they observed that over the previous two decades a quiet methodological revolution had been occuring in the social sciences and that disciplinary boundaries were becoming increasingly blurred. A common focus on an interpretive and qualitative approach to research and theory, they felt, was drawing the social sciences and humanities closer together.

The handbook has now been reissued as a second edition (Denzin and Lincoln 2000). They observe that there is still a need to demonstrate that the practices of qualitative research can change the world in positive ways. Remarkably, even in this new weighty volume, children do not appear in the index and their part in the research process is given scant attention. They claim that at the beginning of the twenty-first century the promise of qualitative research should be 're-engaged as a form of radical democratic practice' (Denzin and Lincoln 2000, p.x). Among the innovations in methods they suggest are developments in reflexivity, multiple voicing, literary styling, performance, reframing validity, situated knowledge and rhetorical/political deliberations.

Changing the Subject also came out as a second edition some 14 years after the appearance of the original collection (Henriques *et al.* 1998). This also caused the authors to reflect on what had been happening to this transformative approach. They felt that in the intervening period the problem of identity and subjectivity had become even more urgent. The authorial team still felt very committed to challenging and changing the way the subject is understood and in this they do include children. What has changed, however, is the way they now engage with these problems and the contexts in which they operate. They stress that despite onslaughts from a number of quarters, notions of the single unitary subject still survive, informing assumptions that shape various dualisms. These dualisms they list as: 'social and cognitive; content and process; the intentionality of agents as opposed to determination by structures; the subject as constituted or constitutive' (Henriques *et al.* 1998, p.ix). The original intention of the book was to push for the recognition of the complexity of the relation between culture and the psyche in the production of subjectivity and identity. This theme, they felt, more than a decade after the appearance of the original volume, still needed to be emphasised. Research on children's power and the exercise of their rights cannot be blind to issues encompassed by this theme. In the intervening period the world has become, in their view, increasingly globalised 'in which everything has been speeded up, with the insistent push of technology compressing time and space' (Giddens 1990; Harvey 1989). Although some accounts of these processes have been put forward using cultural theory and sociology, they have not been engaged with identifying the processes and dynamics that constitute particular subjectivities or how those particular subjectivities manifest themselves in life in the form of particular personalities or selves. This is what, the authors claim, one would have expected to be the domain of social and developmental psychology.

I had thought I would be able to find, amid these influences on my research and thinking, some way forward by using 'radical democratic practices' while working with children on power and powerlessness. I had hoped that there would be ways of working with children where the research itself became a source of empowerment. In fact there was little to be found in the immensely complex language of constructing subjectivities and exploring qualitative research that could be harnessed to my purposes. Yvonne Lincoln's approach to facilitating the expression of marginalised individuals' understanding of the social world provided one possibility. Participation in decision-making processes has also, in practice, proved to be a way in which the child's view of the world is explored and incorporated in action. Similarly, autobiography has been used in various ways; notably material prepared for the UN Summit on Children in 2001 (Save the Children 2001) has tried to incorporate children's stories about their lives in informing views of children's realities.

Accessing children's worlds in authentic ways has called for ingenuity and skill. Their world has partly come to us via creative research techniques such as those described in Chapter 6 with child workers. There has been a variety of relevant work in the UK on listening, including Barnardo's monograph on *Listening to Children*, currently being revised, which has also provided useful guidelines for research work with children facilitating the exploration of their views (Alderson 1995). Ann O'Quigley's (2000) summary of findings and recommendations of recent research on listening to children's views, produced for the Lord Chancellor's Advisory Board on Family Law, points out that children are not used to being listened to. It provides suggestions for facilitating the child's voicing in relation to court proceedings. These are but two examples of a growing body of work.

Morrow and Richards (1996), reflecting on the ethics of social research with children, made some suggestions as to a way forward in methodological and practical terms. They suggest:

> A more social-anthropological approach that allows data to be co-produced in the relationship between researcher and researched, rather than being driven by problem-oriented adult questions, may be useful in child research... Time is also of importance, and research projects need to be designed to allow a relationship to develop between researcher and the researched. Children are not used to being asked their opinions and to relate their experiences to unknown adults, and probably need to have some familiarity with the researcher. (Morrow and Richards 1996, p.101)

This seems fairly obvious *if* children are being treated with due respect as fellow citizens. Morrow and Richards give examples of anthropological research using ethnographic observations of children's daily lives and warn against over-reliance on one type of data. In keeping with the 'revolution' in qualitative method just described, they advocate using a variety of creative methods as ways of counteracting bias and further exacerbating the powerlessness of the child subject.

Within the discipline of sociology a discrete subdiscipline, 'a sociology of childhood', is emerging which has moved from a narrow focus on socialisation and child development 'to a sociology which attempts to take children seriously as they experience their lives in the here and now as children. However, as yet there has been little discussion within sociology of the ethical dilemmas that researching children raises' (Morrow and Richards 1996, p.92). This they feel contrasts with the increasing use of research ethics committees by developmental psychologists. I have already indicated the sources of the psychologists' discomfort while working with direct experience. Sociologists, for rather different reasons, had fewer empirical research studies based on data collected from children themselves, although this is rapidly changing and there are a few notable ones. Pressure to use participatory methods in the research process comes from developing countries where the difference in power relations between adult and child is often blurred since children are often important contributors to the family economy. Young people have also been used as research assistants and data collectors and in interpreting data in the way Judith Ennew has done in Lima and Jamaica. Sharing the research findings with the young people involved has often been a step that the researcher has skipped, revealing that the children were not fully participants. The ability to present the findings, possibly in several forms such that the young people can be involved, is crucial. Alternatively if the young people can be involved in presentations about it then they remain quite clearly stakeholders in the project. I was delighted that, although it took several years to publish the papers from the World Conference on Research and Practice in Children's Rights we held in Exeter in 1992, the Young People's Evaluation Panel who were intimately involved in that conference wrote the foreword to the first of the three volumes relating to that event (John 1996a).

Some accounts of children's activities recounted in this book will throw some light on how children themselves are challenging the received wisdom that they do not 'count' – children involved in Youth Councils; in the Children's Parliament in Rajasthan; as child soldiers and workers; as important consumers; as influential people in the media; in various local projects. These among other examples serve to illustrate in this book how, although the research community may not have turned its gaze upon them with sufficient interest and ingenuity, children themselves are exercising power and claiming their rights in ways which for some might be so threatening as to need to be ignored.

PART II

Children and the Economy

CHAPTER THREE

Counting

INTRODUCTION

Children may be rendered invisible not just because they are at the weak end of (invested) power relationships but by practices employed in collecting data about them and in the presentation of such data. I have argued that to acknowledge children's power it is necessary to ensure methods of research and enquiry are such that they tap into children's realities and lived experience. In the popular consciousness the starting point in trying to understand children's lives might seem to be gathering statistics about them. This is by no means straightforward, is not necessarily helpful and may not provide any insight whatsoever into children's lives. In this chapter I will explore the extent to which children do count. Just as language is important in underscoring the importance or otherwise of children in the social world, so too numbers play their part in establishing their place in the pecking order. I will therefore examine factors contributing to their disappearance in statistics and what helps to make them visible. I will go on to look at the challenges children face in remaining visibly alive and countable, by a consideration of nutrition, and finally I look at their visibility within the economy by homing in on poverty. Poverty influences directly and indirectly the children's ability to exercise their rights and operate powerfully in this new century.

COUNTED OR COUNTING
The invisibility of children in statistics

Even in child studies, children are sometimes invisible, as they are perceived as 'becoming adults'. Information is scattered because it is collected from the viewpoints of the family, the school, women's activities and opportunities, professional and/or bureaucratic interests etc., and is therefore adult-centred. The nature of children's representation in research and documentation thus becomes a significant token of the nature of children's participation in real life. Children's near absence in public statistics and social accounting signifies their lack of importance in the minds of authorities and adult society in general. A description of children that takes seriously their own life expressions might question the validity of conventional wisdom. (Qvortrup *et al.* 1995, p.1)

Children do feature prominently in population studies, particularly in the 'central triad' of mortality, migration and fertility. 'Estimates of child/infant mortality, fertility and family migration have been used to inform understanding of population growth, population projections and models of population change. Children have served population geography well...' (McKendrick 2001, p.470). Nevertheless, '...the population geography of childhood is a mirage, in that children are ever-present but never really there.'(p.461).

Collecting statistical information about children is no straightforward matter. There are many pitfalls in searching for data: where the data is sought; the choice of sources of information; the way the raw data is assembled and presented; the way raw data is converted into indices and indicators; the way that data is understood and compared with data from other contexts. Moreover, 'children' cannot be seen as a homogeneous group even when they share the same ethnic identity. Age, sex, culture and specific context are all important. However, as we shall see in the next chapter, commercial organisations that target children as consumers have taken the task of collecting childhood statistics very seriously. The accuracy of their data is vital to their marketing goals.

To build up a clear picture of children's lives at the beginning of this new century we have to plunder many sources and be guided by a whole variety of professionals such as statisticians, sociologists, demographers, campaigners, charity workers and investigative journalists. Even such interdisciplinary data is not enough. The best possible informants are children themselves but they are all too often not consulted. Slowly a picture is emerging which displays children as one of the most neglected of the world's many minorities. Even the childless Virginia Woolf uses one of her pieces to comment wryly on what awful lives children live and not only that, but on the fact that they can't tell anybody about how awful their lives are (Woolf 1937, p.129).

It is largely true that until recently they have not been able to 'tell' anybody – nor has anyone had the information, both of the collective picture and at the level of individual experience, to act as their informed advocate. Moreover, while statistics may offer some initial glimpse of the situation, statistics in themselves are not meaningful enough to point to solutions to the problems that they sketch. In the papers that were prepared for the postponed UN Special Session on Children held eventually in New York in May 2002, statistics were provided to underline why children matter. The last global meeting dedicated to children was the World Summit on Children in September 1990 at which more than 180 countries took part and signed a final declaration and Plan of Action. Following that Summit 155 countries drew up national programmes aimed at ensuring the survival, protection and development of children. The pressure that has been mounting since that World Summit has provided a deeply troubling statistical picture, even with all the shortcomings of that sort of data, of the state of the world's children. They are now said to make up 40 per cent of the world's population, which amounts to the largest generation of children there has been at any time in history. Hair-raising statistics were provided illustrating 'A World Unfit for Children', on child soldiers, child labour, child poverty, health, education and overseas aid (Save the Children 2001).

The numbers given by Save the Children, alarming as they were, were probably a very conservative estimate of the actual statistics for reasons I examine below. One can also question how useful this picture is in working towards ameliorating the situations these figures seem to circumscribe.

Even when relevant numbers are sought or quarried out of the available data, numbers alone do not speak for themselves. In many ways the scale of a problem does not define its unacceptability. Whether there are 10 or 10,000 children dying of malnutrition, from each of these children's points of view the situation is equally terrible. Numbers do not 'tell' anybody how awful it is for the individual child. Ten terminally malnourished children are ten too many. More does not make it more important but rather locates the problem and perhaps points to systematic causal factors. It is therefore essential to realise that the size of the problem does not change the qualitative nature of it except where there are simple linear resource allocation issues. A large number of children become visible when there are resources to be shared but then, if there are a large number of them, there may be less food to go round, changing the nature of the experience by competing demands upon resources. One of the fundamental problems about looking for statistics in order to get a glimpse of what the world of the child might be like is that mere numbers distort the child's world in a further way. What statistics often provide, even when they can be found, is a picture of the child's needs, and baseline needs at that, rather than his/her aspirations. They therefore tend to be negative in their connotations about the child. When basic survival is at stake they may be important in pleading for resources but beyond that the world of the child is actually more than a simple list of deficits. There are needs for intervention which are not located in the child, however, but rather in the policies or accepted practices of a particular government. Statistics in this situation tell us something about how children are valued.

Foundations of statistical knowledge

In evaluating the degree of helpfulness or otherwise of statistics, the foundation of statistical knowledge as outlined by Saporiti (1997) is important to grasp. He teaches us that this is a three-stage process: first, there is the raw or untreated data which may be pure numerical indices; second, the treatment of this data may provide indexes (percentages and the like) such as to render the data comparable in terms of a scale or unit of measurement point of view; third, both raw data and indexes become indicators when they are attached to a positive or negative value. Adamson underscores this final point. 'All indicators are statements of values, carrying with them implicit messages about what is considered good or bad, positive or negative, to be encouraged or discouraged' (Adamson 1996, p.43). To this Saporiti added pointedly, 'they also carry with them the question of who is in charge to establish what is to be considered good or bad, positive or negative, encouraged or discouraged' (Saporiti 1997, p.305). Therefore indicators of this kind and statistics cannot, of themselves, be informative as they are interwoven with cultural, social and political factors.

First, looking at the way raw data may be collected, Angelo Saporiti, generalising from examples of the situation in Italy, demonstrates how misleading the picture of childhood is if the traditional ways of counting families and seeing children merely as an attribute of the family are used (Saporiti 1997). He points out that if the data collection is family oriented, children's lives are not captured in that sort of statistical accounting. For instance, he demonstrates that data collected from couples and one-parent families about the number of children they have might lead one to believe that 42.1 per cent of these families have only one child. This would imply that there are a very large number of Italian children (42.1%) who have no sibling to play with. If, however, the information is collected in a quite different and rather unusual, child-centred way by asking children how many brothers or sisters they have, we find that only 24.1 per cent of these children have no brothers/sisters. As Saporiti points out, this is a children-centred statistic in that it considers children as the unit of observation and so counts children as individuals in their own right (Saporiti 1997, pp.296–297).

Nevertheless Saporiti claims that children are still a long way from being 'recognised and considered as a social group deserving to be represented independently from their families' (Saporiti 1997, p.299). This situation has contributed to the invisibility of children and childhood in social statistics. It has also affected the perceived identity of the child by attributing to the child the status and characteristics of his/her family. Finally, in Saporiti's view this has resulted in the imposition of an adulto-centric model of data collection and tabulation.

Saporiti goes on to assert that it has only been in the last decade that real efforts have been made to establish some quantitative information in such a child-centred way. While some progress has been made in the industrialised world in this respect, it is still certainly true that great mysteries surround the realm of 'Third World' children and their lives. These mysteries have not been entirely vanquished by the formidable work undertaken each year by Carol Bellamy, Executive Director of UNICEF, in providing a picture of the 'State of the World's Children' (Belamy, 1998, 1999, 2000, 2002a).

> In the European context and in other affluent societies, the basic information on children was (until a decade ago) certainly more advanced than in the rest of the world. And yet there were no statistical data set comprehensive enough to capture the broad meaning of childhood as a social group; nor did we possess adequate statistics, allowing us a complete

picture of the condition of children within the substantive areas of their daily life. (Saporiti 1997, p.298)

The presentation of children this way in statistics does have consequences that frequently disadvantage children individually and in that
official statistics are often the basis on which resources are allocated or
reallocated. Saporiti and others see that the failure to use children as a
basic and distinct unit of observation by subsuming them within the
more general category of the family is a reflection of a process of exclusion in society generally.

Child-focused counting

McKendrick suggests that the first stage in constructing a population
geography of children is 'to problematise our assumed knowledge'
(McKendrick 2001, p.467). One of the methods of doing this is to look
at the ways that children differ from adults. While acknowledging that
the differences between adults and children go well beyond physiologi-
cal and psychological maturity differences, these two developmental
differences are often regarded as the most significant. They are also,
falsely, often presented as 'natural' differences. McKendrick notes that
such a view is problematic in two ways: it minimises the importance of
differences rooted in institutions and social systems; and often age is
used, inappropriately, to indicate developmental stage. 'Yet mental and
physical capacity is also shaped by gender, ethnic background, national
residence and so on. Specifying, let alone understanding, children is far
from straightforward' (McKendrick 2001, p.467).

Hill and Michelson (1981) identified seven 'geographically relevant' ways in which children differ from adults, relying very much on
the world of the Northern child. The differences revolve around:

- behaviour (most of children's energy is channelled into play
  and formal education)
- land use (children use different facilities and, where they share
  the same facilities, they often use them differently)
- territory (adults have more expansive lifeworlds)
- age-specific environmental threats – e.g. stranger-danger
  (Valentine and McKendrick 1997), traffic (Hillman *et al.* 1990;

Roberts, Smith and Bryce 1995) and the home (Rosenbaum 1993)

- economic position (children tend to be positioned on the margins of economic systems)
- political exclusion (most children have no parliamentary voting rights)
- perspective (children's interpretations of situations often vary from those of adults).

It has only been during the last two decades, however, that some attempt has been made by researchers to organise their research in such a way that it addresses the problems of appropriately child-focused research. Such problems include: the need for a conceptual/theoretical attitude which views children as a distinct but diverse social category; a methodology which focuses on the child as the unit of observation and analysis such that, for example, the situation of children in one country can be compared with another. Also required are: an approach to data collection and analysis, which has as its aim uncovering and revealing the 'world' of children as compared with the 'worlds' of other social groups, particularly other minority rights groups who also struggle for recognition; and, finally, an acknowledgement of agency and power. Some of the research work with child workers reported in Chapter 6 gives some exciting examples of how this might be achieved.

The United Nations Convention on the Rights of the Child has acted as a catalyst for the coming together of a number of discipline groups and interdisciplinary groups with a specific focus on childhood as a social category. A number of international agencies have also demonstrated, since the Convention was ratified, a growing awareness of the need for a much fuller, more detailed and informed picture of childhood. Childwatch International has been ingenious in working towards the provision of indicators that provide some picture of the culture of childhood across the world, illustrated in the final section of this chapter (Dia *et al.* 1995; Ennew 1996; Ennew and Miljeteig 1996). More recently, Save the Children and UNICEF assembled statistical data, accompanied by illustrative material from children themselves, to present as part of the materials for the UN Special Session in 2002 (Save the Children 2001; UNICEF 2002).

The last two decades have seen the development of several research groups which have also been looking into ways of gathering fundamental statistical data concerning children in their own right. One such group of researchers with a common focus was the 'Childhood as a Social Phenomenon' group (Qvortrup *et al.* 1994) of which Saporiti, referred to earlier, was a part. This European project concluded its series with a technical appendix which demonstrated how statistics on children could be improved (Jensen and Saporiti 1992). The activities of a group set up more recently, 'Monitoring and Measuring the State of Children – Beyond Survival', have been outlined in a report by Adamson (1996). They included an attempt to develop more appropriate indicators which would also permit comparison of the condition and wellbeing of children in developed industrialised countries. Other groups have made great efforts to develop useful and meaningful statistical pictures of the situation of children (Ben-Arieh and Wintersberger 1997). There is an increasing awareness in the international research community of the need for a change in the approach to collecting statistics, which give some framework for the development of a more authentic picture of the lives of children.

Methodological challenges

While there have been these international and global attempts to get some detailed picture of the world of the child, at the national level initiatives have started and progress is being made – albeit slowly. In writing a 1997 postscript to his 1990 article on 'A Voice for Children in Statistical and Social Accounting', Qvortrup (1997) said that, in his personal experience, when statistical offices in various countries have their attention drawn to their omissions and conflations, he found they were anxious to remedy this situation. He uses as an example of this responsiveness and concern the Nordic Statistical Office. This office, within the framework of the Nordic Council of Ministers, invited members of the European Centre Project (i.e. the European Centre on Childhood as a Social Phenomenon) to produce an expert technical report on the possibility and practicalities of producing childhood statistics. Denmark, Finland, Norway and Sweden have all produced special publications about children, with children being used as the units of observation on a few selected issues in current statistics, and special files and databases have been set up. There are now children's

statistics available in Israel, Canada, the UK and the USA. In the latter
case, in a book entitled *America's Children*, Hernandez (1993) has provided a model of presentation of statistics in a way that makes children
really count. It is important in this example to emphasise once more my
caveat in Chapter 1, that it is important for knowledge and meaning to
meet. Statistics, even good ones, alone are not enough. Even when a
statistical report itself is careful to focus on the child as the unit of observation, interpretation by the media or in a press release can distort findings. This happened in the case of a Danish report, which was
exemplary in its treatment (Talom Born 1996), yet the press release from
the Ministry of Social Affairs fell into the familiar trap of putting the
family once more at the centre. The interpretation of statistics and setting them within the political and social context do matter. Later in this
chapter, with the aid of some of the insights provided by a tireless, campaigning, investigative journalist (Pilger 1998), we will be dwelling on
statistics on, for example, children in poverty and children involved in
armed conflict and, as counterpoint, the way in which these statistics are
often ignored or thought to be of little account. Sometimes even bald
statistics should be heeded.

> Statistics is an important, necessary, indeed indispensable
> research instrument to give expression to children's life
> conditions; [...] Though risk is always there for over inter-
> preting aggregate statistics, used with care, it remains a help-
> ful tool. (Qvortrup 1997, pp.104–50)

One way to improve the tool is to seek information from a very broad
range of sources, not to be simply restricted within one discipline, institution or cultural group. It is by putting together information from disparate sources that we are able to grasp more clearly the situation of the
child. Networking and composite picture building is therefore important, and in this way quite a considerable amount of knowledge is being
built up about the child's world. While there are positive aspects (as
Saporiti, himself a professor of statistics, notes), one of the problems
with information about children being distributed in various places –
institutions, research establishments, academic, policy and campaigning
groups – is that the information is not only fragmented but also often
marked by redundancies and discrepancies (Saporiti 1997). It does not
neatly overlap, as sometimes the basis on which the data has been collected is substantially different and so may even contradict existing

material. The result is that we have neither qualitative nor quantitative data which is at the moment comparable and adequate.

Although arguments have been produced earlier in this chapter that children need to be brought out from behind the shadow of the family, we nevertheless have to interpret the information which has been collected in a child-centred way with reference to other indicators that fill in the context. Such data might be information on fertility rates, for example, as these may give some indication of the value of children and their meaning at the individual, societal and cultural level. McKendrick (2001) feels that the emergence of a (social) geography of childhood does hold out the hope of enriching our understanding of population patterns and processes. To ensure this, the new population geographies involving children should fully engage them rather than use them as a simple routine contribution to the comprehension of population dynamics. This, he emphasises, involves a theoretical engagement with children and childhood. In this he sees 'a need to value the child's perspective and to appreciate the agency of children in shaping their own population futures'(p.470). In other words he acknowledges the power of children to shape understanding in social geography.

Rendering children visible: the journalists' approach

Elisabeth Nasman (1994), looking at the issue of individualisation and institutionalisation of children in today's world, examines the extent to which children are identified and made visible as individuals in public statistics. While it is true that in the population registers children are identifiable in terms of a name, a registration number, sex and place and the exact date of birth, nevertheless in published statistics this individualisation of the data on the child is frequently not used. Abramson (1996), in examining the invisibility of children, does not simply rummage around for statistics but looks at turns of speech and clichés that – whether well intended or not – make children and adolescents invisible. He sees the children's rights movement as one which must work on attitudes. Among the attitudes he identifies as important sites for re-education and action are those which cause invisibility. He provides several illustrative quotes, from the language of human rights issues, which totally exclude children and adolescents. He identifies 'men and women' and 'the majority' quotes in which young people play no part.

Moreover he asserts that when children do get mentioned, it is in the same breath as women, as in 'women and children' – distinct from men.

One way in which statistics have been used to render children visible has been the way they have been used by investigative journalists. Journalists use the statistics that they can find about children and make those meaningful as part of the case they are trying to draw their readers attention towards. We could look at children around the globe at the present time and wonder whether children ever matter, especially in war. Afghanistan was ranked fourth worst in the UNICEF infant mortality statistics in 2001 with 257 children in every 1000 dying under the age of five – a statistic often regarded as a critical indicator of the wellbeing of children. One can only shudder to think of what has happened to even that inadequate statistic now, within a largely migrant population fleeing and on the fringes of bombing and warfare. It will take years before investigative journalists worry away at the fragments of information to give us a picture of what happened to those children. Foremost among the journalists campaigning to draw attention to the costs of war for children has been John Pilger.

> The children of Iraq are 'Unpeople'. So, too, are the half a million children who, according to UNICEF in 1989, die beneath the burden of unrepayable debt. There is little reason to hope that this statistic has changed for the better. One Filipino child is said to die every hour, in a country where more than half the national budget is given over to paying just the interest on World Bank and IMF loans. (Pilger 1998, p.3)

So wrote John Pilger in developing his account of how, in Iraq, the fate of children following the introduction of sanctions after the first Gulf War has been what he refers to as 'the slowest of news'. This means news which does not particularly capture the imagination of journalists or news which happens while their attention is otherwise engaged, as on a Sunday or a holiday period. He says, 'It is generally agreed that the media show cannot go on whilst the cast is away' (Pilger 1998, p.1). Basing his information on data provided by the Food and Agriculture Organisation of the United Nations (FAO 1995), he points out that few people are aware, as it was 'slow news', that as a direct result of the economic sanctions imposed by the West, 560,000 children lost their lives. (The World Health Organisation confirmed this figure – *New Statesman and Society* 1996. A field worker, Jean Lennock, interpreted this statistic graphically in pointing out that this was equivalent to the unnecessary death of one child every six minutes (Pilger 1998). Many of these lives could have been saved with simple antibiotics. These sanctions, Pilger claims, were not aimed at toppling Saddam Hussein or rendering him powerless to build a nuclear bomb but rather at stymieing the market competition of Iraqi oil by forcing down the price of oil produced by Saudi Arabia, 'the West's most important Middle Eastern proxy, next to Israel, and the biggest arms customer' (Pilger 1998, p.53).

In looking more closely at these deaths Pilger refers us to a letter to the Security Council from Ramsey Clark, who had carried out investigations in Iraq since 1991.

> [Most of the deaths] are from the effects of malnutrition including marasmus and kwashiorkor, wasting or emaciation which has reached twelve percent of all children, stunted growth which affects twenty eight percent, diarrhoea, dehydration from bad water or food, which is ordinarily easily controlled and cured, common communicable diseases preventable by vaccinations, and epidemics from deteriorating sanitary conditions. There are no deaths crueller than these. They are suffering slowly, helplessly, without simple sedation to relieve pain, without mercy. (Pilger 1998, pp.53–4)

Nevertheless an urgent appeal to governments for aid was launched by UNICEF in October 1996 emphasising the fact that over 50 per cent of women and children were receiving less than half their calorific needs and were therefore close to starvation. Despite the urgency and gravity of this appeal, only the government of the Netherlands made a contribution (UNICEF 1996). Pilger continues his chilling interpretation of what was happening, further underscoring my argument here that children do not count even when the statistics reach horrific proportions and simply signify the complex harrowing tale of human suffering, yet fail to move governments. It is worth staying with Pilger's view longer as it is highly relevant in understanding at least one view of how children are positioned in relation to global power struggles; how, while they are not just numbers, they become so – expendable ones. Pilger, using all his determination and passionate curiosity, looks behind the numbers to the arrays of official complacency.

The claim is that the UN tried to broker an 'oil for food' arrangement. The details of this deal were to be that Iraq would be allowed to sell $1 billion worth of oil every three months on the world market, half of which would be allocated to war reparations in Kuwait and to the Kurds in 'safe havens'. The remainder would be set aside for the purchase of food, medicines and to buy the basic spare parts for water and sewage treatment facilities. Pilger claims (Pilger 1998, p.54) that the American representatives on the UN Sanctions Committee used every opportunity to obstruct the plan. Although the plan had the approval of the Secretary General, nevertheless it appeared frozen. In an item reported in the *Socialist Review* (1997), Madeleine Albright, at that time US Ambassador to the United Nations, replying to a question as to whether or nor the lives of half a million Iraqi children was too high a price to pay, said, 'I think this is a very hard choice, but the price we think is worth it'.

Pilger suggests that to really grasp the suffering of these Iraqi young people and to report the real reasons why children are dying there is to 'bracket Western governments with dictatorships and totalitarian regimes. Thus the victims become unmentionable' (Pilger 1998, p.55). In trying to get at the real reasons why this happened, Ramsey Clark, a former US Attorney General, suggested:

> The United States has forced this decision on the Security Council. Three of the five permanent members – China, France and the Russian Federation – have sought to modify the sanctions. (The US) blames Saddam Hussein and Iraq for the effects (on the Iraqi people). [...] If Iraq is spending billions on the military, then the sanctions are obviously not working. Malnutrition didn't exist in Iraq before the sanctions. If Saddam Hussein is building palaces, he intends to stay. Meanwhile a whole nation is suffering. Hundreds are dying daily and millions are threatened in Iraq because of US-compelled impoverishment. (Clark 1992, p.10)

To journalists at press conferences about the first Gulf War the Allies claimed that they were progressively knocking out Scud missile sites in Iraq with 'smart' weapons. Most of the bombs were actually old-fashioned 'dump' bombs and notoriously inaccurate: the 88,500 tons of bombs dropped on Iraq and Kuwait – the equivalent, according to Pilger (Pilger 1998, p.48), of more than seven Hiroshimas – missed their targets completely and many fell in populated areas with widespread civilian casualties, many of these children and young people

(Clark 1996). This did not reach popular attention, as it was simply not reported. There was even rather a blasé view of what might possibly be happening, with some journalists claiming, 'There are certain actions that a civilised society can never contemplate. This carpet-bombing is undeniably terrible. But that does not make it wrong' (*Independent on Sunday* 1991).

In this way the killing of many, many innocent children by military bungling is excused – because in warfare, as in so many other fields of life, statistics, when used to make children visible, as they relate to child deaths simply do not count.

STAYING ALIVE

Malnutrition: starving by numbers

Malnutrition is one of the most pernicious forms of oppression as for children there is rarely any way of resisting it; it can disempower or destroy them and cast its long shadow over later generations. In UNICEF's annual report for 1998, *The State of the World's Children* (Bellamy 1998), the focus is on malnutrition. Economic and social statistics are provided on the nations of the world with particular reference to children's wellbeing. To illustrate the discussion on the use of statistical data, it is useful to follow what is presented in this publication. It makes it clear that such data that we have, however inadequate it may be, is not the complete story, as such statistics have long-term consequences. Moreover, numbers alone are not enough, as we have seen, to influence global attitudes and policies. Even when statistics and meaning meet, not only are the cries of children rarely heard but neither are the voices of their advocates – advocates of the stature and authority of the Secretary-General of the United Nations. Kofi Annan, in the preface to the UNICEF 1998 report on *The State of the World's Children*, draws our attention to one of the ways that children were still suffering.

> Over two hundred million children in developing countries under the age of five are malnourished. For them, and for the world at large, this message is especially urgent. Malnutrition contributes to more than half of the nearly 12 million under-five deaths in developing countries each year. Malnourished children often suffer the loss of precious mental capacities. They fall ill more often. If they survive, they may

grow up with lasting mental or physical disabilities.
(UNICEF 1998, p.6)

By 2001, almost 160 million children under five were said still to be
malnourished (White 2001). Since the early 1970s children's welfare
both in the South and in the North has often been the major casualty of
a recession in the world economy. Additional factors which exacerbate
these difficulties are protectionism in industrialised countries, declining
terms of trade, excessive military spending and the ever-present massive
external debts. There are also differences between rural and urban children. In rural situations children may be out of sight and have no
fall-back position, while in a urban setting they are more visible, they
may be able to scrounge scraps from the rich and there may be more diverse sources of food such as bazaars. Rarely, if ever, do structural adjustment policies ameliorate the plight of the youngest and weakest, namely
the children – the inheritors of this impoverished and impoverishing
world. Many of these individual trends have been analysed and moni-
tored, yet the complex interacting way in which, taken together, they
impact the lives of the young and vulnerable is rarely appreciated.
Children simply do not 'count'. In Chapter 1 of the 1998 UNICEF report the 'silent emergency' is addressed, putting forward the argument
that malnutrition is rarely regarded as an emergency even when it is on
the scale signalled by Kofi Annan.

The reasons for this are that the children affected are not necessarily
facing famine; they betray few or no obvious signs. It is all the more surprising to learn therefore that this largely invisible crisis of malnutrition
is implicated in *more than half* of all child deaths worldwide. This proportion, as the report observes, is unmatched by any infectious disease since
the Black Death – yet malnutrition is not an infectious disease. It affects
children's rights and their power to exercise these rights in many and
profound ways. Most significant are the effects on their mental and
physical growth, which then has an effect on perpetuating poverty by
restricting these children, as they grow up as citizens, in the contribution they can personally make to the economy. The scale of this is alarming, yet fails to alarm sufficiently those in power, or indeed capture the
popular conscience. One out of every three children is affected. The report points out the ways in which, as a result, the productivity and abilities of entire societies are lowered. 'More attention is lavished on the
gyrations of the world stock markets than on malnutrition's vast

destructive potential – or on the equally powerful benefits of sound nutrition' (Bellamy 1998, p.9).

Causes of malnutrition

When the scale of malnutrition and the complex interplay of factors that
cause it are examined, the picture is not as one would expect. The consequences of famines, wars and other catastrophes, which would commonly be supposed to be major contributing factors, turn out to be
responsible for only a tiny proportion of the global malnutrition crisis.
Moreover it is not simply a matter of whether a child has enough to eat.
A child who eats enough to satisfy his/her immediate hunger can still be
malnourished. 'Three quarters of the children who die world-wide of
causes related to malnutrition are what nutritionists describe as "mildly"
to "moderately" malnourished and betray no outside signs to a casual
observer' (Bellamy 1998, p.9). The child's body is not necessarily the
place to look for the ultimate cause. Causes include poor health services,
discrimination against women and ignorance of the significance of
micronutrients – minerals, essential amino acids, fatty acids and
vitamins.

    The causal chain in malnutrition is complex. For example, the inter-
play between the two most significant immediate causes – inadequate
dietary intake and illness – creates a vicious circle. In such a circle the
malnourished child may have little resistance to illness and if he/she becomes ill the malnourishment worsens and it becomes a fatal spiral.
When talking of adequate dietary intake it is stated in this report that vitamin and mineral deficiencies are estimated 'to cost some countries the
equivalent of more than 5 percent of their gross national product in lost
lives, disability and productivity' (Bellamy 1998, p.13). The report goes
on:

> Iron deficient children under the age of two years show prob-
> lems with co-ordination and balance and appear more with-
> drawn and hesitant. Such factors can hinder a child's ability to
> interact with and learn from the environment and may lead to
> lower intellectual abilities. (Bellamy 1998, p.15)

Thus nourishment that is adequate and appropriate in terms of its con-
stituent micronutrients for the young is vital for the child's power and
agency today and for the workforce of tomorrow. Children neglected in
this way imperil society as a whole; nevertheless, grave as the situation

is, in terms of both relevant statistics and quality of life issues, it is still a 'silent' emergency.

Gender discrimination and malnutrition

Gender discrimination may be surprising as a contributory causal factor, although the report claims that discrimination and violence against women are major causes of malnutrition.

> Women are the principal providers of nourishment during the most crucial periods of children's development, but the caring practices vital to children's nutritional well-being invariably suffer when the division of labour and resources in families and communities favours men, and when women and girls face discrimination in education and employment.
>
> A lack of access to good education and correct infor-mation is also a cause of malnutrition. Without information strategies and better and more accessible action programmes, the awareness, skills and behaviours needed to combat mal-nutrition cannot be developed.
>
> There is therefore nothing simple about malnutrition – except perhaps the vast toll it is taking. (Bellamy 1998, p.11)

Here we have statistics giving some indication of a problem affecting the mortality of children. The statistic itself, apart from revealing the crisis proportions of the situation, tells us little about its cause, or indeed its consequences – nor do they inform us about how the child experi-ences this.

Malnutrition: consequences and costs

It is possible to provide horrifying information in a statistical form about malnutrition in the developing world demonstrating that huge numbers of children suffer from multiple types of malnutrition. However, malnu-trition is not limited to developing countries and its meaning here for children living in the great wealth divide may be quite different. The picture is sketched by the following information.

- It is estimated by researchers that one in every four children under the age of 12 in the United States (i.e. 13 million children) have a difficult time getting all the food they need – a problem which is at its worst in the last week of the month when families' benefits or wages run out (Bread for the World Institute 1997, p.8).

- Over 20 per cent of children in the United States live in poverty (Bread for the World Institute 1997). This is more than double the rate of most other industrialised countries.

- A recent study indicated that in the United Kingdom children and adults in poor families face health risks linked to diet. The health risks indicated were: anaemia in both adults and children; premature and low-weight births; dental diseases; diabetes; obesity and hypertension (Philips *et al.* 1997, p.1545).

- In the Russian Federation, as an example of the way in which in Central and Eastern Europe the transition to market economies and the associated economic confusion and reductions in state-run social programmes are affecting the most vulnerable, stunted growth is increasing. Between 1992 and 1994 this increased from 9 per cent to 15 per cent (UNICEF 1997b, p.43).

In the papers associated with the planned UN Special Session in 2001 Marcia White reports that indeed, since the World Summit in 1990, there have been some improvements. More, she claims, was done for children:

> …over the last 10 years than in any other period in history. For example, 3 million children were able to survive in 2000 who would have died from preventable disease in 1990: polio and guinea worm disease among preventable diseases claiming the lives of 15 million children a year have almost been eradicated; and while access to clean water has improved it still evades a third of the world's children. (White 2001, p.4)

These are 'improvements' as measured by numbers. Have the surviving children felt significant improvements in their quality of life? White goes on to comment that although there have been some improvements since the first summit, 'day-to-day life for most children remains the same. The gap between the rhetoric and the reality stark' (p.4).

While our concentration in my book is largely on what is happening to children now – this their 'insistent present' – one cannot overlook the fact that the effects of malnutrition cross generations such that women who are themselves underweight and malnourished are likely to give birth to small babies (Bellamy 1998, 1999, 2000), which means that malnourished children growing up will likewise probably have babies of low birth-weight regardless of later malnutrition (Bateson and Martin 1999, p.110ff). In *Design for a Life* Bateson and Martin discuss this in terms of the 'thrifty phenotype' adaptation to harsh conditions. Their hypothesis is this – if maternal physique and health are poor then this has consequences both for the growth of the foetus and its later health and development. In poor conditions it is almost as if a 'weather forecast' from the mother's body means that her baby is born adapted to the meagre diet it will face. Such adaptations include a small body, a lower metabolic rate and reduced behavioural activity. When food is in short supply all these features help to reduce energy expenditure. So the malnourished child may have a built-in resilience to endure the diet that is his/her lot. They point out that this should not make the rich complacent about the poorly nourished. When environmental conditions are bad and likely to continue to be so, adaptations occur to make the best of it. While not disregarding the influence of social and economic conditions on wellbeing, they go on, surprisingly, to produce evidence that social and economic conditions do not account for everything. Relationships between low birth-weight and subsequent health are still found among babies born to affluent homes. Their data is based on studies of severe food shortages and famine during wartime in the Netherlands and in the siege of Leningrad. Babies born to mothers who suffered starvation in the last trimester of their pregnancies were of low birth-weight and as they grew up had difficulties in dealing with high levels of sugar and had an increased risk of developing diabetes. It seems that they were less well adapted to a world markedly different in its plentiful supply of food from that of their foetal life. Women who had been foetuses in the last three months of their intra-uterine life during the famine, despite the fact they had grown up in much richer condition, nevertheless gave birth to abnormally low birth-weight babies. (Bateson and Martin p.112–113). This second generation effect suggests that malnutrition casts a long shadow from present hungers into the future in ominous ways. The size of the problem here is also worrying in that, according to UNICEF, in South Asia, where half of all children are underweight, 60 per cent of women of child-bearing age are underweight. In South East Asia the proportion of underweight women is 45 per cent, and 20 per cent in sub-Saharan Africa. These are worrying figures in themselves and in their bearing on the health, wellbeing and survival of future generations of children. Gathered with considerable ingenuity and difficulty from disparate sources, these statistics paint a devastating picture of the state of the world's children at the end of the twentieth century – a century of unprecedented economic and technological advance – and serve to underscore the central question of this chapter: do children count? This dismal picture drawn by Carol Bellamy for UNICEF in 1998 is not entirely unrelieved in that evidence is also included on projects which demonstrate the power of good nutrition, making clear that, despite the fact there is still much to be done:

> ...There is also growing reason to believe that improving the nutrition of women and children will contribute to overcoming some of the greatest health challenges facing the world including the burden of chronic and degenerative disease, maternal mortality, malaria and AIDS. (Bellamy 1998, p.17)

Much of this information charts children's needs and how they are being, or indeed failing to be, met. Does it tell us anything really about the lives of children as defined by them or throw any light upon these children's aspirations? They are presented as a series of 'parts' to be serviced; although it is true that the recent edition of the UNICEF's annual survey (UNICEF 2002), which this time concentrated on the theme of leadership, has made a big effort to get to grips with the global movement of young people and include their voices on important topics. It has taken a long time to achieve this sort of recognition but it does hold out great hope; the way the world is changing, leaders are now aware that they must listen to children and take them seriously.

What statistics I have chosen to reproduce reinforce the view that the huge incidence of malnutrition in all its forms urgently needs to capture the imagination of the policy maker and financier and so it recently has. At the UN Special Session on Children in May 2002 the Global Alliance for improved Nutrition (GAIN) was launched. It is an alliance of public and private sector organisations, foundations and governments that are committed to saving lives and improving health in developing countries through the elimination of nutritional deficiencies. UNICEF Executive Director Carol Bellamy said at the launch 'For decades people in industrialised countries have avoided vitamin and mineral deficiencies because their food has been fortified. Through

GAIN we will be making sure that children in developing countries have those same benefits.' Proctor and Gamble is one of the private sector partners in the alliance. It will be sharing its technical expertise in food fortification and food technologies with local producers in developing countries so that they can use it to fortify their own food products. Which products will be chosen for such treatment, whether milk, sugar, rice or maize will depend on the country concerned. One of the major contributors ($50 million) to GAIN is the Bill and Melinda Gates Foundation. Bill Gates, Chairman of the Microsoft Corporation said 'We are creating a virtual cycle; better nutrition means better health, which means more children survive, which means that more women will choose to have fewer children, which means more children will get a better education and so on' (www.unicef.org/special session/activities/gain.htm.) The approach to sharing expertise and money by these two members of GAIN illustrates the intelligent generosity of a food giant and a multi-millionaire. As importantly it has the potential to transform the way power has been traditionally wielded by divesting it in the interests of making sure that everybody counts. There is also the dark possibility that it may prove to be another instance of 'uppers' making decisions about the lives of 'lowers'. It is hoped that this might result in the redirection of resources. A picture is glimpsed through these numbers, but not the whole story or the children's aspirations. Malnutrition remains a global problem and statistics on the massive scale of such disadvantage provide material for cosmic grief and for campaigning groups and lobbyists. They are numbers, gathered with some ingenuity and skill, about children and do not necessarily reflect children's views of the world. In Brazil, street children were provided with food from a soup kitchen set up by concerned adults who worried about their nutrition. This was not what they wanted. Their own priority was protection from police harassment (Marcus 1998). Meaningful statistics have to be connected with context and culture to show a full understanding of what is going on. This can be approached in a number of ways, none of them easy. Putting the full narrative line on the statistics is far from straightforward. Work in the sociology of childhood and population geographies has identified what some of these difficulties are. As we have seen, accounts by investigative journalists sometimes make the leaps of interpretation and understanding that the professional researcher is reluctant to make given his/her training in caution about speculation beyond the data. In trying to build up a picture of what children's lives are really like, we need to listen to children. We also need to understand, at the other end of the spectrum, the pressures they are under in industrialised nations from ruthless advertising about diet and nutrition, a topic further developed in the next chapter. There is growing concern in the UK and in the USA at the present time about serious obesity in children and the early onset of type 2 diabetes. These seem to be, according to Marion Nestle's timely analysis of the origins of the obesity epidemic in the United States, connected with lifestyle and diet (Nestle 2002). Also the power some girls exert in shaping their own bodies as in anorexia could lead us into considerable debate about power, agency and diet in countries where food is plentiful.

In the developing world it should not be forgotten that what we know about malnutrition among the young is played out against a situation in which: there are an estimated 1.4 million children under the age of 15 living with HIV worldwide; more than 13 million children aged 14 or younger have been orphaned by AIDS; the virus has killed the most productive members of society, teachers, farmers, civil servants and many breadwinners; 80 per cent of children under the age of 15 living with HIV are children living in Africa; half of all new cases of HIV occur in young people aged 15 to 24 years old. This would be to begin another story, part of an epitaph for the children under the age of 15 who have died from AIDS since the beginning of the epidemic: 4.3 million and counting...(UNICEF 2002).

> Most of the campaigns don't involve young people in the design... Maybe this is why they don't work, because they are just adult ministry of health campaigns. They are just not 'cool' (Youth, Africa). (UNICEF's 'Voices of Young People', UNICEF 2002, p.40)

LIVING IN POVERTY

I have indicated that poverty, like malnutrition, is not simply confined to the developing world. It features in the lives of children even in some of the richest countries on the planet. However, the evidence is hard to find and receives little publicity – it often has to be quarried out from oblique sources. Comparing child poverty in rich nations 'in the league table of relative child poverty: the bottom four places were occupied by UK, Italy, USA and Mexico' (UNICEF 2001). There has been a steady growth in child poverty in the UK. According to the Department of Social Security (DSS 2001), in 1979 one in ten children lived in poverty compared with one in three in 2001. Poverty rose twice as fast for families with children (21%) as for those without (10%) (Howard *et al.* 2001). Malnutrition and stunted growth were to be found in up to two million British children – a consequence, according to the Milk for Schools Campaign (1997), of the reduction of free and cheap school meals, a provision which had taken a century to establish. Further evidence that malnutrition is not just a Third World phenomenon is provided by research in West Yorkshire which, looking at children in school, found that poor children were four centimetres shorter and weighed less than their richer classmates (Mills 1996). The experience of a doctor in Bristol claims that a quarter of the young inner-city patients aged between 14 months and two years he sees are anaemic from lack of iron. This shortage affects mental and physical development and is normally only associated with children in some of the poorest conditions in the world (Mills 1996).

The effects of poverty on these children's futures should be a matter of great concern yet singularly fails to be recognised or capture the popular imagination. They simply do not count or the picture is dismissed as a media hype about people who are regarded as 'scroungers' and swept up into the dismissive arguments about welfare 'fraud'. Government statistics quoted in the *Socialist Worker* in 1997 throw into question the popular belief in massive welfare fraud. It reveals that in 1996 between £2.3 billion and £3.5 billion of benefits, were not claimed either because people were too proud or because they were unaware of their eligibility for such benefits. Stereotypes abound and while we are all aware that, in Britain, factors that contribute to economic hardship have been the abolition of the national housing programme, unemployment and the gradual running down of the social services, there is little real discussion of the causes of poverty and its consequences for the citizens of tomorrow's world. The facts as we know them about poverty and the increasing divide in Britain between the rich and poor receive scant attention. According to an analysis of the Child Poverty Action Group, since Margaret Thatcher came to power, more than £63 billion has been transferred in subsidies from the poor to the rich (Oppenheim and Harker 1996). As yet there are few indications that this trend will be substantially reversed under the Labour government, although the

Chancellor's initiative to reduce child poverty, launched in the summer of 2000, targets the estimated four million British children in families living on less than half average earnings.

The quality of poverty

Some statistics are used as indices of poverty. The choice of factors and the conversion of measures combined to indicate a general state in this way includes values and beliefs about what is involved in poverty and what aspects of life contribute to that concept. Poverty is not just about income and living at or below subsistence level. The Child Poverty Action Group made it clear that defining poverty includes psychological, social and physical needs. They included, in these needs, goods if 80 per cent or more UK households have them (Child Poverty Action Group 1999). The point of this was to include costs which combine to ensure health and socially inclusive living at the turn of the century. Thus in looking at poverty in new ways we are not just counting money but rather looking at the nature of inclusion/exclusion and the implications of that for quality of life and personal contentment.

An innovative, long-term, international research project is investigating the changing nature of child poverty in Ethiopia, India, Peru, Vietnam, South Africa and the UK. This international study of childhood poverty is exciting in that it tries to address some of the problems I have identified in this chapter about data gathering. The project aims to link research and policy makers and planners so that the information produced is used to improve the quality of children's lives. The participating countries were selected from over 20 who expressed interest, in order to illustrate the effects of a range of policy, social and economic issues on child poverty and wellbeing. They were also selected because these countries reflect a range of geographical, social and cultural contexts.

The project arose from the Department for International Development (DFID)'s and Save the Children's concerns to monitor progress towards meeting the International Development Targets and the changing situation of children. It has secured funding until 2003 but hopes to run for 15 years. It was also set up to try to gain some insight into how key development policies affect child wellbeing. The issues to be studied include:

- economic liberalisation
- indebtedness and debt relief
- conflict and natural disasters
- inequality
- government and civil society commitment to poverty reduction.

It is not clear yet the extent to which child-centred and child-negotiated indicators will be used in the project. The first working paper of the project on 'Comparative Perspectives on Child Poverty' (White, Leavy and Masters 2002) makes clear the need to go beyond a concentration on income and a narrow range of measures of health and education if a comprehensive picture of child welfare is to be grasped. As an antidote to all the caveats stated earlier about the use of statistics, this attempts to provide a realistic portrait of what matters to children, pointing out that material wellbeing is only part of that.

Measures of child poverty in developed countries have been dominated by income poverty, although health and education are often included. The rights and sustainability perspectives underscore the need for child welfare indicators that reflect the special position of children. The rights perspective calls for an approach which reflects things that children care most about, and the child development perspective calls for an approach that recognises positive developmental outcomes. The project emphasises that 'good monitoring systems collect data on both outcomes and determinants' (White *et al.* 2002, p.2). Broad definitions of poverty encompass security and 'empowerment' indicating the degree to which an individual has control over his/her own life – control here varying from local to national contexts. Since 1990 the United Nations Development Programme (UNDP) has promoted this broad approach in its Human Development Reports. It was also adopted by the World Bank's *World Development Report* of 2000–01. 'The debate as to whether, say, lack of voice is "really" poverty is semantic and should be set aside. We are interested in people's welfare or well being, and lack of welfare we call poverty' (White *et al.* 2002, p.3).

Child welfare indicators

What 'child welfare indicators' did they use? Non-income-poverty measures are differentiated between 'conventional' indicators and subjective
approaches. Conventional indicators are seen as including social indicators such as health and education status, the most common indicators of
these being life expectancy and literacy. The usual indicators of these
that are regarded as child specific and are widely used in addition to income poverty by international agencies such as UNICEF are infant and
child mortality and school enrolments.

The set of indicators used in developed countries is slightly broader.
In 1999 the UK Department of Social Security (now called the Department for Work and Pensions) proposed using 'income indicators' and
'indicators capturing other aspects of well-being'. Four of the indicators
relate to income, two to living standards and one to family structure.
The latter includes teenage pregnancy which can be seen as a health
measure rather than a child-welfare measure (Department of Social Security 1999). It is interesting to examine what has been included as, in
addition to basic milestones in education at various ages, 'reduction in
the proportion of truancies and exclusions from school' is, for example,
included.

Poverty indicators have also been approached in a subjective way
which might relate to poverty specifically, or more generally to aspects
of wellbeing. In relation to the ongoing discussion on power in my
book, the measure that is of most interest is the self-perception of
wellbeing. The question aimed at analysing teenagers' life satisfaction –
'On the whole, are you satisfied with the life that you lead?' – has been
used from 1973 to 1995 in the twice-annual Eurobarometer survey of
people aged 15 to 64. From this, indices of European teenagers' life satisfaction have been analysed (Micklewright and Stewart 1999). The
Canadian National Longitudinal Survey of Children (NLSC) takes a
comprehensive approach to wellbeing, having eight modules altogether
with subjective indicators. These modules or 'subjective welfare indicators' cover: friends and family; school; about me; feelings and behaviours; my parents and me; puberty; smoking, drinking and drugs;
activities. The emphasis is on how the child feels in some of these areas.
As regards school, for example, the child is asked 'How do you feel
about school?' (I feel safe at school/on the way to school. I feel like an
outsider.) In questions 'about me', the child is asked to comment. (In

general, I like the way I am./A lot of things about me are good.) The ac-knowledgement that such subjectivities are important in the child's sense of wellbeing is to be welcomed. There are, inevitably, problems of interpretation in what the questions mean to children and thus how they answer them and how their responses are interpreted by adults, so it is necessary to be aware of this and continually seek to problematise the data so gathered.

While some income and expenditure surveys ask rather vaguely whether the respondents consider themselves poor, the approaches to establishing self-perception of wellbeing give a more finely nuanced understanding of how children feel. Some researchers have looked at the relationship between income-poverty and child-development out-come measures, arguing that material deprivation matters. Some, for example Luthar (1999), have included not only competence and self-esteem but also behavioural and emotional indices of psychopathology. Others in their examination of child poverty and wellbeing in the UK include some measures of parental behaviour which they feel has an im-portant influence independent of income (McCulloch and Joshi 1999). Looking at the broad range of factors that have been identified as hav-ing child development outcomes underlines the need to look at the whole quality of the child's life rather than home in on a few isolated factors. Research has made it clear that in a fully rounded study of child poverty, social and psychological variables colour the nature of child welfare and well being and should be taken into account. Is it possible to use such a broad-based approach in developing countries or is the focus there necessarily on absolute poverty and its fundamentals such as mal-nutrition, illiteracy and mortality?

The work of Howard White and his colleagues, on which much of the above material has been sourced, asserts '…such a view is short-sighted. Child development concerns are at least as important in developing countries as developed ones (if less well understood)' (White *et al*. 2002, p.ii). Work with child workers described their methods of looking at the whole quality of such young workers' lives as well as their rights. A rich review of work on measuring child welfare in the developing world is also provided by the Young Lives Project (White *et al*. 2002), which stresses the multidimensional nature of poverty. Chambers (1997) presented a powerful case for taking into account the perceptions of poor people themselves. Recent work in developing countries has placed considerable emphasis on social outcomes and on participation.

In Zimbabwe, Senegal, Nicaragua, Thailand and Vietnam, Childwatch International's project has been to identify indicators of the rights of the child which can be measured and to augment this work with case studies in each country. The work has been sensitive to local situations in that the project has grouped the articles from the United Nations Convention on the Rights of the Child, giving an indicator to each constellation of Articles (Childwatch International 1996). White reports on one of the largest and longest-running studies of child health and development in Africa and one of the few large-scale longitudinal studies in the world (White *et al.* 2002, pp.16–18). This study of *Birth to Ten to Twenty,* the KwaZulu-Natal Income Dynamics Study (KIDS), covers a vast number of physical, social, psychological and welfare measures. Material is collected, for example, at individual level on membership of relevant children's social groups such as a youth group, church group, sports group, etc. This means that there are some indices of the child's social capital – an issue that I have discussed in Chapter 1 in relation to the child's resilience. Material was also gathered anonymously on whether a member of the household has been a victim of intra-household assault, which means that there is some indication of the child's security within the home. Extreme deprivation can clearly result from the disintegration of the child's secure home environment. There is a wealth of data on projects measuring outcomes (including child-welfare outcomes) of economic status in both the developed and the developing world.

In looking at the recent overview of these studies that the first Working Paper of the Young Lives Project provides, it is clear that income poverty, while important in itself, needs to be appreciated beyond a narrow range of indicators as affecting a much broader domain of the child's life and welfare. While the move towards trying to measure what matters to children inevitably has some flaws, what matters most about the efforts going on around the world is that they try to gather some insight into children's worlds from their point of view and recognise that children do count – as people rather than numbers.

Concepts deriving from statistics, poverty and malnutrition can be subtle sources of disempowerment, but at the same time can be highly sustainable stratifiers. The statistics trap substitutes numbers for people and people's lives; the poverty trap denies a route to education and the professions; the malnutrition trap is more pernicious since it stunts development and prevents escape even when power is divested. In this new century we should be counting on a world that is set on banishing such entrapment of children and ensuring they are the people who count.

CHAPTER FOUR

Spending
'Cool' Consumers:
Purchasers or Purchased?

CONSUMPTION, CHILDREN AND POWER

In shaping national and global economic and monetary policies, the impact and consequences for children are rarely regarded as important. In contrast, young people are recognised as powerful players in their role as consumers and as a significant source of influence on adult purchasers – power popularly known as 'pester power'. Children consume and their choices determine and are determined by the gigantic corporate machine. The extent to which children address and are capable of understanding relevant information at various ages in making these choices is worth further consideration. When it comes to what to buy, however, the weakest young reader seems expert at reading the writing on the wall in the subculture of desire. It is impossible to consider the issue of the economic power of children without tiptoeing through the interpretative minefield of 'consumption' (Gabriel and Lang 1995). Young observes sadly that things have now become more complicated than in the old days when consumption and production were separate and discrete. He suggests:

> Nowadays the roles of production and consumption are blurred and with the advent of postmodernism a whole new language is to be conquered. Meanings are 'contested' or 'negotiated' rather than defined, relationships are more or less 'problematic', and discourses rather than empirical facts are the stuff of discussion. (Young 1998, p.653)

It seems true here that production and consumption are intimately connected – one large confectionary manufacturer reports that in planning the size and cost of a new product it is axiomatic that the average amount of a child's pocket money is a significant factor (Wall's 2001). The detailed examination by Gabriel and Lang (1995) suggests that often 'the consumer' is treated as a collective and given more attention than individual consumers. In this chapter, while examining the corporate construction of childhood, the values, identities and meanings children themselves display in their consumption will also be examined. In relation to the theme of power that runs throughout this book, children, in exercising their choices in the purchases they make, are displaying their own view of the world and what is important to them in it, rather than accepting other people's realities.

At least, that is what they think they are doing but, as we shall see, when the corporate construction of childhood is discussed, what is in fact evident is the world as the marketeer wishes them to see, and process and respond to. The corporate construction of desire is about the shaping of children's values and consciousness by commerce and big business. For example, the fact that McDonald's has managed to keep its attractive carefree image with young (and many older) consumers around the globe may be due to the success of its public relations strategists, 'If any organisation has the power to shape the lives of children from Pretoria to Moscow, it is McDonald's' (Kincheloe 1997, p.251). Steinberg and Kincheloe and their colleagues (Steinberg and Kincheloe 1997), through their researches and writings, have been at pains to expose the specifics of this process of cultural domination – of which more later. Children's 'power' in the economy therefore lies at the intersection of other powerful interests anxious to recruit them. Who children are, what they become and what they believe is far more at the mercy of such large corporations than many of us can comfortably acknowledge. Moreover, their spending power is not seen simply as immediate and possibly modest, but as part of an entrainment into later brand loyalties and spending habits. Advertisers do, in fact, see children as consumers in training (Fischer *et al.* 1991).

This relationship between advertisers and children can easily be oversimplified (Seiter 1993). Children's TV watching is a complex affair. Children at the beginning of the twenty-first century are not passive and naive TV viewers. Advertising professionals are probably more aware than most that children are active analytical viewers. As viewers, they make their own meanings of the commercials and the products being promoted. The social and psychological dynamics between advertiser and child have not yet been analysed in sufficient detail. What does emerge as a significant feature of these dynamics in the work undertaken so far in America is that children feel very dismissive of the middle-class view of children being individuals in need of constant protection. Various well-intentioned advocacy groups such as ACT (Action for Children's Television – the leading voice in America against corporate advertising for children) promote and campaign for such protection.

> By drawing upon the child's discomfort with middle class protectionism and the accompanying attempt to 'adjust' children to a 'developmentally appropriate' norm, advertisers hit upon a marketing bonanza. If we address kids as kids – a dash of anarchism and a pinch of hyperactivity – they will love our commercials even though parents (especially middle-class parents) will hate them. By the end of the 1960s, commercial children's TV and advertising were grounded on this premise. Such video throws off restraint, discipline, and old views that children should be seen but not heard. Everything for example, that educational TV embraces – earnestness, child as an incomplete adult, child in need of correction – commercial TV rejects. In effect commercial TV sets up an oppositional culture for kids. (Kincheloe 1997, pp.255–6)

What children are enticed to buy is not the end of the story. The purchases are signifiers in themselves, affecting their power in the microcosm of the social world that is theirs. The power of the peer culture, within the oppositional culture referred to above, is probably better understood in marketing than in any other discipline in sensitising tastes at a discrete and immediate level. In the run-up to Christmas, not just TV commercials but even a detailed study of the Argos catalogue provides an insight into the new language and lore of schoolchildren in the UK at the turn of the century.[1] The nursery rhymes and the time-honoured street games, which the Opies so carefully researched and recorded as part of an important transmission of oral history in the culture of childhood during the middle of the twentieth century, seem to have been displaced by retail concerns. They concluded optimistically:

> Having now spent some length of time watching the rising generation, the first in the new Elizabethan age, we cannot but feel that it is a virile generation. The modern schoolchild,

> when out of sight and on his own, appears to be rich in
> language, well-versed in custom, a respecter of the details of
> his own code, and a practising authority of traditional self-
> amusements. (Opie and Opie 1959, p.ix)

This ability for self-amusement, nearly 50 years later, seems less in evidence. Now children, not just the middle-class and affluent, in the playground and on their mobile phone from their homes are well-versed in
the 'must-haves' of their culture, the markers of their identity and
hoped-for social ascendancy. The streets have become perceived as dangerous places for children. The retreat into the home seems marked by
an oral culture of virtual shopping. Christmas celebrations seem to forget the celebration of a penniless baby's birthday; instead they are
marked by a frantic rush by parents to supply the next source of
amusement. There is great anxiety for such parents as Teletubbies or
Playstations sell out or the Argos warehouses nationally run out of 'My
Model Styling Head' or 'Henna Tattoo Making Sets'. The linking of desire with childhood insecurities about identity seems to have had profound effects in getting children to see the world in ways commercially
advantageous to big businesses; children in effect become powerless
pawns in a powerful game.

Since the late 1970s, young people's lives, irrespective of gender or
ethnicity, appear to have become dominated by consumption. Redhead
observes that in the UK, 'by the 80s "Youth Culture" had become an industry in itself and it was even argued by some that youth was no longer
about rebellion or revolt but constituted merely a marketing device and
advertisers' fiction' (Redhead 1993, p.43). Interpersonal relationships
within the peer group are apparently governed to a large extent by con-
sumer-controlled self-presentation. An ICM poll of 500 children between the ages of 11 and 15, reported in the *Guardian*, quotes one
young person: 'If you don't look good you can get tormented at
school...if you wear old track suit bottoms without a name on them like
Adidas, you get bullied' (*Guardian* 1996). Advertising and the mass media have arguably become the most important forces in shaping the culture of young people today. It is an influence that provides both
solidarity and disunity. Young people, in order to fit in with and be
recognised by their 'mates', are pressured into adopting the rapidly
ever-changing images of fashion promoted by the relentless advertising
machine (Goffman 1979). Conformity in fashion is important for

teenagers, and as early as preschoolers too. The 11- to 15-year-old sample reported in the *Guardian* (1996) demonstrates just how critical clothing and image are. Bullying, reported as a common problem by 63 per cent, is often not just associated with physical appearance but, as has been noted, with clothing. Among boys in particular, footwear seems a particularly significant focus. In the survey it emerged that teenagers thought it right to spend £70 on a pair of trainers (this was in 1996 – the relative price is now considerably higher). Such a sum was quite clearly beyond the scope of families on a low income. Similarly, Dennehy, Smith and Harker (1997) suggest that young males frequently demand the latest football team kit, which changes every year. The 1997 cost of the whole kit, they report, is over £50 and many of the areas with the biggest following of football fans (a significant proportion of which are in the 11 to 19 age category) are located in Merseyside and the North East areas of considerable financial deprivation (Dennehy *et al.* 1997, p.26). Young women are the targets for rather different products, many of them to do with enhancing body image according to the current fashions of the day. Nevertheless these all denote a similar culture of belonging.

> The most powerful, and perhaps the most alarming, aspect of image making through the media is the transient nature of images of beauty – a term which appears to be as problematic as health and poverty. But these images are dependent to a great extent on money, and the ability to buy the necessary commodities. (Dennehy *et al.* 1997, p.26)

They go on to point out how music has always played a role in youth culture but that even this sort of 'membership' costs money. It has been noted earlier in Havel's description of the outlawing of the Plastic People of the Universe in former Czechoslovakia that this was regarded as the last straw in interfering with personal freedom. If young people were not free to play the music they chose, what did 'freedom' mean (Havel 1986)?

CHILDREN'S ECONOMIC RESOURCES

In an article in the popular press entitled 'The Rise of the Pocket-money Moguls', Deborah Hutton suggests that although children's pocket money is often thought of as a pittance, taken nationally, in Britain, the sum involved is huge. British parents, she asserts, hand over £1.5 billion to their offspring each year and children do not regard that as enough (Hutton 2000). For the past 28 years Wall's Ice Cream has been conducting surveys of children's purchasing power, the Wall's Pocket Money Monitor. That it should be a large commercial enterprise with very much a child-oriented product that takes this sort of research so seriously reinforces much of what has been said earlier. Their surveys show that during the past few years of economic boom and five decades in which the country as a whole has become steadily more affluent, children have apparently done best of all. The average income has doubled since the 1970s. Children's pocket money is ten times higher than it was in the 1970s. This does not hold for children from families on income support and in homes where parents are unemployed, families in which pocket money is a rare and infrequent phenomenon; attention will be given to this section of the community in a moment.

Just as Wall's has conducted regular studies in the UK of children's financial resources, so also in the United States McDonald's and other fast-food advertisers (Fischer *et al.* 1991) found that at the end of the 1980s children were already spending $4.2 billion of their own money. They were also found to influence spending, by their households, of an additional $131 billion each year and of this $82 billion was spent on food and drink. Nineteen out of every 20 children aged between 6 and 11 years old visited a fast-food restaurant every month (Kincheloe 1997).

Staying with those fortunate enough to have regular pocket money, while the population of 0- to 15-year-olds has remained relatively stable since 1991, the Wall's Pocket Money Monitor revealed that Britain's 12 million plus children had an average weekly pocket money of £3.10 in the year 2000. This was a massive rise on 1999 figures of 29 per cent (70p) – this being 14 times the rate of inflation. As a percentage change, year on year, this is the highest it has been since the Pocket Money Monitor was launched in 1974. Forecasters have worked out that if the present rate of increase continues, the average weekly pocket money, which now averages £3.10, will be nearly £40 by 2010 (see Table 4.1).

Table 4.1 Parental Weekly Pocket Money: Past, Present and Future	
1975	33p
1980	99p
1990	£1.49
2000	£3.10
2010 (projected)	£39.00

Source: Wall's Pocket Money Monitor (2001)

Comparisons are not straightforward, however, as sometimes those receiving larger amounts are expected to fund their own entertainment or buy clothing, such as the trainers that have already been mentioned or even substantial items such as winter coats. Children receiving smaller amounts may have these items bought for them.

Not only is pocket money increasing, but children are also managing it more professionally. Research by the Bank of Scotland (2000) revealed that children are increasingly getting their pocket money paid into a bank account. Both Omnibus Wave Four findings (Bank of Scotland 2000) and research conducted by BMRB International (Bank of Scotland 2000) on behalf of Wall's suggests that girls are more likely to save than boys. Looking at children between the ages of 7 and 11 years, two-thirds of them have at least one bank account, some even have two, and in the last four years the number of automatic deposits has doubled. It is arguable that once money is paid directly into a child's bank account, power is transferred from parent to child. Becoming financially independent can be seen as part of a developmental sequence of empowerment. For many children the change from a relatively token sum of pocket money to an allowance marks an important transition point.

Some parents see pocket money as part of becoming financially aware and set the amount with this in mind. It is not only the parents who are concerned about financial management. In a poll of more than 3000 children by MORI, 48 per cent said they wanted more detailed lessons about managing money. This compared with 31 per cent wanting more information on careers and surprisingly, given the interests of the young, only 27 per cent wanting more information on the environment (MORI 2000). Since this poll, many schools throughout the country have incorporated financial education in their personal, health and social education (PHSE) classes and it has become an option in the National Curriculum. A website is available: '15 Ways to Teach Kids About Money' (www.familyeducation.com/article/0,1120,37-6106-0-1,00.html). This attempts to get children to share their parents' values about money so it is not exactly individually empowering to the child. It provides a model of exemplary prudence that is distinctly 'uncool'. Children do seem to be more skilled about financial management than many of us would give them credit for. One child in five, according to the Wall's research, saves some or all of his/her pocket money and children have become far more sophisticated in charging for their services. This research revealed that while for the last two years, the average weekly income from outside work earned by many children has continued to fall, incomes from other sources have continued to rise, many of these being within the home – keeping their rooms tidy, babysitting a sibling, etc. Annual research by the analysts Datamonitor suggests that in this area children's negotiation skills are becoming increasingly sophisticated in putting a price on their time or services (Datamonitor 2000).

What does the pocket money buy?

- Five to eight years old: 50–80p per week buys sweets.

- 10 to 12 years old: £2.50 per week buys the above plus video rental or CD/Game Boy games (saving required).

- 12 to 13 years old: £10 per week buys the above, plus cinema outing and takeaway.

- 15 years old: £50 per month buys small items of clothing, magazines, occasional computer games and presents and covers the mobile-phone bill.

- 16 plus: £70 per month buys above, plus stationery, travel and meals out

(Hutton 2000)

In the United States, as indicated earlier, in the early 1990s, McDonald's and other fast-food advertisers discovered an enormous and, what was then, an overlooked market (Fischer *et al.* 1991). There is every reason to believe that this potential market has increased substantially since then.

Thus children have a spending power and an influence on spending that is sizeable. Children are no longer reckless spenders and are a serious source of income for the corporations determined to colonise their purchasing consciousness. It is no mere chance that some of the biggest research operations into children's resources, their spending habits and their management of money have been conducted by industries with products they wish to sell to children.

Children from low-income families

If it can be called 'fortunate' to be the easy prey of advertising and the greedy, ruthless marketing of big industrial conglomerates, then some children are not so fortunate and have life experiences which further exacerbate the deepening chasm between rich and poor in this country. A survey by Jules Shropshire and Sue Middleton of the experiences and attitudes of children from low-income families towards money reveals a very different picture from that described above (Shropshire and Middleton 1999). While over one-third of British children were living in poverty towards the end of the twentieth century, little was previously known about what effect this had on their understanding of the economic world or upon their value systems and aspirations. This study described the immediate effects of growing up in poor families, drawing on a survey of lifestyles and living standards of children undertaken by the Centre for Research in Social Policy at Loughborough University in 1995 (Shropshire and Middleton 1999). This was based on information from a random sample of 1239 children stratified by age, birth order and family type. The following is based on responses to an administered questionnaire by 435 children aged between 5 and 16 years (27% from income-support families, 43% from lone-parent families, and 22% from lone-parent families on income support). It is worth considering in some detail.

The picture revealed was that children living in lone-parent families and in families claiming income support were less likely to receive regular pocket money and had less experience of handling their own money than did other children. They were likely to receive pocket money only infrequently and only when their parents felt they could afford it. Experience of part-time work was also less likely. Of the two-fifths of children who did have part-time jobs, however, those living in lone-parent and income support families worked for longer hours and for lower rates of pay than did other children. Most of these children were never told about family income or spending and if such discussions did take place then they were more likely to be about spending than income.

Discussions of family finances were more likely to occur in lone-parent families than two-parent families, possibly because lone parents were sharing their anxieties and concerns about money with their children in the absence of another adult with whom to discuss such matters. Discussions of family income were also more likely in families claiming income support than other families. Two-thirds of children in lone-parent families or income-support families said they were frequently told their family could not afford what they wanted; less than half of other children said this. These experiences affected children's beliefs, behaviour and aspirations in that two-fifths of the children living in income-support families and lone-parent families worried that their family did not have enough to live on, compared with less than 10 per cent of other children. In lone-parent households many of the children learned at a young age not to ask for things they wanted. In order to examine this further, these children were asked what they would ask for if it were their birthday next week. While generally children did identify much the same type of items and services as were chosen by children who were less disadvantaged, the estimated cost of the items chosen by children living in lone-parent and income-support families was significantly lower than items named by other children. 'Regardless of the cost of the desired item, a significant number of children from lone-parent and Income Support families had learnt to accept that they might not get what they wanted for their birthday and to cover up their disappointment' (Joseph Rowntree Foundation 1999, p.3). The children's experiences have the ring of forlorn sadness, worry, disappointment and resignation about them.

Children's knowledge and experience of the financial circumstances of their immediate family and of the wider economic world outside were thought likely to affect the children's own economic futures. To date there has been little information about the experiences and attitudes of children living in poverty. This research was focused not so much on children's pocket money or their desires for material goods but rather more generally on whether they learn to be poor. Sadly it seemed to indicate that they do. The opportunities for children living in lone-parent or income-support families to learn to manage a sum of money of their own, in the absence of a regular amount of money as pocket money or as money earned from paid work outside or within the home, are fewer than for children from less disadvantaged families. The research suggests that for such children this sort of early learning constrains not only their expectations in the immediate future but also, even more depressingly, reduces their aspirations for the future, which seems to imply an acceptance of continuing poverty. As regards their future aspirations, these children were asked what they would like to do after they left school. Children in lone-parent or income-support families had much lower career aspirations than children from two-parent or non-income-support families. The former children were more likely than other children to say that they wanted jobs requiring minimal training and generally few academic qualifications. Very few of them hoped to join the labour market in professional occupations defined as socio-economic group four. In a sense these children have been socialised into accepting continuing poverty and powerlessness and implicitly collude with the inevitability of it all.

These experiences in childhood seem to have a long-term effect on children. Interviews of cohorts participating in the National Child Development Study by Gregg, Harkness and Machin (1998) looked at certain characteristics at selected points in the lives of children born in 1958. It was found that young adults who, as children, had suffered financial hardship were in trouble with the law or played truant or had significantly greater than average chances of earning lower wages, being out of work, spending time in prison (in the case of men) or becoming lone parents (in the case of women). This was noted regardless of the socio-economic background or their other experiences in early childhood. Lower educational attainment was only partly responsible for these outcomes. The research concluded that parents who had themselves been disadvantaged in childhood were more likely to have children who did poorly early on at school.

Therefore, although children seem to be an important 'market' as spenders and future spenders, maybe this is an area of the culture where envy and desire provide a vicious antisocial cocktail of disadvantage, powerlessness and retaliatory violent power from the social under-wolves. The marketeers see to it that what children can buy plays a larger and larger part in what they feel they are, in their self-representation and who they are acknowledged to be and the treatment they consequently receive. Earlier and earlier, money also buys drugs and can be amassed from dealing. This adds another layer to the dynamics of envy and desire, a form of resilience, a way of dulling the pain of life as it unequally is and through dealing a repositioning in the peer-group hierarchy.

THE CORPORATE CONSTRUCTION OF CHILDHOOD

Steinberg and Kincheloe coined the term 'Kinder-culture' to describe the corporate construction of postmodern childhood as 'primarily a pedagogy of pleasure' (Steinberg and Kincheloe 1997, p.5). They iden-tify new sites of learning with business and industrial corporations as educators. Their examination of this phenomenon is set within an ex-amination of what they point to as a 'contemporary crisis of childhood' (p.3). This crisis is characterised by views frequently voiced in the popu-lar and academic press that children are growing up too fast, that child-hood has been lost, that children have become tormentors and tormented in broken homes and dysfunctional communities. Indeed, my book opens with an example of boys murdering a toddler in the United Kingdom. Steinberg and Kincheloe illustrate their point by out-lining the worst American nightmare about postmodern childhood and use the film *Halloween* graphically to illustrate their point. The real hor-ror is that no-one is there to help the child as there is separation from both parents and the 'community', which is virtually non-existent (Steinberg and Kincheloe 1997, p.3). Although there are many ways this crisis can be thought about, they suggest that the common signifiers are the horror of danger faced in solitude, and the absence of any sense of power, control and support. The isolation of the postmodern child, they believe, is very real. In the United States, for instance, they suggest that the community is fragmented to the point where even the safety of children in Halloween festivities cannot be guaranteed (Ferguson 1994; Paul 1994). Steinberg and Kincheloe go on to argue: 'Kinderculture and the popular culture in general constitute a social dynamic that contrib-utes to violence by young people' (1997, p.22). The way in which such antisocial exercise of power is scored and orchestrated by the corporate culture is worth further examination.

We have discussed in other parts of this book issues relating to the development of 'resilience', a component of which is the social capital the child feels he/she can call upon. Here it is claimed there is none. The child is bereft. Since the 1960s in the United States, the number of children living with one parent has tripled and since the late 1960s the amount of time parents spend with their children has dropped from an average of 30 hours per week to 17 (Galston 1991; Lipsky and Adams 1994). With a lot of parents working, many children are home alone, fending for themselves, and these children have turned to TV and video games to help pass this time or 'kill' the boredom that is frequently the malaise of the postmodern child.

The relevance of this crisis of childhood to the ongoing concerns of the present chapter is in the way these researchers look for some of the contributory causes and find that the influences in this diet of TV and videos show evidence that a greedy market and financial gain form part of the picture. They acknowledge that there are indeed a number of other causal factors. The complex factor their research has focused and examined in particular has been the corporate production of popular kinderculture and the impact of this kind of socialisation on children. This they see as 'cultural pedagogy' (Steinberg and Kincheloe 1997, p.3), by which term they emphasise that education does not just take place in school but is a process which takes place in a number of social settings, some of which have a very powerful, pervasive and long-lasting influence. Such 'pedagogical sites' they identify as 'those places where power is organised and deployed' (p.4), which are the cinema, the library, books, television, video games, comics, newspapers, magazines, toys, advertisements, sports and such like. Giroux (1994) argues that if we are to really make sense of the educational process in the late twentieth century it is essential that we turn our gaze beyond activities in school to examine also this wider culture. This sort of learning is effective and profound in that it enlists desire and yearning, and in doing so brings about substantial changes in identity. They talk of the 'cultural curriculum', which is determined not within the conventional education system aiming in some general way at producing good citizens, but rather by commerce and industry, the aims of which are profit rather than social and personal wellbeing (Steinberg and Kincheloe 1997).

The concerns of industry frame this cultural pedagogy and these commercial values and aims infiltrate and subvert both adult and child consciousness. What adults and children dream about and yearn for has been carefully shaped by the advertising of products by commercial concerns and the lives and values promoted in the cinema and videos.

Commerce and industry appear to have studied very carefully ways of exploiting the wants of children and adults, of captivating their interests and capitalising upon their insecurities. These industries seem to have become, on the basis of their diligent research, very skilful in tutoring tastes, desires and wishes by using techniques that are stunningly effective in 'teaching' children what they must have and *be*:

> The worldviews produced by corporate advertisers to some degree always let children know that the most exciting things life can provide are produced by your friends in corporate America. The economics lesson is powerful when it is repeated hundreds and thousands of times. (Steinberg and Kincheloe 1997, p.4)

The argument is put forward that professionals, parents and members of society have a responsibility to become literate about what is going on. They should analyse and understand the brainwashing that is taking place under their very noses. They should study the curriculum of big business and take an informed look at the political and social consequences of this highly professional form of education and subversion. Cultural pedagogy is a form of domination but, since it is seen as the 'pedagogy of pleasure' (Steinberg and Kincheloe 1997, p.5), disconnecting child addicts from it is no simple matter. The refraction of reality by the distorting lens of corporate culture means that asserting one's own view of reality – that is, becoming 'powerful' as positioned throughout my volume – is not a possibility; the child has been sucked into an illusion so compelling that it becomes his/her own reality. Hence branded trainers at a phenomenally 'unreal' price become the 'norm' in the child's mendaciously tutored world-view.

Moreover the commercial imperative is often cloaked in a spurious sort of legitimacy – note the American Eagle and flag on billboards and retail outlets apparently contributing to the pure all-American patriotism of some products in the USA. McDonald's advertisements use home and family symbols which appear to position them as the defenders of the American way of life. Kroc believed that McDonald's public image should be a 'combination of YMCA, Girl Scouts and Sunday School' (Kroc 1977). The teaching packs sponsored by Shell, McDonald's and many other such strategies, one could argue, promote the same message of wholesome benevolence. Steinberg, Kincheloe and their colleagues argue powerfully for cultural studies to take on the challenge of studying the broadly based nature of childhood education, including how the power dynamics that characterise kinderculture produce pleasure and pain in the daily lives of children. They point out that the study of children has been largely neglected by cultural studies on the grounds that it is regarded as a low-status academic activity. They argue for work to promote an understanding of kinderculture because not only does it subtly give insights into children's consciousness and into the culture in general, it also reveals at a very basic level what it is that unsettles us in our everyday lives and why this is so. Their claim is that such a study within the ambit of cultural studies could lead to:

> ...democratic pedagogies for childhood at the cultural, familial and school levels. Cultural studies connected to a democratic pedagogy for children involves investigations of how children's consciousnesses are produced around issues of social justice and egalitarian power relations. Thus our analyses focus on exposing the footprints of power left by the corporate producers of kinderculture and their effect on the psyches of our children. Appreciating the ambiguity and complexity of power, our democratic pedagogy for children is committed to challenging manipulative and racist, sexist, and class-biased entertainment for children. It is equally opposed to other manifestations of kinderculture that promote violence and social and psychological pathologies. Children's entertainment, like other social spheres, is a contested public space where different social, economic, and political interests compete for control. Unfortunately, Americans are uncomfortable with overt discussions of power. Such unease allows the power wielders to hide in the recesses of the cultural and political landscape – all the while shaping cultural expression and public policy in their own interests, which may conflict with those of less powerful social groups such as children. (Steinberg and Kincheloe 1997, pp.6–7)

Strategies of resistance have been suggested, which have been dealt with elsewhere in this book. In looking at children and economic power perhaps we ought to look at cultural pedagogy a little further. Children developed highly proficient skills in media literacy without many adults being aware of it or acknowledging it. Such literacy, it is argued, is a basic feature of a child's entrainment into the social and commercial world, yet little acknowledgement has been made of the importance of media literacy – it is generally thought of as not a topic for children (McLaren and Morris 1997).

Giroux (1997) reflects on the blurring of the boundaries between entertainment, education and commerce such that messages are being delivered to children in a Disneyesque way; this is far more in the interests of the commercial sponsor than the welfare and development of the child. Kinderculture is seen as a social force that influences the child's understanding of the meaning of the world such that interpretations are within a constrained range of possibilities (Donald 1993; Mumby 1989; Thiele 1986), which hinder the development of the child's full understanding of civic society in serving to feed the divisions of envy, inequalities and greed. 'Affective moments of power evasion' (Fiske 1993, p.27) provide a space in which the child can reread the culture in a more critical mode – looking, for example, at Disney films, analysing them in terms of gender bias. This is an exciting beginning and in kinderculture we are taken not only through the terrors media culture holds but also through various steps towards the favoured 'democratic pedagogy' in countering it.

CHILDREN'S CONSUMER DEVELOPMENT

Changing perspective from the culture to the child's cognitive equipment through which the media are processed, Deborah Roedder John reviewed 25 years of research that had been undertaken on the consumer socialisation of children (D.R. John 1999). A model is proposed in which the child's ability to process information coming from the corporate culture is viewed in terms of stages. This stocktaking of research assesses what has been established about children's consumer thinking. She identifies a developmental sequence in the emergence of knowledge relevant to consumption, in the values implicit in all this activity. The framework which is presented involves a series of conceptual stages, with children moving on from one stage to another as they mature both socially and cognitively. These stages are examined, looking at the research on children's knowledge of advertising, branding, products, shopping, choices and prices. The motivation for purchasing and the influence of parents on consumption are also considered in a very different way to the kinderculture analyses just discussed. There is a considerable body of literature from very different perspectives on children as consumers (Moschis 1985; Moschis, Nelson and McGrath 1995; Young 1990).

Looking at children as consumers in an age-related way it is possible to argue that the way that children process advertising relates to their cognitive abilities at their particular stage of development. Piaget's theory of cognitive development proposes four main stages of cognitive development and forms the basis for this model (summarised by Ginsberg and Opper 1988). The first stage when consumption becomes sharply focused is during the pre-operational phase, which lasts from about the age of two years to seven years, when children are able to distinguish television advertising as separate from programmes. They are able to do this, claims John (D.R. John 1999), on the basis of very concrete features, such as advertisements being shorter, rather than on the basis of the intent of such advertisements. This kind of understanding comes much later, around eight years old, when children begin to grasp something about the persuasive intentions of the advertiser. Although the child might, by the time he/she reaches this age, be *able* to discern the purposes of advertising, he/she rarely uses this knowledge in evaluating advertising messages. John (D.R. John 1999) cites information providing explanations for this disjunction, identifying children's inability between ages 8 and 11 years to retrieve and use information – an ability which she claims is still developing.

Cognitive development is not the only feature of children's growing awareness of the commercial world and their role as consumers.

> Social perspective taking, involving the ability to see perspectives beyond one's own, is strongly related to purchase influence and negotiation skills, for example. Impression formation, involving the ability to make social comparisons, is strongly related to understanding the social aspects of products and consumption. (D.R. John 1999, p.6)

It is claimed that children's abilities to understand perspectives other than their own – that is, to take an intersubjective view – also progress through a series of stages (Selman 1980). The social and intersubjective aspects of consumer understanding, as is explained in D.R. John's review, hinge on the child's ability to understand the advertiser's intent, which is crucial to reading the corporate culture and, indeed, resisting it. Selman suggests that children are not usually able to spot the persuasive intentions of the advertiser until they are about eight to ten years old. This ability to weigh up information from many sources and perspectives is indicated, so it is claimed, in thoughtful, flexible and appropriate decision making. The model presented is so designed that the stages overlap within the age ranges to accommodate the fact that these complex, multifaceted abilities may be more clearly evident towards the end of a stage than in the middle when they are still developing.

D.R. John's (1999) review of 25 years of consumer research acknowledges that the developments do not take place in a vacuum but within a social context of parents, peers, friends, mass media and marketing institutions. The role of the marketing institutions seems underplayed relative to the discussion in the preceding section, which illustrates the ways in which business and industry have subtly but unremittingly courted their young consumers and in so doing have researched the nature of 'the ground' in which they wish to create a 'need'. John states that these influences are not incorporated into the suggested framework due to the primary focus on age. While this is a plausible excuse, one might wonder whether this is another example of the way in which the academic community has chosen to be relatively blind to the cultural study of childhood and to the power that the corporate socialisers wield. 'One of the most enduring concerns about consumer socialisation is that our culture encourages children to focus on material goods as a means of achieving personal happiness, success and self-fulfilment' (D.R. John 1999). What makes this sinister is that the corporate socialisation of children involves powerful and sophisticated techniques of schooling desire.

ECONOMIC POLICIES AND CHILD IMPACT

While children are being mercilessly recruited as consumers, economic policies seem blinkered to the effects of such policies on children. 'Today's dominant economic paradigm (globally and in the EU) has a pronounced adult bias' (Save the Children 2000, p.27). This was the conclusion to the International Save the Children Alliance Europe

Group's review of *Children, Economics and the EU,* looking at the situation of the European Union's (EU's) 90 million children who make up one-fifth of the EU's population. Economic policies form the framework within which children thrive or falter; such policies can, for instance, influence how many children are doomed to live in poverty and the extent to which it is possible to ensure secure home environments for children growing up. Some national economic decisions can facilitate the combining of work and family life while others make it virtually impossible to juggle the two. The possibilities of young people entering the labour market for the first time can also be profoundly constrained by government policies. In regions of great disadvantage, economic policies can strike at the lives and emotional and material security of whole generations of children in irreparable ways. Government economic decisions are not neutral as regards children's wellbeing, yet child impact is rarely a consideration when such decisions are made. In developing countries macroeconomists design structural adjustment programmes which totally disregard the interests of the child and can even be quite harmful to them. Moreover children's voices are never heard – their point of view as regards their life experiences is not sought or taken into account, which further serves to reinforce their powerlessness. Some ways of hearing children's voices in policy making have been found at various levels, with different degrees of success, as described in Chapters 7 and 8. These have ranged from the Voice of the Children international involvement to the work of Youth Councils pressing for child-impact statements in the introduction of new policies at local government levels.

So little systematic work has been done to analyse the effects of economic policies on children that the International Save the Children Alliance Europe Group commissioned Save the Children Sweden to co-ordinate a review of the situation (Save the Children 2000). This was intended to bring child-impact issues to attention in the following ways.

- By drawing the attention of policy makers, economists, academics and NGOs and others concerned with children's rights issues to the links between children's rights and economics.

- By encouraging decision makers to take a grip on the effects of economic policies on children by putting pressure on

European economists to develop tools by which child impact can be analysed.

- By encouraging NGOs working in children's rights areas to take on board the importance of integrating economics and economic analysis into their work.

- By encouraging an analysis of direct and indirect effects on children by the analysis of direct measures such as EU expenditure to the far more indirect and subtle effects of EU trade agreements.

- By examining the fundamental objectives of EU economic policy making and the pressures and changes it is facing and what the response to these challenges might mean for children's rights and welfare (Save the Children 2000).

To this end, Save the Children in Romania, Spain, the UK and Sweden held group discussions with young people aged 15 to 17 years old. In inflation, employment or unemployment, savings, investments, fiscal surpluses and deficits – that is, macroeconomic broad-canvas policies – children rarely feature. A country's non-monetary fiscal policies tend also to be 'child-blind'.

> Financial markets have come to play an increasingly im-portant role in determining the scope for macro-economic policies in most countries in the world. But financial markets react to short-term events, and do not consider the interests of children. Children take too long to develop to be interesting. To a currency trader to whom 'long term' may mean one week, the rate of return on investments in children's health and education is not worth considering. Clearly, neither financial markets nor the majority of macroeconomists are renowned for taking the interest of the child as their point of departure. (Save the Children 2000, p.16)

Why this blind spot? In Chapter 3, some of the reasons why children do not count have already been examined. While one would argue that the protection of the rights of the child is primarily to be justified in moral rather than economic terms, the financial arguments are nevertheless strong. Prevention of antisocial behaviour through education and vari-ous child-welfare provisions is obviously better than remedial action post hoc and it is also cheaper. The Swedes, who were part of this Save the Children study, have observed that the total costs to Swedish society of a single life of crime – beginning with petty crime in childhood and continuing through spells in prison amounting to about ten years in total, with long-term unemployment in between – is estimated to be the equivalent of 2 million euros. Investing in child education and welfare therefore can be thought of in terms of how much money it saves if a long-term view of the situation is taken.

This, of course, takes an oversimplistic view of the carefully calibrated corporate lens through which the child has been tutored by business interests to 'see' the world. This is a 'world' in which TV and the cinema have made violence, crime and various forms of delinquent behaviour captivating and alluring and relatively commonplace. In emphasising that there are no economic policies that are 'child neutral', Save the Children produces evidence which indicates that policies which appear to have very little impact on children do in fact influence children for better or worse.

Policies, legislation and expenditure which are quite explicit in targeting children embrace most of the Articles of the UN Convention on the Rights of the Child. These direct influences cover public provision for education, day-care centres and primary health care and regulations against exploitative child labour. These are all measures which are decided in the European Union at member state level. They are all explicitly designed to protect children's rights. Policies which are less directly focused on child welfare come to affect children via their effects on the family. They include social security arrangements, welfare policies and social and regional policies which affect the family. Responsibilities for these policies may be shared between the EU and the member state – as, for instance, in the case of employment and regional policies.

Even less directly we encounter policies which, while profoundly affecting children, are not primarily designed with them in mind, and so these consequences are largely indirect. They include monetary policies, overall fiscal policies and the formation of the European Monetary Union (EMU) itself. Finally, least direct of all, trading provisions aimed at the opening up of markets also have effects on children. Included here are the EU's trade policies, the establishment of the single European market and the wider context of the process now commonly referred to as 'globalisation'.

It is important that this work (Save the Children 2000) draws our attention to the indirect effects of these policies on children, as this is so often overlooked by civil servant advisers and seriously forgotten by many policy makers. This study shows how the situation of parents is intimately connected with economic and social processes generally. The effects that proposed developments have on them in turn influence the sort of life children have as they grow up. All these policies and measures have consequences for children's power in a world which is increasingly defined in economic terms. It becomes very clear how important it is to improve our understanding of the mechanisms by which economic policies come to have an effect on children and on alleviating the poverty trap. Save the Children argue that there are tools to consider child impact, and other tools could easily be developed. It is emphasised over and over again throughout the work that 'these studies provide further evidence of the view that no economic policy can be assumed to be child neutral and that it *is* possible to design economic policies that can be much more explicitly child friendly' (Save the Children 2000, p.109).

Looking at economic policy and children in Europe is complicated by the fact that some decisions affecting children are taken at the member state level, so decision making at both levels must be considered. Member states continue to set their own budgets which have effects – direct and indirect – on children and their families. Nevertheless the EU has its own budget and a range of economic policies, both of which have effects at various levels on children's lives. A detailed discussion of the way in which some of the EU policy areas have affected children can be found in Ruxton (1999).

European Monetary Union

Examining the European Monetary Union from the point of view of the best interests of the child, there are indeed some things to be said in its favour. Direct benefits include the ways in which contributions of the EMU to growth, stability and employment in the union would have potentially positive effects on children. These would come about as a result of more certainty and predictability in the exchange rate between countries, which affects profits. Investment funds would become more mobile as currency risks are removed. Obviating the need to switch between national currencies would not only make travelling but also payment much easier and less costly within a highly mobile Europe. Common pricing is also expected to increase competition and hence productivity and wealth creation. All of these things serve to enhance economic activity generally. It is also predicted that low stable inflation will be a consequence of adopting the euro. Children would benefit from all these things as household members; households would indirectly benefit from these economic gains by means of higher wages, promotions and salary increases redistributed through the tax and benefit system. It is also anticipated that competitive pressures will bring down the costs of rearing children in terms of food, clothing, equipment, etc. The effects of mega-policies linked to the EMU are, however, unpredictable in their outcomes in relation to the poverty trap within the diverse cultures they encompass. However, it is to be hoped that a predictable stable economy would also mean that parents could plan ahead more confidently in terms of housing and other family-related expenditures. Stabilisers which have been introduced to work towards convergence in the Stability and Growth Pact reveal consequences with ominous implications for families. 'Initial evidence (from convergence criteria implementations) suggests that social expenditure will be cut to keep to budgetary targets, which will harm the poorest and particularly children in poorer regions – an experience similar to structural adjustment programmes in developing countries' (Save the Children 2000, p.38). Volume 2 of the Children in Charge Series (John 1996b) discussed the adverse impact of policies in South America introduced to deal with foreign debt on child care, infant malnutrition and mortality (Chavarria 1992; Duron Segovia 1993).

Single market

The single market, has an impact on children in ways which are both potentially positive and negative.[2] There are indirect benefits in that families and their children have freedom of movement within the EU because of the comparability of legislation, employment, training and consumer protection. While this is all theoretically possible, few families in fact benefit from the freedom that such harmonisation provides. There are two areas, however, in which the consistency of labour laws has helped children. There has been a harmonisation of standards that has outlawed harmful and exploitative child labour, contained in the Young Workers Directive 1994/33/EC. The recognition of maternity rights and the need to provide child care has also affected children's lives for the better. The Pregnant Women at Work Directive, adopted by the Council of Ministers in 1992, has been seen as a family-friendly and progressive step. Guidelines and national action plans for employment drafted in 1999 have earmarked as a priority, in order to facilitate the return of parents to the labour market, the need to develop policies and implementation programmes for the care of children and dependants.

While measures have been introduced or planned with very positive direct and indirect effects on children, the single market has had costs for children. As regards legislation within the single market on products, children do not seem to have been consistently thought about. The protection of children was not given explicit consideration in the drafting of the EU Directive on misleading advertising and distance selling. In toy advertising the EU's position even undermined the attempts of one of its member states to protect children. The Greek government, as part of its determination to promote the best interests of the child, had banned the television advertising of toys. Toy manufacturers appealed to the European Commission who ruled that such a ban breached single-market rules. Similarly in Sweden, TV advertisements are prohibited for children under 12. A UK television station, however, beamed advertisements across to Sweden and under the free market of goods and services this was deemed legitimate. It is clear, therefore, given these two examples, that measures introduced to protect children within a member state can be circumvented in quite legitimate ways within the EU. A further worry has arisen in connection with the free movement of people across the EU in that this freedom has extended to drugs, crime and child trafficking. It has not only allowed the free movement of goods and services but also enabled child abusers and paedophiles to move around freely, covering their traces, and also to exchange pornographic material, as had recently been revealed by the cracking of a big international paedophile ring.

It is clear that in the development of economic policies at any level, child-impact assessments need to be made. Economic interests should not overrule children's welfare, whether it is in the relative prosperity of the European Union or in developing countries saddled with massive debts and operating adjustment policies which are 'child blind'.

The rights of children living within the EU 'have developed in a piecemeal way and in some instances children's rights have had to be established by taking cases to the Courts of Justice' (Radda Barnen 1998, p.20). The Save the Children study concludes by recommending that a comprehensive reference to the rights and interests of the child should be inserted in the next revision of the Treaty on European Union. The existing Treaty should, in their view, include a specific amendment to articles on consumer protection and product standardisation to ensure that the specific interests of children are considered.

CHOOSING

Children as consumers are caught in a web of variable institutional protection in family, property and vulnerability to commercial pressures, the general thread of which is to constrain their freedom. Institutional policy, whether mere economic or regulatory, fails to take children into account in ways which award the child scope for informed consumer choice and overall empowerment. Internal contradictions abound; coercive advertising may contain representations which are evocative and liberating. Conversely, well-meaning regulation may restrict competition and drive up prices.

This chapter has focused very largely on children in the developed world. By doing so, it is hoped that the counterpoint between this perspective and material in other parts of the book which looks particularly at children's lives in the developing world will emphasise that wealth does not necessarily mean power. While in some of the wealthiest nations in the world it would seem that children are free to make choices, we see that this 'freedom' is an illusion. I have looked at the corporate entrapment of children in a consumer society. A life of consumer compulsion, of orchestrated desire and subtly controlled 'choices' leaves our children as fodder for the marketeers' mill. Wealth and riches, I have tried to demonstrate, do not necessarily provide protection from a form of exploitation that is as subtle as it is powerful. Thus children who, on the face of it, seem to be a powerful magnet for business are in fact relatively powerless when within the thrall of that 'magnetic field'. Teaching them to read the text of their culture, to scorn the advertisers' claims with the dismissive 'As if' of disbelief, is not easy. Acceptance within the peer group compounds the strength of the consumer lures. I have illustrated in Chapter 3 how more comprehensive indices of poverty now include, in measures of wellbeing, inclusion. I have pointed out here how poor children try to modify their aspirations to reality. Among the more affluent, inclusion is still a major anxiety for children them-selves. For my grand-daughter, at three years old it was important to have a 'Barbie' birthday cake to keep her edge with the gang at the play-group. These are not poverty traps but the childhood entrapment of a rich consumer society in the Western world. Children are not choosing freely but are hostages, conscripted into consumption and rendered powerless in powerful ways.

Endnotes

1.   Argos is a major British retail warehouse which promotes its wares through the distribution of large free pictorial catalogues.

2.   The single market is the name given to the European Union's internal market. It is a unique example of a regional trading block, where 15 member states have consented to taking a range of economic decisions at European level. This means that in certain areas of macroeconomic decision making, national sovereignty is relinquished in the interests of integration of the market and the facilitation of its growth.

PART III

Enduring and Surviving

CHAPTER FIVE

Whatever Makes You Stronger...

Reflections in your mind
Troubles you have been through
It shows
In the mirror, in the water
Misery through your body
Happiness through your heart
It all shows in the mirror in the water
Reflections of thy brain.

(An eight-year-old child's poem)

I have suggested in Chapter 3, by means of examples drawn from around the world, that children count for little or nothing in a world intent on conflict or aggrandisement of various kinds. Taking a global perspective this is probably true. Narrowing down the focus to a national level, maybe children, while not 'counting' as they should as fellow citizens, are not a negligible force in the structure, practicalities and politics of a society. Children's position is intricately woven into the unique fabric of their culture both as witnesses of it and as contributors and agents for change within it. This counterpoint between passive and active roles shapes this chapter and the next, providing a theoretical model around which the whole book implicitly or explicitly revolves. These two aspects of children's experience, I argue, are pivotal in a psychological approach to the understanding of human development.

If children are to be meaningful citizens in a social world, what then is their own power base – from which they can exercise their rights – and what are the social and cultural factors which constrain and shape such a springboard? More than ten years on, has the United Nations Convention on the Rights of the Child proved to be a useful tool in establishing the child's position in society? Is the child's voice now a voice to be heard? I have already hinted at ways children have been viewed as 'the new dangerous classes' (Ingleby 1985) or, worse, as 'witches' (Douglas 1970) who threaten the status quo and government and parent hegemony. In the UK there have been a succession of enquiries as to how and why children have been neglected, tortured and killed by people 'caring' for them and their situation overlooked or ignored by the various services supposed to intervene when parents or carers come under suspicion. Milan Kundera, in an interview with Ian McEwan, memorably said:

> People always see the political and personal as different worlds, as if each had its own logic, its own rules, but the very horrors that take place on the big stage of politics resemble, strangely but insistently, the small horrors of our private life. (Reynolds 1995, p.218)

POWER RELATIONS AND SURVIVAL

A recent example of the 'small horror' of private life was that of Victoria Climbie, a little girl sent in 1997 from the Ivory Coast by her parents to stay with her great-aunt in the hope that, in the UK, she would have a better chance in life than her parents could offer. She stayed with this great-aunt and the aunt's boyfriend who subjected her to torture and abuse. She died early in 2000, aged eight, having been beaten and starved for months on end in their flat in London. The couple were able to inflict terrible injuries despite the repeated involvement of the authorities. The whole catalogue of ways in which alarms were raised about her plight went unheeded. At least 12 chances to save her were missed by agencies that should have protected her. The child's parents concluded that the only people who had truly tried to help their daughter were members of the public who contacted the authorities. Their lawyer said:

> It is regrettable that the most that was done for Victoria was done by those who were not paid or trained to protect her. In this case the most striking conclusion to emerge is that the profession systematically ignored the evidence of child abuse which was glaringly obvious to those who stood outside the system. (Judd 2002)

It might seem that this child did not matter to anyone in contact with her. The sheer venom with which she was treated by her 'family' in the UK raises many questions about what function children serve within the domestic setting. They occasionally have such a significant role that their obliteration, for some carers, seems the only way of coping with the interpersonal dynamics. The indifference that this child's situation met with within the social services casts a further sinister light on the case. The suggestion is that the death of this little girl at the hands of an aunt and her partner was partly the dreadful consequence of a sort of political correctness. The social worker assigned to her and the superior of that social worker (described during the inquiry as having been developing a serious psychotic mental illness at the time) were both black. The implicit understanding, therefore, was that their work must not be questioned for such a criticism might be construed as 'racist'. This is further compounded by the notion that:

> ...social workers are taught – in the name of ethnic awareness – to treat the customs of other countries, other races with respect. Certain cultures accept violence towards women and children. If the child had been severely disciplined, well maybe it's the custom in her African village, don't interfere with cultural norms. Let well alone. (Lambert 2002)

Thus it is even suggested that political correctness was a contributory factor in what poor little Victoria had to endure and her eventual murder. While children are noticed within the complex dynamics of the 'family', the extent to which they are significant has been seen by Judith Ennew as relating to their position in a matrix defined by gender, race and class. She saw power relationships as crucial. 'Adult power over children is so absolute that in a sense all children are abused and all adults abusers' (Ennew 1986, p.24). She believes that the two axes of the power relationships as they influence children's lives are:

- power relations between men and women (as children are so often bound up in problems faced by women)
- power relations between adults and children (Ennew 1986).

Race and class further complicate these two factors. Spelling this out further means that although a boy child may have a more powerful position than a girl of the same age and ethnic origin, if the girl is white and he is black this may not be so. On the other hand if the boy is older and black this imbalance may be changed. If he is younger and black but of a higher social class he might well overcome the power advantage that age confers. It is not an entirely simple picture and has important implications. It is also further compounded by cultural ideologies as I describe below.

CHILDREN IN THEIR CULTURE

I could catalogue a huge number of examples which demonstrate that within the 'family', in whatever way that might be constituted, and within the peer group and immediate society, children do count and signify powerful forces at work in the dynamics of relationships within those settings. Within these dynamics they often have to endure appalling treatment that they have little or no power to change. Leaving 'home' with all the perils that entails might be the only solution. The Children's Society report in 1999 estimated that one in nine young people will run away overnight before the age of 16. This suggests that around 77,000 young people under the age of 16 will run away for the first time each year (Child Poverty Action Group 1999). Of the 80 children murdered in the UK in 2001, a third were murdered within the family. This chapter is not the place to examine those particular issues further, other than to remark that to the extent that psychologists have acknowledged and studied children's experiences they have become somewhat obsessed with children's suffering. I hypothesised earlier that it has been the psychologists' reluctance to work with children's experiences that have made them notably absent from researching and indeed championing children's rights. Their concern and entry into such debates is welcome, but concentrating on the suffering of children can distort popular conceptions of children and indeed their own perceptions of themselves. Often a picture of children as dependent, relatively powerless and in need of protection is, albeit unconsciously, reinforced by such a preoccupation. This may lead to psychologists and other caring professionals adopting a helping role which, at best, may 'help' but, very likely, may usurp the agency of the child. Moreover, looking backwards at the sweep of suffering, rather than at the way the child in the present manages hard times and what the future prognosis might be, is also the legacy of the genetic fallacy I have discussed earlier in this book (see Chapter 2). Psychologists' work on endurance, however, is relevant as it is based largely in the present and is forward-looking.

Children do indeed suffer as in the example I have just cited, yet they often cope with adversity in a manner which frequently belies their years. In what ways do children manage the challenges that their lives can present to them and how do they themselves, by their actions, turn some of those challenges to good effect? This does not involve a power over oppressors but rather a power to endure. It is in such circumstances that children demonstrate self-determination, a sophisticated grasp of their situation and, often, considerable courage. The International Resilience Project (Grotberg 1995) was briefly described in Chapter 1 with the factors identified as 'I have', 'I can', 'I am'. That project took a particularly individual orientation, not looking so much at the peer group – 'We have', 'We can', 'We are' – that is, it did not look so much at the surrounding culture of the child as at the child's individual and personal resources. Social capital was considered very much from the individual's point of view, yet taken collectively it can be a great resource and shapes responses in particular ways. Schucksmith and Hendry (1998), listening to the concerns adolescents expressed, found that they stressed the importance of peer acceptance and parental love.

Judith Ennew has provided, in much of her writing (Ennew 1986, 1995), evidence that the preoccupations of the culture colour the way the child interprets the world, makes sense of it and shapes how he/she defines himself/herself. In one of her examples in Peru, her conversations with children had as a major recurring theme the 'happy family'. The Peruvian children referred to happiness a lot when they were discussing the family. In contrast, when she was researching in Jamaica, she found that the children there were always talking about suffering. She detected a pervasive concept of 'the sufferer' in Jamaica coupled with a belief that this suffering had to be stoically borne. It may be that these ideologies helped the children to cope with the demanding lives they led and to structure and rationalise their personal worlds.

Such pervasive concepts may also subtly serve as a form of control. The Peruvian child may feel that for acceptance it is important to be seen as a happy person, while the Jamaican child has to put up with suffering to be an accepted member of Jamaican society. Ennew emphasises that it is important to look at the broad philosophical and ideological background against which views on childhood and child-rearing are formed. She believes that the individual is partly a product of these implicit ideologies (Ennew 1986). Moreover the power the child can wield and how that child views the prevailing ideologies and values of the culture in which he/she is located shapes his/her own potency and self-determination. The child is seen by cultural anthropology as mirroring the power struggles of society as a whole. Martin Woodhead has made a strong case that any cross-cultural child-development programme must take account of differences in social and cultural assumptions about the values and goals for childhood which pertain within that specific setting (Woodhead 1990, 1999b). He found that in Trinidad and Tobago the achievement of language and motor skills might be given less priority by parents and by teachers than the child's spiritual development (Woodhead 1996). A child's development in those localities is more likely, therefore, to be judged by the extent to which the child has developed spiritually rather than linguistically.

Traditionally childhood has been studied within the framework of adults' notions about children and their understanding of them (Christensen and James 2000). Children were rarely called upon to express their views. Research was primarily *on* children or around them rather than *with* them but, thanks in part to the thinking behind the United Nations Convention on the Rights of the Child, approaches have changed (Verhellen 1993). In fact it has been suggested that a new paradigm has emerged in childhood studies (James and Prout 1990).

> This suggests that children can and should be viewed as social actors, as people who can take an active role in any research relationship and, therefore, as people who are self-determining and possessed of a particular perspective on the social world of which we as adults need to take account. (James 2000, p.172)

James identifies this as a paradigm shift to 'the new social studies of childhood'. Formerly research on children had been coloured by a whole set of assumptions about children and childhood. Some of the questionable elements of these assumptions were the extent to which childhood could be seen as universal and the nature of the part played by cognitive and biological changes. Social competence had been seen as a function of biological and cognitive stages, and age was seen as an important index of development. I have examined earlier in this volume problems associated with this sort of developmentalism. Priscilla Alderson (Alderson 2000), in a volume in the Children in Charge Series, has also examined in some detail the problems of such developmentalism being present in trying to understand young children. Age and stage become irrelevant. The problems with this approach had become clear – it was no longer tenable to disregard the social factors in children's development or to be blind to the context of cultural assumptions in which such development occurs contrary to the abiding myth. Children could no longer be regarded as passive recipients of the socialisation process. Developmental psychology, as I have indicated in Chapter 1, was taking, in the 1970s, a much more interactive and dynamic social view of childhood. As I shall argue later, the challenges children experience in adjusting dynamically to their own specific culture is what shapes their development.

A recognition of the importance of the immediate social context raises questions about the extent to which it is possible to talk about childhood in any sort of universal way. While sociologists were emphasising children as social actors within varying cultural and social frameworks (James, Jenks and Prout 1998), psychologists were mostly silent. The reasons for this have been suggested in earlier chapters as relating to psychologists' anxiety to reinforce the position of their discipline within the natural sciences, being therefore reluctant to deal with direct experience. Psychologists were busy categorising while sociologists were naturalising. Social and developmental psychologists are now beginning to contribute useful insights about the *quality* of the experiences that children have in terms of endurance and resilience, which may, despite cultural contexts, have some universal characteristics (Grotberg 1995; Hendry and Kloep 2002; Suedfeld 1997).

CHILDREN'S POWER AND PARENT–CHILD RELATIONSHIPS

The prevailing ideologies and values of the culture shape perspectives within that culture and, importantly for my argument here, the relationships that form the context in which the child is reared and has to survive. The child's power base in recent years has reflected changes in parent–child relationships and value structures surrounding these relationships.

In Mozambique for instance, Palme, in Volume 3 of this Children in Charge Series, points out tensions that arise between children and their parents as a result of 'progress'. While there is a desire to send children from rural villages to the towns so that they will benefit from the educational opportunities the urban setting offers, there are also fears.

> The educational project was not only costly but hazardous…it was far from unproblematic, as witnessed by numerous stories of ungrateful relatives whose behaviour once they had disappeared to the city, showed little respect for their group of origin and its needs. The 'secrets' of school and of formal education, to which the educated young man (or woman) were considered to be initiated, then, also represented a potential danger to the moral values which guaranteed the unity of the group… The transformation might be accepted for boys but represented a considerable risk for girls. An educated girl would not be able to marry a man with less education than herself. (Palme 1997, p.206)

In a matrilineal society this raised complex problems. In Mozambique, after 15 years of civil war, the migration of many rural families to urban settings created further disruptions of family bonds and structures.

In Europe an analysis of the values of contemporary European modernity (Therborn 1995) suggests three important influences of post-1960 tendencies, all of which have served to weaken family collectivism. This is a context which affects not only the parent's sense of being in control but also the child's sense of personal power. These have been important changes as, although they have an indirect effect, they relate to the intra-family value system in positioning the child on the dependence–autonomy continuum.

The first of these influences has been the entry of the mass media and television into children's lives. Neil Postman, a professor of media studies, in the early 1980s had attracted some considerable attention by claiming, in a somewhat overgeneralised argument, that the appearance of television meant that childhood had disappeared – that is, the divide between the adults' and children's world was dissolved (Postman 1983). Therborn, one of Europe's foremost sociologists, in an overview of the trajectory of European societies, East and West, since the end of World War II, saw that the advent of the mass media opened up another, rather special world outside the home and neighbourhood. Whether the main effect has been a 'global media moulding' or an extension of individuation, the forming of the individual, he says, remains an open question. He states, 'The coupling of the opposite alternatives is only yet another manifestation of the dialectics of modernity' (Therborn 1995, p.290). While Therborn does not mention this, the growth of the Internet in recent years has extended this profound effect on the power base of the child. We find (EU 1999) that Internet use in the EU almost doubled between 1998 and 1999 according to a survey released by the European Commission on 20 July 1999. An average of 8.3 per cent of private households in the EU had Internet access at the end of 1998, which was up from 4.4 per cent in 1997. The level of Internet usage varies widely from 39.6 per cent of the population in Sweden to 10 per cent in the UK and 3.9 per cent in Greece. Of these users it is not clear how many are children. Children, however, have found the Internet an amazing tool in their own emancipation both in gathering information and in exchanging with contacts through e-mail systems. This is a powerful tool as it is not clear that the user is a child and moreover information not easily available to children by any other means can be accessed. Since the time high-school students in the United States used this means to gather information required for making bombs and gathering weapons to attack pupils in their school, attempts have increased to include safeguards to prevent children roaming through the Internet freely. The use of chat rooms by paedophiles has also increased the pressure for controls on this medium; the Internet has been liberating for children but, like so many freedoms, protection from danger is now placing restrictions on it.

A second influence on parent–child relations is seen as relating to the prevalence or otherwise of extra-parental day-care and pre-primary schooling. This was spearheaded in Eastern Europe, becoming pronounced in Scandinavia after 1970, but much less important elsewhere, although to a certain extent visible in the French, Italian and Belgian 'maternal schools' and in the German kindergartens (OECD 1990a). These two influences, the media and daycare/preschooling, are both seen as 'reversing the parental home-centredness which followed upon the constitution of modern childhood' (Therborn 1995, p.291). Therborn examines comparative parental values in Europe and beyond. Clearly, to fully understand the implications of much of this data, it is necessary to read it in the national and historical context; nevertheless in a very broad brushstroke way it provides for interesting comparisons between countries. It has also to be borne in mind, however, that there is a possibility that the questions are understood differently in different cultures.

Table 5.1 World views on parenting

Qualities of children to be encouraged – independence or obedience? Parental duty to do their best for their children even at the expense of their own wellbeing, or should parents have their own lives and not be asked to sacrifice? *Dominance* scores, i.e. the percentage agreeing with the former of each pair of questions minus that agreeing with the opposite statement. Unweighted national averages.

Region/Country	Independence	Parental Sacrifice
North-Central Europe[1]	29	34
South-West Europe[2]	-9	60
Eastern Europe I[3]	41	26
Eastern Europe II[4]	0	25
North America	15	52
Latin America[5]	-11	64
Ex-Col. Zone[6]	-40	70
East Asian EIM[7]	55	(16)[8]
Turkey	-12	39

1. Austria, West Germany, the Netherlands, Denmark, Finland, Iceland, Norway and Sweden.
2. Britain, Northern Ireland, France, Italy, Portugal, Spain.
3. Bulgaria, Hungary, East Germany, Estonia, Latvia, Lithuania.
4. Czechoslovakia, Poland, Belorussia, Russia.
5. Brazil, Chile, Mexico.
6. India, Nigeria.
7. East Asian countries of externally induced modernisation: China, Japan, South Korea.
8. An average makes little sense here: China score 42, Japan 12 and South Korea -5.5.

Adapted, with permission, from Therborn (1995) p.292

Data source: World Values Survey 1990–1991, Variables 225, 227, 236

Two questions (among others) were asked of parents.

- What qualities should be encouraged in *children* – independence *or* obedience?

- Do *parents* have a duty to do their best for their children even at the expense of their own wellbeing, *or* should *parents* have their own lives and not be asked to sacrifice?

The percentage agreeing with the former of each pair of questions minus that agreeing with the opposite statement is shown in Table 5.1. Therborn comments that the patterns of cultural values do not correspond very well either with continental or with social systemic boundaries. The countries were therefore grouped with regard to both cultural/historical proximity and the diffusion of parental ideologies. Deviations from these clusters are noted at the bottom of the table.

In this context, a consistent family individualism involves an encouragement of both the children's and the parents' independence – and a consistent family collectivism involves the opposite. Other possible combinations may be seen as child-centred or parent-centred individualism rather than 'inconsistent'. The encouragement of the child's independence is likely to be empowering in increasing knowledge of the world and mastery of it. Therborn detects 'two Europes' (1995) – one which is more individualist than most of the world and one not. These are not, surprisingly, the traditional clusterings. The countries which embrace child independence and were relatively restrained in demanding parental sacrifices were Central Europe, except for Czechoslovakia (as it was then) and Poland, but linking up with Bulgaria and the Baltic and North Atlantic areas. The strongest individualism was noted in Denmark and West Germany and, on the Eastern fringes, Latvia, Lithuania and Bulgaria. It is interesting to note that Lithuanian respondents were the only ones in the survey where a majority accorded parents priority to their own lives, while the South Koreans were the only other people in the world doing that. In the North–Central European grouping, Sweden comes out as a relatively low scorer. In the South-west of Europe, from Belgium to Portugal, including the UK, family values are distinctly collectivist. A marked preference for obedience over independence is demonstrated in Portugal, followed by France and Northern Ireland, whereas the other countries in this group are about evenly split. The marked Franco–German difference is a reversal of old stereotypes.

> With regard to Europe we may conclude that sharp contrasts in family values persist between blocs of countries which for all practical purposes must be regarded as all modern. But that family, or private world, individualism, more in the New Worlds and probably more than anywhere else on the globe, is clearly held in a strong, central, part of Europe. (Therborn 1995, p.293)

When looking at the mainsprings of children's power or powerlessness, a concentration on Europe alone is obviously too narrow. Therborn, in taking stock of the trajectory of European societies, is aware of this. He points out that Europe can no longer be regarded as the most prestigious club in the world although he feels its boundaries are still important and that it is the most developed club of states. Since the Cold War and in a post-European world, the European project cannot possibly be to preserve a division of Europe. He regards it as a significant supra-state social organisation that could be a major contribution to the twenty-first century, a view reinforced by Hutton's recent analysis of *The World We're In* (Hutton 2002). In wondering whether Europe's politicians will be up to the challenges facing them, Therborn states that an empirical sociological discourse 'may end at the doorstep of politics. The future of modernity, however, cannot be left to the politicians. It hinges rather upon dialogues between intellectuals and peoples' (Therborn 1995, p.295).

He sees two issues as crucial in such a dialogue – issues which are both important in terms of the place of children within concepts of modernity. The first issue relates to questions about the relationship between reality and truth and the search for truth about reality. Are such concepts themselves meaningful and, only if they are, do any notions about progress, growth, development or emancipation make any sense? 'Is the occurrence or not of child exploitation, rape, torture, and murder a potentially universal truth, or only one "local knowledge" or one "narrative" among many?' (Therborn 1995, p.365). Thinking about children's rights is predicated upon a belief that there is a potentially universal truth, although I have discussed earlier Ennew's views that the United Nations Convention on the Rights of the Child relates to Western 'indoor' children (Ennew 1995). Martin Woodhead (2000) further questions a view of universals about childhood development.

The second point Therborn cites, in summing up the future of European modernity, relates to whether illumination, autonomy, maturity, emancipation and liberation – the Enlightenment tradition – can be separated from its base, the history of which was principally a base of economic growth and transformation. 'Sustainable development', a central concept in modernity, is seen as requiring self-limitation particularly by Europe and North America. The question Therborn ponders is whether such economic self-limitation will be compatible with collective democracy and with personal and social emancipation. He sees making these compatible as the great progressive task of the future. In Chapter 8, I will describe the Indian Children's Parliament in Rajasthan, which, in the tradition of Gandhi, provides an example that captures sustainability, rural regeneration, personal responsibility and democratic action – all undertaken by children in one of the poorest regions of the world.

SURVIVAL AND INDOMITABILITY

From a sociological point of view, family values and the way families operate in Europe and more widely provide the context within which children develop and survive. There has been little research on the psychological processes by which these values have their influence and on how children do manage to carry on despite extreme adversity. How do children learn independence and self-determination and what are the processes of individuation?

It is useful to turn to ongoing work by psychologists in what, at first glance, seems an apparently unrelated field. A recent analysis by Peter Suedfeld of this work, based on a wide range of examples (so far only with adults, and much of it outside mainstream social psychology), raises some highly relevant points about survival and coping strategies (Suedfeld 1997). He uses as his point of departure the poem 'Invictus' written in the nineteenth century by the British poet William E. Henley[1]. The thread running through the poem is that of human courage, of remaining unbeaten and unconquerable, of triumphing over adversity and disaster and the strength of the human spirit in such circumstances.

Beyond this place of wrath and tears
Looms but the Horror of the shade,
And yet the menace of the years
Finds, and shall find, me unafraid.

(Henley 1875)

Suedfeld introduces his argument by suggesting that the attitudes captured by this poem have received scant attention in psychological research and theorising. It is interesting that he should have been drawn to this poem, which is indeed the focus of his research on survival, given his own childhood experiences. Having been born in Hungary in 1935 he had had to survive the Holocaust as a hidden child in Budapest. Maybe his interests resonated with the stoicism and endurance that had characterised much of his own early childhood.

Suedfeld's suggestion is that while for the caring professions the amelioration of suffering is often more dramatic and rich in its possibilities for helping, it may lead to an undue concentration on the negative consequences of adversity. Such an emphasis can overlook responses of independence and self-determination and, in his view, become one-sided, leading to scientific inaccuracy serving to confirm self-fulfilling prophecies. This, he feels, is a very negative approach to the human condition. A recent trend by psychologists is to take a more positive point of view. Such an approach is articulated by the dictum commonly attributed to Nietzsche, whatever does not kill you makes you stronger, which also inspires the title of this chapter. These psychologists, while not wishing in any way to diminish the reality of human suffering and the integrity and importance of those who help, have provided by their research a powerful antidote to a culture of victimhood now seemingly escalating in Western cultures. It heralded a new approach. A recent book on *Lifespan Development* considers the challenges that are faced, the resources that we possess and the risks that are taken throughout life (Hendry and Kloep 2002). This book emerged from the Centre for Child Research in Trondheim – a centre that has attracted a distinguished group of international scholars from a wide variety of disciplines. Hendry and Kloep, in looking at human behaviour across the lifespan, use as an integrating framework the 'challenge-risk' model. Such a model moves away from a 'distress and disorder' approach. This new research concentrates rather on the resilience and resourcefulness of the individual within the social context. The life course is seen as a process of continuous responses to challenge.

The focus on surviving in difficult circumstances shifted the emphasis from distress and seems initially a long way from concerns with children's lives. Suedfeld's research work drew on studies of human behaviour in challenging environments (Suedfeld 1997). The first of these were experiments on reactions to sensory deprivation provided by prolonged periods of confinement in a small room under conditions of complete darkness. When Suedfeld looked at the studies on which the wisdom about sensory deprivation had been based he was surprised. It seemed that the experience had been so extremely unpleasant that many subjects quit the experiment prematurely. Added to this, such studies had given rise to something of a furore in a number of relevant quarters suggesting that the experiments were dangerous if not unethical. The period of confinement was commonly between 4 and 24 hours. What is surprising, he pointed out, is that most of us spend around eight hours a day lying fairly still in a darkened room. His curiosity increased when, faced with being a subject in such a study, he himself became so anxious that he quit after about four hours. He eventually concluded that what was happening was in effect a self-fulfilling prophecy, in that the set up was such that subjects *expected* bizarre, disturbing experiences – an expectation that was reinforced by various aspects of the experimental conditions. This was consistent with early research in social psychology (Festinger 1950; Moscovici 1976), which indicated that high uncertainty increases vulnerability to suggestion. This has also happened in our views of development. We have been socialised into thinking of challenging circumstances as having negative effects. Various means of familiarising these experimental subjects with the situation, providing reassuring and low-key instructions, meant eventually that the procedures became standard and even enjoyable.

Many years later the procedure, now known as the Restricted Environmental Stimulation Technique or REST (Suedfeld 1980), is considered highly enjoyable and deeply relaxing and is even used for stress management. It is possible to extrapolate REST to non-experimental locations that involve confinement, monotony, reduced stimulation and solitude. Such experiences feature naturally in real life and indeed the mixing of sacred odysseys with personal resourcefulness form the core of some spiritual quests. Various forms of retreat in many cultures mark transitions and rites of passage. In parts of the Outward Bound courses, for example, the challenge of surviving alone in the bush or wilderness teaches teenagers that they have the necessary ingenuity and resourcefulness to survive. Potter describes the self-imposed solitude of such religious leaders of Moses, Jesus, Mohammed and the Buddha and the significance of this retreat from the everyday world (Potter 1958). There are many examples of how individuals have sought out challenges and personal solitary quests and odysseys as a spur to fresh thinking.

Second, Suedfeld took inspiration from studies of how people adapt in the Arctic and Antarctic, polar regions both remote from the accustomed spaces of most human beings and rich in unexpected crises and potential privations, disasters, freezing, drowning or starvation. While there are indeed such privations, Steel (1994) found that the challenge also brought out fortitude, perseverance, ingenuity and comradeship. Polar workers tend to form a strong emotional bond with the place. They return as often as they can, and express great distress when asked to imagine that they could never go back again. Palinkas reports compelling evidence for the beneficial effect of polar experience revealed when two groups of naval personnel were compared. One group who wintered over in Antarctica was compared with a group of sailors who had not been so assigned. The groups were comparable in other variables deemed relevant. It was found that the winter-over group had fewer hospitalisations, and showed lower short- and long-term rates of mental disorders and accidents, leading to a conclusion that 'the lessons learnt in coping with the stressful Antarctic environment may be utilised in coping with other stressful experiences as well' (Palinkas 1990, p.247). They 'showed "eustress" – that is positive stress, rather than distress or negative stress' (Suedfeld 1997, p.332). These transferable skills are thought to relate to having developed behaviours which reinforce people's feelings of being in control of themselves and their environment. This is where it becomes relevant to my concerns here with children's coping skills, and their ability to influence their environment and gain some control over it. The Antarctic sailors, in adjusting to the stressors they were presented with, not only prevented themselves from becoming ill but also actually became stronger and healthier. The studies on stress were not restricted to the Antarctic but also included studies of solitary confinement in modern prisons, brainwashing, shipwreck castaways and civilians brutally imprisoned during wartime as, for example, in the Holocaust. Some even consider that the Holocaust experience made them stronger and more sensitive to others (Lomranz 1995). The message seems to be the same: ingenuity, co-operation and good leadership are crucial to survival. Social support seemed also crucial to survival, as is a perception of being in control. This means that everyday stressors are better tolerated, though not necessarily avoided, if people can work out ways of exerting some control over their environment regardless of how non-responsive that environment might be.

It may seem that all of this material, while interesting, does not relate very well to the situation of children. Maybe we think of stress as a 'grown-up' concept. Evidence to the contrary, however, has come from many studies of children in extreme circumstances. For example, in 1990 a nationwide survey of grammar-school children in Japan showed that 63.2 per cent were suffering from high levels of blood cholesterol, 36.2 per cent from ulcers, 22.1 per cent from high blood pressure and 21.4 per cent from diabetes (Arita and Yamaoka 1992, p.14). Even very young Japanese children were responding to the educational pressures they were experiencing with symptoms normally associated with stressed business executives much later in life (Field 1995). Field adds to these stories the comments of a spokesperson from the leading artificial hair transplant manufacturer, who said that wigs were finding new customers among schoolchildren suffering from stress-related baldness. This was thought to be attributable to the pressures of cram-school attendance or bullying in their regular schools. Field adds these comments to other reports which include a new pervasiveness of eczema and chronic constipation, further to years of stories of school violence (which, on my visit to Japan early in 1998, had included beheadings of pupils by peers and violent attacks on teachers), leading her 'to believe that childhood itself is at risk in Japan today, and not because of war, disease or malnutrition' (Field 1995, p.53).

While clearly stress can be taken to extremes, maybe the idea of childhood as a stress-free period of our lives is a myth and perhaps understanding childhood in terms of such culturally assumed myths is what has made us treat children as we do and fail to take them seriously. While sociologists, cultural anthropologists, ethnographers and psychologists have all exposed the nonsense of myths about the passive child being acted upon by the culture, perhaps endurance is a primary characteristic of childhood that has been thrown out with that 'bath water' rather than being seen as the dynamic positive characteristic that it is. Endurance is not a passive concept but one of a certain sort of mastery – of gauging the possibilities, controlling as much as one can and living within those parameters. Perhaps the day-to-day endurance of unremitting marginalisation is the true mark of courage and indeed of childhood. Whereas we have dismissed universal notions of the concept of childhood, maybe if we reframe and see children within the category of minority rights groups, the experiences of children do have some recognisable unity around a concept of endurance – an experience that is common to the whole group of marginalised individuals.

ENDURANCE

Myths about childhood are perhaps what have clouded our vision of the realities. In the Introduction to James Joyce's *Ulysses*, Declan Kiberd (1992) looks at the role of mythologies in the writings of both Joyce and T.S. Eliot – mythologies which serve as a reference point in literature in the way I would argue mythologies do, in conceptualising childhood and the experiences of the child. One of the persisting myths is that childhood is somehow stress-free – that children are learning and growing rather than enduring and surviving. Looking at Joyce's *Ulysses* here is not as irrelevant as it might at first seem both to the developing theme of stress, survival and endurance and to childhood. T.S. Eliot, in what is regarded as a seminal essay on '*Ulysses*, Order and Myth', regards the literary method used in the writing of *Ulysses* as having 'the importance of a scientific discovery' so that 'instead of narrative method we may now use the mythical method'. This was an attractive method in that it was 'a way of controlling, of ordering, of giving a shape and a significance to the immense panorama of futility and anarchy which is contemporary life' (Eliot 1923, p.5). This is interesting as it gives us an oblique clue as to why myths persist about children. Maybe such myths serve to order and control in our minds what is mysterious and possibly threatening about the presence among us not of 'unpeople', as some might wish them to be, but of sentient beings – witnesses to much of the 'futility and anarchy' of adult lives. These beings can thread their way skilfully through adult views of reality, while still holding on to their own. For Joyce, exploring linear and circular views of historical development, however, 'everything changed even as it remained itself, and so the differences gave the repetitions point and purpose, allowing him to redefine heroism as the capacity to endure rather than inflict suffering' (Kiberd 1992, p.xxviii). He used myths to remind us of what man had in common across the ages but used 'real life to demonstrate that real bravery was perhaps mental rather than physical – Yeats suggesting that Joyce had a "heroic mind"... In fact the traffic between ancient myth and current reality always ran along a two-way street' (Kiberd 1992, p.xxix). Perhaps the indomitability Suedfeld described earlier in this chapter is about mental courage. It is the theme of endurance which must engage us here – endurance as true bravery. I would argue that the 'silent' power many children wield is that of resilience and endurance of putting up with very challenging circumstances in quite sophisticated ways. In trying to understand children, stressful experiences (as part of children's engagement with the world and their responses and their survival) have only recently begun to figure, if somewhat obliquely, in developmental psychology.

Myths about what is 'best' for children have been constructed as excuses for tyranny which has made us overlook the everyday heroisms. Children used to be seen, and indeed in some cultures are currently seen, in terms of their economic usefulness and their duties and obligations. More recently there has been a tendency, in common with the history of other minority rights groups, to define children in terms of their needs, as defined by people other than them. Often, concern about such needs is completely out of touch with the world and how children perceive it. Providing for children's needs has become a contemporary 'myth'. Woodhead describes early frustration with the indiscriminate use of the concept of needs in professional discourse and policy statements. In fact he believed that the rhetorical device of 'the needs of children' has served to define power relationships between experts and families, service providers and consumers, in ways that have little to do with the children themselves (Woodhead 1997). It is also an example of power over children where children are provided for in terms of adults' views of reality. There are resonances with what happened to other minority rights groups – women, disabled people, ethnic minorities – where professionals of various kinds defined what their needs were, thereby depersonalising them.

Such groups have not wished to define their own 'needs', which they see as a negative deficit concept, but rather state their aspirations and exercise their rights. These 'myths' have often been challenged or overturned by children. It is interesting that while the concept of rights has been seen as a powerful antidote to 'needs', changing as it does concepts of protection and dependence, rights have been interpreted in culturally biased ways. This has revealed some tensions in the 'rights' concept as embodied in the UN Convention on the Rights of the Child, which is seen by some as based on a very Western way of constructing adult–child relationships. Article 32 of the Convention refers to child labour, outlining the right of the child to be protected from economic exploitation and from performing any work that is likely to be hazardous or to interfere with the child's education. Boyden and Myers have pointed out that children's survival and the survival of their families in some countries is dependent on the child's labour; to outlaw this is to put their lives and their families' lives in jeopardy (Boyden and Myers 1995). Miljeteig (2000), looking at children's participative rights in this regard, states that it is only when understood as civil and political rights or as democratic rights that these rights to participation will become meaningful. Working children provide an example here as in the first International Meeting of Working Children in Kundapur, India, from 27 November to 9 December 1996. In the Declaration from that meeting they show sophistication about their aspirations that took many of the people involved in child labour debates completely by surprise. It emphasised in a very practical way the argument that to fully understand child-labour situations, working children and young people and their families have to be involved (Miljeteig 1999; Woodhead 1999a). Miljeteig argues that 'we will not see a genuine child rights approach emerge until working children and youth are allowed to influence policies and programmes through active participation and partnership, and until we have fully realised the important resource they represent' (Miljeteig 2000, p.303).

The Kundapur Declaration gives us a glimpse of what the children endure and how they are trying to exercise control in this situation.

Kundapur Declaration

1. We want recognition of our problems, our initiatives, proposals and our process of organisation.

2. We are against the boycott of products made by children.

3. We want respect and security for ourselves and the work that we do.

4. We want an education system whose methodology and content are adapted to our reality.

5. We want professional training adapted to our reality and capabilities.

6. We want access to good health care for working children.

7. We want to be consulted in all decisions concerning us, at local, national or international level.

8. We want the root causes of our situation, primarily poverty, to be addressed and tackled.

9. We want more activities in rural areas and decentralisation in decision making, so that children will no longer be forced to migrate.

10. We are against exploitation at work but we are for work with dignity with hours adapted so that we can have time for education and leisure.

> (International Meeting of Working Children, Kundapur,
> India, 27 November to 9 December 1996)

The Dakar Declaration adopted by the representatives of the Movements of Working Children and Youth in Africa, Latin America and Asia at their meeting in Dakar, Senegal, in March 1998 similarly reflects what working children endure and what their aspirations are. I take up the issue of child labour further in Chapter 7. Judith Ennew argues that 'the structures of domination which trivialise or misinterpret children's voices, remain rooted (and virtually untouched) in patriarchy' (Ennew 1998a, p.xix). In Volume 1 of the Children in Charge Series, Richard Kinsey, in the concluding remarks in his paper on 'Children's Knowledge of Crime in the UK', suggests the prevalence of abiding myths: '...it seems, we are witnessing the elaboration of continuing (albeit contradictory and diverse) metaphors and rhetoric of childhood – a rhetoric which, in its familiarity and continuity with a past, is all the more powerful in a re-structured present' (Kinsey 1996, p.263). He goes on:

> And perhaps, therefore, the object of our research should not have been young people but the continuing representations of childhood and the 'techniques of neutralisation' employed by those adults who commit offences and incivilities against

young people, who (routinely) push past them at bus queues
or at the supermarket counter and who similarly ignore them
in the definition of policy priorities. (Kinsey 1996, p.263)

I would argue that the hallmark of childhood experience, throughout
the world, is surviving, tolerating and enduring circumstances and experiences that are frequently intolerable. It is in their sophisticated management of often dreadful treatment and in elaborate choreography of
tolerance that children show their similarities with other minority rights
groups. Such groups have had to live through being ignored, being
treated as subhuman, being treated as parcels rather than people with
agency, being regarded as of little or no account. They have endured this
in a way that is often nothing short of heroic.

Another myth is that children know and understand little. They often do know, do understand, yet rarely have the power to change their
lot – they must endure it. The fact that they grasp only too well what is
going on is what makes them so dangerous. They *know* and are witnesses
to what is going on around them. This has been captured often in literature in a way that is immediately recognisable. Seamus Deane, for example in *Reading in the Dark*, provides a compelling evocation of childhood
that we immediately identify with. He writes about secrets – secrets that
elude adults in the story but are grasped by the child in all their complexity (Deane 1996). Margaret Drabble, reviewing Lorna Sage's
award-winning autobiography *Bad Blood*, in the *Guardian* (2000), said,
'It is a vividly remembered honest, generous, shocking story of a 1950s
childhood and a teenage love affair… A fine transformation of pain into
something redeeming – I don't think that is too grand a word'. Such
books and others like Gosse's *Father and Son* have captured childhood as
it is lived and endured– an adult world observed and succumbed to as
there is no other way to survive, but the children are not deceived, nor
do they forget. The material in Chapter 3 has given concrete examples
of difficult lives that children live now. Material produced for the 2002
UN Special Session on Children (UNICEF 2002) further describes the
real lives of children from various parts of the world in all the challenging detail and immediacy of their experiences (Bellamy 2002a).

MODEL OF DEVELOPMENTAL CHALLENGE

A concern with our knowledge about what is involved in surviving, about endurance and about indomitability is therefore highly relevant to a consideration of children and power, although so far very little attention has been given to this pervasive and positive aspect of children's behaviour and experience and perceptions of being in control.

> It matters not how strait the gate
> How charged with punishments the scroll,
> I am the master of my fate;
> I am the captain of my soul.

(Henley 1875)

Moreover it is by turning to apparently irrelevant studies of endurance that we come across a model of understanding, which throws some light on understanding children's power and the nature of their powerlessness (Hendry and Kloep 2002). Responding to challenge/risk has a long tradition in developmental psychology although it has only been recently that this has been put together as a model in an attempt to explain the processes in lifespan development from birth through to old age. The theoretical framework is based on a 'challenge-risk' model that moves away from traditional distress and disorder approaches, instead considering the resilience and resourcefulness of the individual within the social context. Although they do not use the words 'eustress' and 'endurance', this is implied in their concepts of resilience and resourcefulness (Hendry and Kloep 2002). Their central model ties together different stages of the lifespan.

Importantly these psychologists compare theories of development in terms of how they deal with response to challenge in a new and helpful way. The work of Freud, Piaget (with a sidelong glance at Riegel, Rogers and Maslow), Levinson Erikson, Vygotsky, Skinner, Bronfenbrenner, Elder and Baltes are compared in order to emphasise ideas of development in its cultural context. From this comparison similar elements are distilled, from which emerges what they claim to be an explanatory model of lifespan development – their model of developmental challenge. The least familiar of the theorists they chose to compare are probably Elder and Baltes. Elder they regard as 'one of the pioneers of life course theory'. His study *Children of the Great Depression*

(Elder 1974) inspired him to look at social change, life pathways and individual development in new ways as modes of behavioural continuity and change (Elder 1997, 1998). In common with the other developmental theorists compared, he sees the importance of 'life transitions', in other words challenges in shaping development. He said, 'People bring a life history of personal experiences and dispositions to each transition, interpret the new circumstances in terms of this history, and work out lines of adaptation that can fundamentally alter their life course' (Elder 1997, p.957).

Unlike the other scholars considered, Elder does not want to focus certain events on certain age stages, regarding them rather, as well as the individual's differential reactions to them, as a function of historical period, place and time during the course of life. Elder was working in the United States. During the same period, Baltes and his colleagues were putting forward their approach to lifespan development in Germany (Baltes and Goulet 1970; Baltes, Reese and Lipsitt 1980). By the late 1990s they elaborated their four central tenets of their approach to lifespan development (Smith and Baltes 1999). In summing up how all the theories compared built up to a model of lifespan development Hendry and Kloep summarise the common key elements. This is something of an achievement on account of the many theoretical contradictions between the various theorists they had chosen for analysis – for example, it would be difficult to render the ideas of Skinner and Maslow compatible. The following elements they see as key principles.

1. There needs to be a challenge (task, crisis, stimulus and loss) to stimulate development.

2. Development occurs through successful solving of this challenge.

3. 'Unsuccessful' solving of a challenge leads to some kinds of problem in meeting future challenges.

4. Solving challenges is an interactional, dialectical process that leads to changes either in the environment, in the individual, or both, and thereby stimulates development.

5. Individuals have differing amounts of resources to meet challenges.

(Hendry and Kloep 2002, p.16)

They point out that there are similarities among the theories they looked at such as the importance of security and early learning. They also reveal that some ideas cannot be combined – as for instance the belief in stages and discontinuous development as compared with ideas about the continuity of development. At this point they take sides and choose ideas evolving in life-course theory from the early 1960s. Their lifespan model of developmental challenge, they claim, is rooted in the broad range of major developmental theories cited above. The idea is that 'lifelong individual development results from the dynamic interactions between potential challenges and individual resources within the ecological context of different psycho-social systems' (Hendry and Kloep 2002, p.17). The significance of their analysis for us here is the emphasis on challenge. I would argue that working out strategies of endurance is how many children respond to crises – strategies that move them on in their development.

Hendry and Kloep consider individual differences in potential resources to deal with challenge, and in what constitutes, as they refer to it, the 'resource pool'. They then examine the dynamic interaction within and between potential resources, and between potential resources and tasks to be faced, considering how we can establish whether a challenge has been met successfully. They also write about stress seekers – individuals who seek out challenges. Later in their book they go on to consider the nature of challenges we face, looking at normative and non-normative shifts. The former is concerned with developmental tasks and the latter with unexpected and often traumatic events like bereavement, divorce or redundancy and ensuing poverty. Individuals at any stage in the lifespan can be engulfed in various ways by these non-normative shifts.

The development and illustration of their model proceeds through the lifespan. It looks initially at the challenges of childhood, focusing their discussion on three areas with all development being both integrative and interactive: first on maturational changes as a challenge to learn psychomotor skills and in this phase they suggest that all social, cognitive and sensorimotor resources are (potentially) available to enrich the 'resource pool'. Second learning as it relates to building up social resources proceeds with the child, according to their model, beginning to learn the various gradations of social relations , from 'vertical' to 'horizontal' by means of interactions with parents, peers and other adults. As regards the third challenge of attending school, they bring into focus the necessary tension between self-efficacy and independent learning with conforming, fitting in and learning from older authority figures. 'This third issue may be important as a forerunner in the development of both conformity (i.e. stagnation) and boundary-testing (i.e. development) in the next phase of the life course, that is adolescence' (Hendry and Kloep 2002, p.80). Here, in this artificial dichotomy, they do not seem to grasp the importance of endurance. In endurance, the boundaries have been cleverly established and the child conforming as and when needed to an adult view of reality is operating powerfully, not stagnantly, within those realities. In looking at adolescence they see the tasks as different from those of adulthood even though they share a number of common features. Puberty, the adolescent body, romance and societal images are seen as presenting challenges here, as are leisure and risk taking. In this quest for adult status they see a task is to resolve the tensions between individuality and conventionality – 'perhaps the major challenge of adolescence, and one which may have important implications for the building up of resources and for the effectiveness of the resource "pool" later in the life course' (p.97). It is acknowledged, however, that this is a pattern of more traditional cultures and in many societies now globalisation has brought about rapid social changes providing severe challenges to former ways of living and to the traditional choices of early adulthood.

As a model of development that extends throughout the life course, it holds a potential which in its present form it does not fulfil. It is useful to think of development proceeding in response to risks and challenges, which require the individual to dig deep into the resources he/she has built up. Nevertheless the model presents a cosy and Western view of that process rather than producing some significant insights into how children and young people do actually cope with the complex, trying lives so many of them lead. Children now represent 40 per cent of the world's population and indeed they are involved in many of this world's troubles but are rarely considered at the global economic and policy level, at the level of national government or often, to their cost, within the politics of the family. A model of lifespan development has been provided at the beginning of this troubled new century, without fully acknowledging that for children a major challenge is to learn how to survive as a marginalised and forgotten group – in developed countries as well as in developing ones. A challenge-risk response-development model is a useful approach but has to be set not just in the immediate social context but also in the political context, as Pilger did in a preceding chapter (Pilger 1998), if such models are to have any edge in gaining insight into children's lives and enduring suffering. We need to know something about the mechanism by which events come to have their impact.

COPING AND COLLUDING

Even in the industrialised world it has been argued that children are not always passively under the control, ownership and direction of adults. A considerable time ago Carolyn Steedman illustrated through some ingenious research how some children have coped with difficult lives (1982). There is little reason to suppose that the processes she illustrates have changed significantly in the intervening years. She suggests that the children colluded with their culture and effectively became agents of their own socialisation. The clues to this process and how children viewed themselves were provided by their own writing. This research was conducted among young children living in deprived and desperately depressing worlds – the fabric of which was despair, poverty, the progression of pregnancies, worries and family tensions. Child and adult worlds were not clearly differentiated. The data was provided by a series of stories that three little girls wrote collaboratively over several weeks and the tape recordings of their negotiations as to what should be included in them. In her book *Tidy House* (Steedman 1982), in which she presents the research findings, she gave some insight into how the girls coped with difficult lives and made sense of these lives. They were not bewildered by what they saw but simply accepted the inevitability of it all and their place in it. They endured it.

> By many external indices, then, the children who wrote the story that is the subject of this book [*The Tidy House*] came from a background of material deprivation. They had, like all children in their class and many thousands of others, to deal with the tension, conflict and anxiety that are the attendants of poverty. It has been observed many times before that children in such circumstances have to deal with problems that would floor many twice their age and that attempts on their part to cope with these difficulties do not merely mirror the

> complexities of adult life that surround them, but are rather a
> measure of the way in which the exigencies of general social
> life become a dominant factor in the growth of their sense of
> self. (Steedman 1982, p.9)

These little girls understood the adult world with a remarkable insight
and a very profound understanding. They were not obviously depressed
by this understanding but rather accepted the inevitability of it all. They
stoically demonstrated their belief that their lot as they grew into adulthood would be to have a life very similar to the one they observed. It
was this recognition that they wove into their stories.

Other children have had to meet the challenges of managing to survive within a sinister, frightening and abusive adult world that they
could barely understand, which robbed them of a considerable degree
of personal agency but which they learnt to endure. They were witnesses and party to secrets that they suspected were dreadful but had to
incorporate into the rhythm of their daily lives. They did not know what
terrors were lurking or would beset them next. In her book on ritual and
satanic abuse Sara Scott describes the most appalling treatment and intimidation of children (Scott 2001). For most of her adult survivor interviewees, ritual-abuse memories remained deeply interwoven with
scenes of everyday domestic life. Six of these interviewees described
home lives saturated by abuse. They believed the purpose of this was to
prepare them for their 'correct' participation in a ritual and to instil in
them a view of themselves as both innately 'evil' and 'special' – that is,
'special' in being chosen for the privilege of extreme degradation. Each
recalled being trained not to cry or respond to pain. One interviewee
described in a matter of fact way her insight into what was going on.

> From about three days before you'd be either starved apart
> from maybe excrement or blood or something... I wasn't be-
> ing fed and was kept in the dark. So all in all I knew what was
> coming off, but I was also very confused and disorientated.
> When you get really thirsty and hungry you start to get
> spacey anyway. (Scott 2001, p.70)

Another interviewee describes how she tried to integrate it all into 'normal life'.

When you got up in the morning it didn't matter what had gone on the night before, you had to behave as if nothing had happened. And that could be difficult to achieve, for Mum could be washing the blood off the walls or whatever and at the same time carry on and get your Weetabix out, you know. There was always so much tension and you had to be careful about everything. But we did like to go to school, and if it were an OK day we would get fed and stuff. (Scott 2001, pp.70–71)

Many of the interviewees described how their loneliness, lack of stimulus and discomforts in their preschool years had led them to develop techniques to 'switch off' and 'disappear inside their own head'. Some of the dissociative practices they described (two told how they could use a naked flame or hyperventilate in order to 'trance out' at will) are the same as the ways prisoners and torture victims are reported to have tried to overcome pain, hunger and cold (Herman 1992). All the interviewees described how they were perpetually anxious and told of the dread of returning home from school and being called downstairs. They were constantly on the alert, a vigilance which in battered women has been described as the 'chronic apprehension of imminent doom' (Hilberman 1980, p.1341). These children were operating as if they were working for the resistance behind enemy lines, having to pass, not drawing attention to themselves and yet fearing at any moment that the worst would happen. These are stories of real courage and great insight by children about how to get by in their own bewildering part of the world where their rights to protection did not operate and only their own ingenuity saved them. They indicate their own strange power of grasping in part these adults' views of 'reality' but managing somehow or another to hang on to their own realities. They were 'endurers'.

Of course there are many questions to be asked about the two examples I have chosen – methodological questions about interpreting children's lives from the stories they write and understanding children's lives by their adult testimonies and possibly adult constructions of what they felt, understood and experienced when they were children. Jean La Fontaine, a senior British anthropologist, was funded by the Department of Health to undertake research into these allegations. She found no independent corroborations in the many cases that she studied. In explaining why these stories continued to be believed she drew parallels with witchcraft accusations in the anthropological literature and also with witch hunts in sixteenth- and seventeenth-century Europe (La Fontaine 1998). Perhaps, then, these were the classic 'myths' (the Odysseus parallels) which re-emerge as the real stories of this mythology (the endurance of Ulysses) today. Sara Scott in her rejoinder reminds us:

> 'Moral panic' and 'false memory' are two of the discourses of disbelief. From different directions they accuse people of having imagined childhoods involving rape, lies, cruelty, and terror, when nothing of the sort occurred. [...] It is my contention that the 'discourse of disbelief' serves a motivated course of social action, supports the interests of particular actors and the silencing of others. (Scott 2001, p.59)

Sara Scott reports these childhoods, despite 'the discourse of disbelief which will sound a powerful note of cynicism throughout my book – a questioning counterpoint to my analysis of my interviewees' life-stories' (Scott 2001, p.60). Such lives, described by the cumulation and cross-matching of material and within an acceptance that some children endure awful experiences, turn out to be 'beyond disbelief'.

Moderate pain and discomfort may serve as challenges that make the child respond by calling on all the resources that he/she has and growing. There are questions as to whether 'indomitability' has limits – whether the weirdness and suffering can be so extreme that the child's resource pool is overwhelmed. Maybe the child is no longer able to retreat into his/her own realities which resource his/her navigation of the adult world. Perhaps the only way the child can continue to endure an adult world he/she can no longer understand or 'pass' in is to identify with the aggressor, a mute compliance with the adult world, and lose his/her sense of self and important childhood realities. Why is it that the voices of survivors are resisted at a time when '...the voices of the youngest of our species are now being recorded, listened to and respected as never before, albeit against a background of hostility. Children are being un-muted. Which raises a fascinating question: why should it be that children's voices and children's participation are being advocated at this stage in history?' (Ennew 1998b, p.xviii). Maybe it is because they are beginning to be people – people who have their own realities and a world that needs to be understood.

Endnote

1. It is interesting to note, given the origins of the present book, that the poem 'Invictus', about courage in the face of adversity, was written when William E. Henley was in hospital in Edinburgh. He suffered from tubercula bone disease for three years, eventually losing a leg. During that time he became a friend of R.L. Stevenson and a model for one-legged Long John Silver in *Treasure Island*.

CHAPTER SIX

Warriors and Workers

INTRODUCTION

> In America a child is reported abused or neglected every
> eleven seconds, is born into poverty every thirty two seconds,
> is born to a teen mother every sixty two seconds, is arrested
> for a violent crime every four minutes, and is killed by guns
> every ninety eight minutes...
>
> Never before have we exposed children so early and
> relentlessly to cultural messages glamorising violence, sex,
> material possessions, and the use of alcohol and tobacco with
> so few mediating influences from responsible adults. Never
> have we experienced such numbing and reckless reliance on
> violence to solve problems, feel powerful, or be entertained.
> Never have so many children been permitted to rely on guns
> and gangs for protection and guidance rather than on parents,
> neighbours, religious congregations, and schools. (Edelman
> 1996, p. ix)

This statement by the President of the Children's Defence Fund introduces a book by Linda Lantieri and Janet Patti (1996) on *Waging Peace in
Our Schools*. There is no reason to think that the picture has become
better since 1996. At the Children's Defence Fund's annual conference
in 1994, Lantieri and Patti presented a practice-based workshop on violence prevention and conflict resolution in schools. They described the
heart of their work in creating safe and caring schools as being: conflict
resolution, valuing diversity, and enhancing social and emotional literacy. Lantieri and Patti, through their highly structured Resolving Conflict Creatively Program (RCCP), now active in several hundred schools
in North America, produce a guide for teaching young people to
empathise, mediate, negotiate and create peace. This is a top-down
approach to empowerment in that the system is taught rather than

developing organically: 'We can help young people realize that the highest form of heroism is the passionate search for non violent solutions to complex problems. Young people can learn to deal with their anger differently' (Lantieri and Patti 1996, p.7). They cite the research on violence, conflict resolution, emotional literacy and diversity education that has informed their practice. Today RCCP's National Centre works with the national non-profit organisation Educators for Social Responsibility in its efforts to make social responsibility an integral part of education by fostering new ways of teaching and learning. This is an approach using an invested power model. The World Conference on Violence at School and Public Policy held in Paris in March 2000 gave researchers and policy makers an opportunity to compare the successes and difficulties of different strategies. Although prevention and intervention practices still vary widely, the scientific community seemed to agree at this conference that studies need to focus on the victims and their social environment (EU 2000).

Violence is one of the most obvious forms of the exercise of power. Its origins and targets are diffuse. Sometimes it forms a reaction to powerlessness, a reach for power and control. Early in this book we considered the violence of two child murderers as possibly located in trying to read the messages of their culture about masculinity (Jackson 1995). Looking at the legacy of young activists in South Africa I suggest that the language of violence and brutality in which they had to operate had long-term effects on school-based conflict. Moreover the level of violence within societies is not just a matter of the young perpetrators but also of the suffering of the bullied, the assaulted, the maimed and killed young victims. It is about what children have to endure as well as what they initiate. Stephen Roth identifies children being in an especially vulnerable situation as central to the issue of ethnic discrimination that is often the core of conflict in civil war.

> The most important aspect for minority groups is the rights of the child. The protection of the family is of existential importance to minorities, just as the rights of the child are vital assurance of their continuity... The oppression of minorities through killing of children has been a frequent historical phenomenon. Indeed the killing of children as a means of oppression goes back to biblical times. (Roth 1992 p.99)

The nature of civil unrest within some countries has been such that for some children the only way to survive has been to volunteer for military service, to kill rather than be killed.

CHILD SOLDIERS

An estimated 300,000 children, some as young as seven, are fighting in conflict around the world. Twenty million children have been forced from their homes by war and two million children were killed in conflict between 1985 and 1995 (White 2001). These statistics confirm that millions of children are not merely bystanders but are targets of war. For the purposes of the present book on power, what is intriguing here are the children who become part of the hierarchy of power by volunteering to fight. Large numbers of boys, particularly in Africa, have become active combatants.

Graca Machel, in her report commissioned by the Secretary General of the United Nations in response to a call from the General Assembly, states:

> ...there is a space devoid of the most basic human values; a space in which children are slaughtered, raped and maimed; a space in which children are starved and exposed to extreme brutality. Such unregulated terror and violence speak of deliberate victimisation. There are few further depths to which humanity can sink. (Machel 1996)

She talks of facing a crisis of civilisation in which 'The world is being sucked into a moral vacuum' (Machel 1996).

Warfare has changed in its nature. After the Crusades, wars used to be about territory, trade routes and material resources. They were adult issues. Now there is a new pattern, partly identified by Francis Fukuyama in the *End of History* argument that wars of that kind are now over since different countries were apparently coming to share increasingly similar political and economic situations, and religious and hegemonic conflicts of a quite different kind have taken their place (Fukuyama 1992). Wars today are not necessarily waged between states but often within them from village to village and from street to street. In Japan, South Africa and in the USA pupils have in one or two notable cases waged war on their schoolmates and teachers. On a broader scale, in conflict these days 90 per cent of war victims are civilians and of these about half are children. 'Others are mutilated by landmines and many more die as a result of the destruction of health centres, water supplies and the tearing apart of families and communities, with untold psychological effects for generations. Even starvation, as in the Sudan war, is now being used as a weapon of war' (Barnett 1999, p.316). Machel says 'children simply have no part in warfare' (1996) yet they are heavily implicated in a number of terrible ways. Children witness rape and other sexual atrocities, often forced between family members, and are sometimes the victims themselves. The Machel report recommends that wartime rape and other sexual torture must be prosecuted as war crimes and in addition that all military personnel, including those engaged in peacekeeping, should receive training regarding their responsibilities to women and children.

Warfare has also changed in significant ways that not only make it easier for children to participate but also makes them desirable and sometimes ready conscripts. The easy availability of weaponry, and the new assault rifles which are of simple design and so lightweight that they can be carried, stripped and reassembled by the very young, has contributed to the recruitment of tens of thousands of boys and girls. The weapons are also relatively cheap: 'in Uganda, for example, an AK-47 assault rifle can be purchased for the price of a chicken' (Barnett 1999, p.316). Hence children are not always the hapless victims of war but have a relatively easy access to what on the face of it seems like a very powerful role in their own societies. There is little more terrifying for adults nor more challenging to their idea of power and competence than when it is reversed and they are in the sights of a five-year-old pointing a gun, yet many of the 'adult' soldiers were recruited as children and schooled in brutality ever since. Western ideas of competence and developmentalism seem to be very much out of place here.

While recruitment of young fighters is now a global phenomenon, in Africa it has been particularly widespread and in over ten years of civil war in Sierra Leone possibly at its most harrowing. Wars tend to be fought by young people. The age profile in African civil wars tends to be especially young and Sierra Leone is no exception. One of the reasons for the use of children and young teenagers is that they are good at warfare that involves the unobtrusive movements of small units and the ambush tactics that characterise bush warfare. Partly as a result of historical factors, which include high rates of population increase from a low historical base deriving partly from the slave trade and colonial epidemics of venereal disease, Africa is now the youngest continent. The present scourge of AIDS has further exacerbated this situation. In most African countries now half or more of the population is under 18. Even if there had not been the economic decline of recent years youth unemployment would have been a major problem. Collier, in a recent study, suggests that the presence of large numbers of young people in the population and economic decline are better predictors of rebel war than dictatorship or inequality (Collier 2000).

Civil war in Sierra Leone

Paul Richards, in recounting the situation in Sierra Leone, examines the complexities of identifying how young people come to be involved in fighting.

> By definition 'conscription' is 'compulsory enrolment for military service (Penguin English Dictionary)'. It is distinguished from volunteering ('to offer oneself spontaneously for military service'). To oppose these terms is problematic in many respects, and it might be more helpful to envisage a continuum of military incorporation, with 'conscription' positioned towards one extreme and 'volunteering' towards the other. Here we deal mainly with 'youth volunteers' and 'abductees'. Neither are 'conscripts' in the dictionary sense but the element of compulsion (whether of circumstances or capture) is never far away. (Richards 2002, p.255)

To understand what being a 'young volunteer' means he feels that it is necessary to understand the historical and social context in which this happens. The decision to volunteer is influenced by a number of factors, including peer and social pressure, danger or desperation or a sense of fate. Sometimes conscription takes place through circumstances. For example, children whose parents or caregivers have been lost or killed sometimes 'become fighters because they need parent-surrogates and training in life skills' (Richards 2002, p.255). Richards reminds us, however, that there is considerable variation across cultures about when children become adults, and in practical terms for children from poor families 'adulthood' (in the sense of material self-reliance rather than *legally*) arrives early. This is particularly the case for children of poor families where half the population is below 18.

We must be careful, therefore, not to deny the agency of young teenage 'volunteers', who are consciously taking 'adult' decisions. Moral opprobrium tends to attach to those who recruit them, but in our experience young teenage 'volunteers' are often doing no more or less than 'beg' for an apprenticeship from a skilled professional whose trade happens to be war. It might be as appropriate to 'blame' poverty, or ideals about apprenticeship, for the phenomenon of young volunteer soldiers, as to place all responsibility on the 'warlord'. (Richards 2002, p.256)

Richards's data is drawn from his team's in-depth interviews mainly with ex-combatants passing through a programme launched in 1994 to demobilise child soldiers. Of these interviews 20 were carried out mainly in 1996–97, prior to and just after the signing of the Abidjan accords. The team interviewed mainly 'volunteers' but also drew on interviews with 'abductees' in the analysis. The interview material is published in detail in Richards (1996) and Peters and Richards (1998a, 1998b), which includes the interview transcripts and describes the methods and more background to the war. It is a complex war to understand. Briefly, the main elements involved are as follows:

- RUF (the Revolutionary United Front) – the main rebel faction
- Liberian Special Forces – some allied with the RUF, some with the government
- army-linked irregulars
- civil defence militia loyal to the democratic government (elected (1996).

There have been two formal demobilisation programmes for ex-combatants – one after the Abidjan agreement in 1996 and the other after the Lome peace accord in 1999, each of which foundered when hostilities recommenced.

At the outset of war in 1991 the RUF enlarged itself through appealing to young people in the border region: 'children from ramshackle rural schools and footloose diamond diggers' (Richards 2002, p.257). Some of these young people, captivated by the populist rhetoric in the manifesto, rallied voluntarily. Others were abducted but came to terms with their fate fairly rapidly as they realised that resistance was futile. 'One tactic to enforce loyalty among the abductees was to compel children to assist in public executions of parents and elders, thus more or less guaranteeing the abductees could never return home' (Richards 2002, p.257). Once scarified or tattooed, persistent runaways were either killed by the RUF or wiped out by opposing forces (Amnesty International 1992). Moreover, assuming that the village children would have been turned against them, adults sometimes begged government soldiers to kill rather than rehabilitate escaped abductees. Richards points out that to anyone from well-founded states, the abduction of children to join the militia might seem particularly shocking and morally repugnant. In societies with a history of colonial forced labour, enslavement and enforced membership of adult associations responsible for security in stateless societies, he feels that abduction seems very little different from and no more or less objectionable than other forms of conscription.

The life of the abductees proceeded very much on the basis of a Darwinian process of selection in that the weaker ones died from the privations of living in the bush, some were used as cannon fodder and those who revealed their scruples were killed by the movement as weak or cowards. The ones who survived were the strongest both physically and mentally, having the least scruples and seemingly having forgotten or distanced themselves from the social world from which they had been snatched. 'Over ten years of "selection pressure", these hardened survivalists have risen to become the backbone of the movement, stopping at no atrocity to stay alive' (Richards 2002, p.257). I have spoken earlier of how children are particularly good at living within two realities – their own and that of the adult world in which they have to pass and conform. In this extreme situation children realised intuitively or otherwise that in order to survive they had to accept the adult view of reality and incorporate it as their own. In this sense they were powerless, yet in the way they identified with the tactics and behaviour of their adult counterparts and overcame whatever remaining squeamishness they had, they became terrifyingly powerful as their own lives depended upon it – under-age cadres of the RUF who seemed to lack all sense of self-preservation. 'They did not know when they were out gunned,' one exasperated but experienced sergeant fighting against them explained in 1992 (Richards 2002 p.261).

In the irregular army many recruits were under-age and linked to the local commander through family ties. Richards describes it as similar to a nineteenth-century organisational model in that they were, in effect, apprentice 'war-boys' trained by a 'master of war'. They fought in short bursts and then were engaged in other work such as rice farming for their commander. Under this system some girls were recruited and proved sometimes to be effective fighters. They were especially vulnerable to abuses including military rape which was a routine punishment for any military failures.

Although the young army irregulars often proved to be effective fighters and were largely responsible for driving the RUF back to the borders in 1992–93, they were vulnerable, as they had no army induction number. If their commander was killed the little band of irregulars had to find new protectors. This was not easy as ungrateful civilians failed to recognise their achievements, lumping them all together as 'rebels'. They became disaffected or disgruntled. Some of them switched sides while others quit and still others used the skills they had learnt by freelancing as armed robbers.

In assessing the demobilisation needs for the 45,000 plus combatants from the war in Sierra Leone several variables have had to be considered. These include the way in which the individual was recruited, gender, age, and social and educational background.

Recruitment

It seems that although volunteering to the RUF tends to be underestimated, nevertheless most of those fighting for the RUF have been abductees. What confuses the picture is that most abductees developed a staunch loyalty to the RUF cause and its personnel. Richards speculates as to whether this has arisen from the social dynamics of group processes, indoctrination or what he calls the 'Stockholm Syndrome'. This syndrome refers to the situation in which traumatised hostages develop a sense of identification with and dependence upon their captors (Richards 1996). Some have been fighting with the movement for as long as nine years from the time they were originally abducted.

> They hardly know any other social reality than the battle
> groups and the bush camps within which they have been
> raised. Having committed many appalling acts of violence it
> is clear that they could only be re-integrated with their
> original communities with the greatest of difficulty, and may
> have to be settled on long-term secure schemes. Having been

> seized in the first instance, and locked within the movement
> by fear of summary execution, many RUF fighters are them-
> selves the victims of human rights abuse. (Richards 2002,
> p.266)

In June 2000 the Attorney General of Sierra Leone announced that under-age abductees will not be charged with war crimes but will instead
give testimony to a truth and reconciliation tribunal. It was unclear
whether this would apply only to those who were currently under-age
or whether it would also include those who were under-age when they
were abducted and the means that would establish this. There are further
problems, as even among the young 'volunteers' some were war orphans
or unemployed and desperate for work with no other choices than to
put themselves forward for military training.

Age

The RUF tends to be an exceptionally young movement, many of its soldiers having been abducted from rural primary schools in a culture coloured by a crisis of national educational collapse, and by a global youth
culture of violence depicted in videos and gangsta rap. Army irregulars
were largely teenagers or pre-teenagers when recruited and the Civil
Defence Force (CDF) extensively recruited under-age fighters. Richards, on the basis of his extensive research in Sierra Leone, argues that
maybe too much emphasis is placed on current child soldiers. The really
worrying ones, he suggests, are the combatants who have been formed
as under-age fighters.

> Many now look fully adult, and society views them as if they
> had always been responsible for their actions. This causes dif-
> ficulties, since a former child soldier is often a formidably
> hard fighter to have survived the experience of abduction, but
> views demobilisation with suspicion if it means being treated
> as an adult war criminal. (Richards 2002, p.270)

Social and educational background

The children that were recruited by the RUF were mainly rural but had
basic literacy as the movement relied heavily on handwritten communications in the bush. Illiterates were rejected for guerrilla training. The
children that volunteered were often the casualties of an education system that had collapsed when teachers had given up, having been unpaid

for long periods of time, or those who had been excluded on failure to pay their fees. Some of these children became 'sand sand' boys labouring in the alluvial diamond pits. The army irregulars in contrast were mainly recruited at the front – some of the child recruits having been orphaned by the RUF atrocities but others stating that they had joined for revenge or to replace lost educational sponsorship. For some of these children the army provided a trade and indeed many were very proud of their skill and competence in handling weapons. In addition the army provided food and clothing and, for those bereaved, some companionship in their grief.

Soldiering on

I have dwelt in some detail on Sierra Leone to provide a glimpse of the complexity of the situation of many child soldiers and to provide some insight into the motives of the volunteers. In a situation that seems hopeless this role offers the child some sense of power and control over his/her fate. As has become clear, the army, whatever faction the child joins, is as much an education or employment agency as a fighting machine. Looking at the child's situation it is evident that there are very limited choices. President Momoh is reported to have told students that education was a privilege not a right. Given this context, Richards says, 'In some respects, war has come to represent a kind of self-help approach to training and employment for many young people' (Richards 2002, p.276). I have included child soldiers in this book on children's rights and power to demonstrate that although children may often be forced to fight against their will, sometimes it is the most powerful decision they can make in the circumstances in which they find themselves. In this case they are warring for themselves rather than as mere agents of an adult power. They are no longer living within an adult's view of reality as they have adopted that version as their own. Richards differentiates between the experiences of army and CDF combatants, who are mainly volunteers with civil society support in varying degrees, and the RUF combatants, who were mainly abductees with no social support beyond the insular world of the bush camps. The latter was more cult than army and as yet the nature of this social experience is not fully understood (Richards 1998a). Further work on understanding these experiences may give us some insights into the nature of the child's endurance. It seems clear that whatever the child's rights in international instruments the RUF would have scant regard for them when they needed to strengthen their own forces. This is probably true of many of the rebel forces in civil wars throughout Africa. What remains a challenging problem is the demobilisation and rehabilitation of children who have spent most of their growing up enduring life as active combatants.

Optional protocol to the Convention on the Rights of the Child

In June 1999 International Labour Organisation Convention No. 182 on the Prohibition and Immediate Action for the Elimination of the Worst Forms of Child Labour – which prohibits, *inter alia*, forced or compulsory recruitment of children for use in armed combat – was unanimously adopted. This was followed, on 25 May 2000, by the General Assembly of the United Nations adopting the Optional Protocol to the Convention on the Rights of the Child on the involvement of children in armed conflict (UN 2000). By 2001, 80 states had signed it and four had ratified it. Ten ratifications are needed to bring it into force. The States Parties agreed to two new Articles. One relates to taking all feasible measures to ensure that members of their armed forces who have not attained the age of 18 years do not take a direct part in hostilities. The second is to ensure that persons who have not attained the age of 18 years are not compulsorily recruited into the armed forces.

By following the detailed case history of civil war in Sierra Leone, one can immediately see how very difficult these recommendations and Articles will be to enforce and, moreover, how they would reduce the life options of many children seeking to exercise some agency within their view of reality in a terrifyingly confused world.

CHILD LABOUR

Soldiering is possibly one of the most harrowing forms of child labour, forcing the child to accept views of violence and brutality as part of daily life. The work that Richards and his colleagues are doing to try to establish how the children themselves experience this form of work is challenging and, although at an early stage, reflects a growing movement in children's rights to establish at first-hand how the children themselves experience their situation and what its meaning is to them. Just as many children have ostensibly volunteered to fight in order to eat, so many children throughout the world have to work in order to support their families and themselves. The degree of choice or compulsion involved is again difficult to establish. The UN Children's Fund estimates that some 200,000 children a year are trafficked in West and Central Africa as slave labour. This plight was brought to the world's attention when in 2001 a ship suspected of carrying a cargo of 200 child slaves was turned away from Gabon and Cameroon (Robinson and Palus 2001).

New research with child labourers is trying to gain some insight into how they view their work. This approach marks a breakthrough in relationships between adults and children. In this book, which has as a major organising theme children's power, the work that is developing in the field of child labour is particularly significant. In other minority rights groups the point at which their activism has started to become effective is when the direct experiences of their members have been sought and listened to. My definition of power uses Rowe's statement: 'In the final analysis, power is the right to have your definition of reality prevail over other people's definition of reality' (1989, p.16). Hence listening to the child labourer's realities has represented a start on a process of empowerment. For so many years there has been worldwide pressure to end child labour, largely based on assumptions made out of context about what is best for children and about their needs defined on the basis of Northern indoor childhood (Ennew 1995). Thankfully this conceptual and cultural imperialism has been challenged by children's own views of their lives and aspirations, what they are prepared to stoically accept and endure and what they think it is important to change.

Signatories to the United Nations Convention on the Rights of the Child, under Article 32, undertake to:

> ...protect children from performing any work that is likely to be hazardous or interfere with the child's education or to be harmful to the child's health or physical, mental, spiritual, moral or social development.

The later Convention proposed by the International Labour Organisation (ILO), designed to target intolerable working situations for children (International Labour Organisation 1996), now prohibits the worst forms of child labour and came into force in many countries in 2000.

Debates persist about what is harmful to a working child's development and what the nature of intervention should be, as it might not necessarily be helpful or indeed in the best interests of the child in particular circumstances. White (1996) cites the case of child workers in garment factories in Bangladesh being thrown out in order to satisfy consumer pressures for child-free products with scant regard for the importance of work in the economic lives of these children and their families. Bourdillon (2001), to cite a further example, described the situation of three companies that export tea from Zimbabwe and the way they responded to pressures from international buyers on the child-labour issue. One company had a policy of not employing children but rather hypocritically did support small-scale growers, some of whom used child labour in exploitative conditions. This company did nothing for children yet had no problems in selling its tea overseas. The other two companies in their various ways had been combining work with educational opportunities for their child workers. Their eventual decision, in response to international pressure, not to employ children had disastrous effects in that the children lost their work and their educational opportunities. Bourdillon concludes:

> It appears that the less people do for children in need the
> more acceptable are their products on international markets.
> To focus opprobrium on child labour instead of child abuse
> has deleterious effects for children. (Bourdillon unpublished)

Woodhead (1998b) points out:

> The case for protecting children from hazard and exploitation
> in every area of their lives (at work, at school or in the family
> and community) all too often becomes distorted by focusing
> on particular issues that offend modern Western sensibilities.
> (Woodhead 1998b, p.125)

Even in the UK we are naive about the role of work in some children's lives (Pettitt 1998). The ILO estimates that there are 250 million children worldwide under the age of 15 who work. Their estimates suggest that 120 million children aged 5 to 14 have full-time jobs and a further 130 million are in part-time employment ranging from jobs combined with education to highly exploitative, dangerous work. Evaluating child labour the ILO identifies the worst forms of child labour as including prostitution, slavery, the sale and trafficking of children, debt bondage and forced labour including the forced conscription of child soldiers (White 2002).

The perspective of the child worker

At the Exeter International Conference on Children's Rights in 1992, Aracelli Brizzio de la Hoz presented a paper on research in Mexico City interviewing children who lived or worked on the street (de la Hoz and Martinez Morales 1997). A census indicated that, in the area under investigation, over 11,000 boys and girls between the ages of 5 and 17 worked on the street, over a thousand of whom had no family connections at all. A selected sample from this population was interviewed. For over half of this population, poverty had impelled them to work, limiting their education. The interviews gave some insight into the experiences of these children and what they felt was important in life as they saw it.

This early work reported from Mexico prefigured a growing trend around the world to seek the views of the child worker. Some years later in Mexico, I met and talked to some of the street workers in Xjalapa, some in schools that had been set up for them with lively Mexican music specially played for them in their breaktime, underscoring their culture and their indomitability. I encountered some of them selling chewing gum or matches in bars in the evenings, some entertaining with juggling firebrands at street corners, and the (now familiar in most parts of the world) windscreen washing at the traffic lights. The adults who had grown up as street children were emphatic about how essential it had been for them to find ways of earning money. I was also taken out into the countryside to see the real hardship of work for some Mexican children from as early as 11 years old. They endured standing barefoot up to their thighs in wet clay all day long, with no cheering music here – only unrelenting damp, extracting clay to make bricks. The cost to many of them was the very early onset of chronic arthritis. I saw there the attempts that were being made to provide educational opportunities that, like the night schools of Rajasthan described in Chapter 8, respected the children's need to work, providing basic relevant education at times and places that fitted in with their working day.

The UN Convention on the Rights of the Child (UNCRC) emphasises that young people below the age of 18 enjoy central civil and political rights. Per Miljeteig outlines the constellation of participation rights that have been extremely important for working children. These include rights to: freedom of thought, conscience and religion; freedom of association; protection of privacy; and access to information. An important innovation brought about by UNCRC is the right to be informed about the rights established by the Convention. In addressing the situation of working children and youth it is important to bear in mind that 'participation rights' include all of these rights.

Acknowledging that children are capable of having views, listening, and taking these seriously also implies that children can act autonomously. They are able to protect their own interests, and act as *stakeholders* in these efforts. In several countries around the world working children and youth have capitalised on these rights, sometimes forming organisations and pressing to be parties to the child-labour discourse. 'Are we ready to take them seriously as *partners* in the further efforts to address the problems associated with child labour?' (Miljeteig 2000, p.301).

The language and stance in this field has changed from that of protection to strong powerful roles for the child as 'stakeholder' and 'partner'. In Peru, Manthoc, one of the most vocal proponents of working children's participation, uses the term 'protagonism' to stress the interactive and responsibility-taking aspects of participation. This word is increasingly being used in English with the meaning it carries in Spanish to emphasise some of the activities not normally linked with participation, such as a capacity to take an active part in defining the choices of a given community (Miljeteig 2000; Swift 1999; Tolfree 1998; Torres 1994).

Miljeteig claims that within the framework provided by UN Convention on the Rights of the Child the discussion as regards child labour has become increasingly focused on the exploitative aspects of child labour and how to intervene to prevent such exploitation through, for instance, education, social mobilisation and poverty-reduction activities. Debates about policy making as regards work that is dangerous, exploitative or abusive and about the possible detrimental effects of work on child development have characterised international concern (UNICEF 1997a; White 2001). It has become widely accepted that it is necessary to include the inside knowledge and views of working children and youth and the perspectives of their families if real understanding is to be reached and progress made (Miljeteig 1999; Woodhead 1999b).

Tapping child workers' experience

A Save the Children programme in Vietnam has begun a series of studies as part of work on child labour to try to ensure that the emphasis in existing projects becomes more child-focused (Theis 1998; Theis and Huyen 1997). As part of this work information has been collected about working children and from children. Interestingly data has also been collected from children by children themselves. The primary aim was to improve understanding of the children's lives, their interests, capacities and needs and this was done by starting off with a determination to listen. The information gathered is set in the context of specific themes – gender, the family, community and society – and linked to country-level statistics. A secondary benefit of this research has been to demonstrate children's ability to participate in research activities. In order to facilitate children's participation, research methods were used that were 'tailored to children's capabilities, disaggregated by age, to the topic of the research and to the conditions of each research location' (Theis 1998, p.82). These participatory methods included semi-structured interviews and discussions, diagramming, listing, scoring and photography. The children proved to be enthusiastic co-researchers, assisting in providing new insights into the lives of these working children and revealing the importance of children's views of their situation. Even in a programme as innovative and progressive as this had been, nevertheless the researchers felt they had tended to underestimate how capable, inventive, ingenious and resourceful the children actually were in protecting themselves and in resisting and evading exploitation and abuse. Paradoxically while involving children in the research they had nevertheless not rid themselves of traditional notions of the child as passive and in need of protection.

Adapting this rural research to an urban setting, the Save the Children Fund (SCF) conducted a further study of child workers in Ho Chi Minh City, which has a population of six million (Theis 1998). The challenges presented by such an urban setting for involving child workers in participatory research bred further innovative strategies, including using a photo-appraisal approach (Hubbard 1991). Members of the community, including children, are provided with cameras with which to document their lives. Photographs produced in this way are then discussed and selected for inclusion in publication, meaning that children are involved in the collection, analysis and presentation of this visual

account of their lives. An audience who would probably not read research reports may be reached and influenced as the pictures have the
potential of raising consciousness among adults about how children
view their own lives. This technique was enthusiastically responded to
by the rural children, although the results were described as rather
'mixed' (Theis 1998, p.85). Acrimonious disputes arose between SCF
and its local government partner concerning the ownership and control
of the negatives.

> This issue demonstrates how sensitive children's participation
> is when taken seriously, especially in a country that does not
> have a tradition of freedom of expression. It also raises ethical
> issues regarding children who are encouraged to express their
> views openly and critically. (Theis 1998, p.85)

Based on the experiences in Vietnam, Theis believes that it would be difficult for children to work in the same research team alongside adults.
His view is that conditions have to be created which enable children to
take greater responsibility for the entire research process. By the end of
1997 this view was taken by SCF which was planning to train a group
of children in Ho Chi Minh City to be involved in research with street
children in their own community, thus empowering the children themselves. SCF sees these benefits as paramount and more important than
collecting good quality data or the production of a polished report. In
my view it is probable that the data will be of the best quality in that it
will be as close as it may be possible to get to children's lived experience
and thus the mainsprings of their personal power. In Chapter 3, I have
made a similar point about data in that statistics of children do not provide the same insights as information gathered by children.

   The aim of the work in Vietnam was to ensure that the work of the
NGO became more child-focused. In Nepal, a multisector Nepalese
team has been conducting child-centred participatory research since
1999 (Sharma, Nepal and Pandey 2001). Adverse publicity on child-
labour issues in the carpet industries resulted in the formation of the
National Society for the Protection of Environment and Children
(NASPEC), aiming to return children from hazardous conditions to a
'normal' way of life and undertake the necessary rehabilitative activities.
The difficulties among these various agencies and for NGOs responding
to international concerns has been to establish what 'normal' life can be
now for these children. Rehabilitation is problematic as, they

discovered, child workers will not necessarily be accepted back into their villages. Making the adjustments to a new 'better' life is not straightforward, especially when their new realities have often been shaped by adults identifying their 'needs' for them. The similarities with what happened in the early history of the rehabilitation of disabled people are striking in that professionals often defined their needs for them. Within a new fashion for collecting evidence, children's views can be gathered and interpreted and this process may be coloured by adult prejudices, views, prescriptions and priorities, even when they all ostensibly share the same culture.

Blagborough (1998), reviewing research with child domestic workers, points out that while it is crucial to collect information from the children themselves, in the case of these children, certain ethical issues arise. They are isolated, and talking about their situation, far from empowering them, might make them anxious and fearful. What they say might well be constrained by worries about upsetting their employer. Interviewing can be stressful and make the child depressed or even result in the child running away. The interviewer needs to build up the child's confidence over a period of time, which poses practical problems. Blagborough found conducting such interviews best if the children are already participating in some existing project. He describes how this has been done in Bangladesh where drawing and storytelling were used by the group for self-expression. In Haiti 'family centres' attended by child domestics provided an appropriate setting for in-depth research. In the Philippines child domestics were sought out in the park where they went on their day off. This work eventually led to the establishment of an Association of Household Workers.

In a climate of increasing sensitivity to the insider perspective, several other studies have tried systematically to gather information from children themselves using imaginative research techniques and context-appropriate strategies. The hope is to find creative solutions to the problems faced by working children as they themselves perceive them using a process of enquiry that can itself be empowering. In a Radda Barnen study (Woodhead 1998b), 300 children (mostly aged 10 to 14 years, balanced in terms of gender and rural and urban locations) participated in research that was carried out by local fieldworkers in four regions of the world (Bangladesh, Ethiopia, the Philippines, and El Salvador, Guatemala and Nicaragua). The children's work included lead mining, firework manufacture, weaving, brick chipping, domestic work, market work, porters, street vending, shoe shining, fishing and its associated activities, and agricultural work. Fifty local workshops were organised where groups of working children were able to share their experiences, opinions and thoughts about aspects which troubled them. Most of the young people participating in this study were not involved in any movement of child workers so had not had their thinking shaped or influenced by such organisations. Whether the children felt that they had to work or whether they chose to do so was investigated, as were issues of the circumstances in which they worked. The group work was guided by a specially designed Children's Perspective Protocol sensitive to local circumstances and conditions. This enabled and encouraged young people to express their feelings and values in a variety of ways that were meaningful to them, such as mapping, drawings, role play and group discussion. The core of the Protocol was provided by a series of semi-structured activities and games, many of which revolved around picture cards, produced locally so that they would be relevant. Key terms in children's lives were explored by sorting, comparing, ranking, etc. Great effort was made to ensure that this work was relevant to the culture and specific setting of these children. A complementary study (Tolfree 1998) was undertaken which focused specifically on the views of working children who are engaged in or supported by Radda Barnen programmes in Bangladesh, El Salvador, Ethiopia, Peru and Senegal.

In the UK, while children's work does not have the same high profile that it has in the developing world, it is significant – in fact it is the norm for children to work (Hobbs and McKechnie 1998). There has been considerable investigation into the extent and type of work done by children (Hobbs and McKechnie 1997; Joliffe *et al.* 1995) but little on what children think about their work. Qualitative research was undertaken by Save the Children in four areas of the UK with young people between the ages of 11 and 16. Although this was a heterogeneous group there were great similarities across gender and ethnicity in their reasons for working and attitudes towards it and the jobs they do. Work played an important part in their lives. The motivation went beyond just money to the social aspects of the work, getting away from home, alleviating boredom and for some gaining experience, confidence and self-esteem. While it was a way of increasing their personal powers there were disadvantages. Often they did not feel they had been treated fairly as compared to adults and some of them had been exposed to dangerous and unpleasant situations. They made various suggestions, the strongest of which was for an official complaints procedure (Save the Children 1998).

Taking account of the children's experience and perspectives is regarded by Woodhead (1998a) as important in four respects: children have a right to be heard; children's working world has a meaning to them which is important to understand; children are capable of expressing their feelings and aspirations in a context which respects their abilities and mode of communication; children are an important source of evidence on how work might harm their development within their specific working environment, family and community setting. I feel that seeking children's experiences also ideally signifies a transformation of adult–child relationships in that it makes clear that the adult's views do not dominate and marks the beginning of a process towards reciprocal understanding.

Working Children and Youth Organisations (WCYOs)

Working Children and Youth Organisations have a long history and are to be found in various parts of the world (Marcus 1998; Miljeteig 1999, 2002; Reddy 1998; Swift 1999; Torres 1994). As early as 1899, Reddy reports, the newspaper boys in New York successfully organised themselves to press for increased wages (Reddy 1998). Children have been organising themselves in order to improve their working conditions for some considerable time. If we understand how capable, ingenious and highly motivated child workers are, this should not surprise us. Another early example is of a Catholic activist movement emerging in 1925 in Belgium, the Young Christian Workers Movement of workers aged between 15 and 25, which later inspired some of the pioneering movements in Latin America (Swift 1999). One of the most vocal proponents of these working children's organisations, Manthoc, sprang up in Peru. Manthoc (Movement of Working Children and Adolescents from Christian Working Class Families) is described by Torres (1994). While working children's movements started to appear in different parts of the world in the 1970s, the point at which such movements came to play a part in discussions about child labour came rather later. Often an NGO linked to them provided support of various kinds and sometimes advocacy with employers. Some WCYOs have grown out of a refusal of adult trade unions to admit young members (Marcus 1998). The peer-group support provided by these organisations has often been important. It has only been rather recently that these groups have begun to be recognised as important contributors to child-labour dialogue.

Miljeteig (2000), drawing on the detailed accounts of Swift (1999) and Tolfree (1998), identifies what it is that organisations of working children seem to have in common, which include: they have a strong foundation in a grass-roots movement with an activist approach; they have grown organically and spontaneously from small beginnings; they have small organisational units; they elect officers democratically. The growth of such movements has been rapid in West Africa and Latin America. What has added to their strength has been the international networking among such organisations globally. It is notable that these characteristics mirror many of those typical of minority rights groups pressing for recognition and social change.

Participation of child workers at local level

It has not been common to find the formal involvement of children and young people in local representative structures involved in developing planning initiatives or policy. While occasionally young people's views are sought, this tends to be in a one-off and informal way rather than leading to the development of structures to ensure their representation. The number of examples of local representative bodies developing more formal structures to accommodate children and young people's points of view on their situation, including work, has been increasing (Miljeteig 1999; Moran 1998). One example of a local organisation has been in Southern India. An NGO called Concern for Working Children (CWC) assisted working children and young people develop their own organisation, Bhima Sangha. Part of this work has been facilitating children to leave work that is dangerous and obtain education or train-ing in relevant, culturally appropriate skills. Bhima Sangha groups have also been supported by CWC in putting their views to village councils where such views have been positively received and acted upon (Marcus 1998). A common goal has been to support children in their day-to-day lives. This is often done through small focused discussion groups in-spired by the Participatory Rural Appraisal (PRA) approach used by many NGOs in developmental work (Chambers 1997). Children who have participated have commented on how the experience has increased their self-confidence. Some have benefited from what they have learnt about their society in such groups. In fact Manthoc has as part of its aims to adopt an educational approach which raises awareness about society and gives information and develops relevant skills. In several such organisations there is informal learning in vocational skills.

Child participation in international policy making

Attempts to regulate the conditions of children's work ideally should involve them as the principal stakeholders as those most likely to be directly affected by hazards and dangers that form a focus of concern. While it seems self-evident that children should have a say in these matters, adults are not always ready to hear what they have to say or to have their workers being listened to on the international stage. It has now become something of a fashion, as it did at one stage in the development of the social movement of disabled people, to have presentations from working children themselves at large gatherings. In 1997 eight representatives of movements of working children were invited by the Dutch government to a meeting in Amsterdam. The Norwegian government has also arranged for a similar direct involvement in meetings in Oslo about child labour (Woodhead 1998b). Child workers have been represented at important meetings in Latin America and in Sweden.

While child labour has been high on the international policy agenda for some time, it is only recently that child workers have been included in these deliberations. The most notable recent example of children's participation in such discussions was the presentation by one young delegate at the UN Special Session on Children in May 2002, elected by child workers in Burkina Faso. This 17-year-old delegate was a member of the Burkina Faso Child and Young Workers' Association. He was assisted in attending by Save the Children, who prepared a film about child labour in Burkina Faso's gold mines for this session. Young people have been getting together there for some time to combat dangerous and unregulated gold mining (White 2001). Participation by children and young workers in international meetings on child labour is a relatively new phenomenon and one that is viewed with some caution by many adult delegates. It does serve to give child labour a face, to provide opportunities for a more finely detailed and immediate understanding of the issues and to challenge common assumptions. It is not always a positive experience for the children. There are often baffling procedures and structures that stand in the way of establishing a dialogue in which children's experiences are heard, and the language used is sometimes an obstacle. A Declaration by young workers addressed to the 87th Assembly of the ILO on the Convention on the Worst Form of Child Labour stated: 'Instead of talking about "rehabilitation" [...] we prefer the phrase "the necessary attention and assistance"; and instead of "return to society" we prefer "active participation in the community and society"' (Miljeteig 2000). Similarly talk of 'abolishing child labour' at these gatherings is seen by the children as discrediting their efforts and trying to get rid of an activity that is meaningful and important to them. There are great parallels with the social movement of disabled people who complained about the control of the naming process suggesting, for example, a significant shift from the disabled individual to the disabling environment.

Working children have brought important information and views to the dialogue. Sometimes it is simply local activities which are presented at international meetings. Children's presentations at international gatherings have sometimes been threatening to their employers. One example is Iqbal Masin, a winner of the World's Children's Prize for the Rights of the Child in 2000 (www.childrensworld.org). Iqbal in 1992 ran away from his work as a debt slave in a carpet factory in Pakistan to attend a meeting with the Bonded Labour Liberation Front (BLLF). He was very influenced by Ehsan Ullah Kahn, the leader. Iqbal was encouraged to tell other children at the gathering about his work experiences. There he found out about the law which forbids debt slavery and the penalties imposed on those who exploit debt slaves, a law widely disregarded in Pakistan. Iqbal spread the word among his friends in his home village and children in other carpet factories that they need not stay with their owners. In the Muridke region, first hundreds and then thousands of children left their rug factories despite the pleadings and threats of their employers. Iqbal went to live at the BLLF in Lahore. On his visits home to his family his former employer threatened him. Threats became increasingly violent. Iqbal was invited to Sweden to talk about his experiences, where, in 1994, his visit received extensive news coverage. He went to the United States to receive a prize from Reebok for having fought so hard for the rights of debt-slave children. In 1995, back in Pakistan, he visited his family for Easter and was murdered. A farm worker was accused for this but in Sweden in 1999 a film *Death of a Slave Boy* put forward the view that he was killed by murderers paid by his former employer in the carpet factory. This illustrates that however courageous it might be for children to speak out locally, nationally or internationally, it can be enormously dangerous for them – they can become too powerful for their own safety.

WORKING IT OUT

Children's power has been illustrated in this brief examination of children's involvement in work and warfare. While it is impossible to be comprehensive, a number of issues which are important to any consideration of children's agency – self-esteem, self-determination, endurance, ingenuity and indomitability – have been raised. Africa has the highest rate of child labour in the world: 41 per cent of 5- to 14-year-olds work (Robinson and Palus 2001). Thinking about child warriors and child workers serves to challenge culturally biased assumptions about childhood. Ideas of protecting children are often out of touch with their lives and also serve to underestimate and diminish them. It is worth reiterating that ideas about when children become adults vary across cultures and often, to our eyes, this arrives early. The denial of agency to young workers or volunteer fighters, who may be taking 'adult' decisions in relation to their own appraisal of their prospects, is often based on an outside, partial view of their lives and choices open to them. Protection in these circumstances may deny their agency and autonomy. To look at their life options as they see them, to consider ways of ameliorating the desperate poverty that restricts these options and the conditions within which children are employed, is probably a more fruitful approach than blanket prohibition of these activities. Most child slaves come from the poorest countries, such as Benin, Burkina Faso or Mali, where up to 70 per cent of the people live on less than 75p per day and there are no options for children – no school and no jobs (Robinson and Palus 2001).

To outlaw child labour in order to prioritise education does two things. It underestimates what children learn about life, family responsibilities and social relations at work among their peers. It also sometimes tries to privilege an education that is neither relevant nor useful for these children and the future that they face. In my autobiographical journey through this book I recall my father's life as a child worker down the coal mine (illegally) at 13 to support a family fallen on hard times. For many of his peers in similar circumstances education was the only possible escape. After very long shifts underground they were taught by the village schoolmaster, all of them eventually achieving great distinction in their chosen fields. The education they received respected the fact they were obliged to work – a fact that was also recognised by the foreman's 'blind' eye as regards their age.

In the various forms of work which children have of necessity had to do they have been important witnesses of inhumane and exploitative treatment, and while they have been ingenious in the ways they have endured it, *their* testimony locally and more widely has brought about change. It has been helpful that children themselves have indicated that the language used in relation to their lives is inappropriate. Minority rights groups as part of their campaigning tried to show how language can 'normalise' their experiences in ways that do not match their emphases and aspirations and miss the point entirely. The interviews with 'volunteers' and abductees who have had to work as soldiers in Sierra Leone have led to insight and understanding which has guided demobilisation programmes. While working as child soldiers they may pay with their life for resisting or questioning the violence which appears unbounded. It seemed that only those children who were strong, had few scruples and for whom their family and kin were a very distant memory could survive and go on to become soldiers who would stop at no atrocity to stay alive. What meaning did they make out of experiences such as these in turbulent times of total role confusion? It is encouraging that research continues, even in these difficult circumstances, to gather information from demobilised soldiers who started as child soldiers on what their experiences have meant to them. This respects their endurance and resilience and educates the uncomprehending adult. This chapter, while it has touched on many issues, has emphasised the centrality of children's direct experiences. As with other minority rights groups, the transformation of power relationships starts with having one's own engagement with the world, the meaning this has and the aspirations one holds taken seriously. In this way disabled people managed to relocate 'the problem' from a deficit or 'need' in them to a disabling environment. Children do not need their realities interpreted for them, or their needs defined by adults who see the world a different way. Their power lies in defining their own world.

In bringing about change, local activities with children or those initiated by them have been significant and have had considerable achievements. The local circumstances are known and understood and so are the children. Representations by working children at international gatherings have helped to give child labour 'a face', an authenticity, and have introduced a detailed subtlety and relevance into the debates. Locally there is not the same need for such illustrative interventions. In their own context, once they have established a role in which they are listened to, children have had useful observations to make. In India one of the suggestions that children in the Bhima Sangha group made to their village task-force related to their concerns about the degradation of natural resources close to the village, which they had noted meant seasonal migrations to find work and long walks to find fodder and food. They also expressed concern over the poor maintenance of the village paths, the consequence of which was that in the wet season the children who did go to school could not get there (Marcus 1998). These children acting responsibly as good citizens were taking a broad view of life in their village.

Local knowledge and familiarity have a dark side too. Exploitative and ruthless employers can take revenge on child workers' relatives as well as the children. In Pakistan, Iqbal's family had been threatened many times before he himself was murdered. The importance of social capital provided by the family and community has been recognised in perverse ways in preventing the desertion of abductees. In Cambodia, as in Sierra Leone, children were used in various ways that exploited their local knowledge and familiarity in order to spy and inform on those they knew. This dirty work endowed children with a terrifying power and in the case of the adult Khmer, after many decades of war, has been said by some to have left a legacy of a fear of children (Boyden 2001). I have written in the early chapters of this book of children even in a relatively stable society being seen as 'dangerous' mainly on the basis of adult uncertainty about how they construe the world and what they are capable of (Douglas 1970; Ingleby 1985). I have also examined the psychologists' inability or reluctance to deal with the politics of experience (Reicher 1996). In the case of the two young murderers in the UK it had been suggested that in trying to read the text of their culture, and what it meant to be 'masculine' in that culture, they killed a child in an attempt to stifle the baby in themselves (Jackson 1995). The act was interpreted by some as a reach for power in a world in which they had been often humiliated, rendered powerless and unimportant. A similar conception is put forward by Gitta Sereny in examining the life experiences of another child murderer in the UK, Mary Bell (Sereny 1995). Such children are seen by others as evil freaks of nature. Culpability and the age of criminal responsibility are issues raised in relation to child soldiers and indeed any 'crime' committed by children. The age at which the child is held morally responsible varies from seven or eight in some cultures to much older in others. It is some indicator of the fear of children. In France, under new legislation, 13- to 16-year-old children who insult people in authority may be sent to a detention centre for up to six months. *La Monde* comments: 'Instead of looking at our young people as the "door to the future" our society seems to be afraid of them' (*La Monde*, 6 August 2002).

In the case of child soldiers the mistrust of children is rooted in what child combatants have been used to do, as instruments of others' power and in the destruction of familiar power hierarchies, deferences and boundaries of behaviour. In Sierra Leone adults assumed that village children had turned against them and so preferred escaped abductees to be killed rather than risk taking them back. Traditional relationships between adults and children have had to be rethought. In stressing the importance of hearing from child workers how they view their situation, Chambers' (1997) questions about whose reality counts come into play. What happens when the hierarchy of adult–child relationships has been inverted? What can we say about acculturation into the mores of a society when a moral order longer exists?

A further aspect of the illustrations given in this chapter is that the concern of researchers to gather material about children's direct experience is a rare acknowledgement, as I have argued elsewhere, of the importance of the 'insistent present' (Whitehead 1932). Children's lives are being appreciated in the here and now, not as part of some causal chain that leads backwards but rather as a point on a life trajectory that incorporates the present and the aspirational future. I have argued in Chapter 2 how important this is if we are to escape the genetic fallacy and recognise that as life is lived forwards, interpretation backwards is not helpful. Concentrating on the child's present forces recognition that a universal view of what childhood and children are about is inappropriate. The immediacy of the present is situated in present practices, beliefs, the present turmoil of a community and locality and the broad politics of culture. This makes it increasingly clear how hard it is to generalise about childhood.

While I have argued earlier that traditionally the discipline of child development has paid little regard to the present in a general sense, it has also relied on a model of development that has a very generalised normative basis. It takes no account of the child growing up in circumstances of civil unrest, warfare, dislocations of communities, atrocities, bereavement and the extermination of family members. The assumption is of the child growing up in a 'normal' environment. The examples that have been given in this chapter indicate how very varied children's lives and environments have been. The testimonies of child workers have served to make it abundantly clear that social context plays a vital part. Jo Boyden (2001) quite rightly, on the basis of work in Cambodia, questions what this recognition means for socialisation theory. She asks questions about how in troubled times children develop a sense of morality and some sense of moral order. In this she contrasts role-centred societies and person-centric societies. She also looks at the roles of adults and the peer group as relationships form a central part of this. Increasingly old ideas of human universals in child development are being replaced by an understanding that, in learning, the situation and the context are crucial.

Bruner has stressed the importance of looking at the way knowledge and meaning meet (1990); however, while we know that children's lives can be far from stable, as yet the meaning of this for reconceptualising our developmental theories has been largely dodged. Wood (1998) has put the case for the central part culture plays in organising human social experience and in actively structuring cognition. Children's experiences enable us to understand the way in which they organise their realities and the way in which the culture colours their meaning-making.

Hendry and Kloep (2002) in summarising modern developmental theories looked for a 'framework of commonality' (p.6) in each theory, looking at them in terms of what common ideas they had about development in its cultural context, especially how each theory handles 'challenge'. They point out that the kinds of challenges, their origin and how this is described vary between theories but they argued that the mechanism of responding to challenge had similarities in all cases. They proposed a model of developmental challenge. In looking at the lives of child soldiers and child workers we have seen some of the ways this model of challenge-risk response has operated alongside individual differences in the experiences that have contributed to the 'resource pool'.

PART IV

Children in Charge

CHAPTER SEVEN

Children at Large
Agency, Participation, Politics
and Democracy

INTRODUCTION

Children do not always have to endure other people's worlds passively however cleverly they may do so. Sometimes they express themselves by actively taking control, by taking charge and having a direct effect on their situation. This refusal to put up with the treatment any longer sometimes erupts in violent and what is regarded as 'delinquent' behaviour. The facilitation of the means by which children do exercise agency and how they do this has become a growth industry in relevant disciplines with the issues of participation, self-determination and involvement in democratic practices becoming foci of concern. After a slow start in the early 1990s, suddenly every practitioner seems to be concerned with encouraging and researching children's participation. Roger Hart's 'Ladder of Participation' (Arnstein 1979; Hart 1992) has provided a frequent framework here but it has been criticised as describing children's participation with the eyes of an adult 'bestower' of rights (John 1996a, p.15). One wonders whether children have indeed been the major beneficiaries of this surge of interest or whether it has been the careers of adults who have captured the spirit of the times which have been most advantaged. This chapter looks at issues relating to the child's right to express a view on the world stage or more locally, the necessary changes in adult–child relationships and the role of school, schooling and peer education. Chapter 8 takes this further by providing examples of young people actively taking part in their societies – making their view of reality influence what happens.

VOICE

In Chapter 2 I mentioned the shortcomings of current qualitative research methods in relation to the voices of children. Children's silences should come under scrutiny by psychologists both from the point of view of the processes that have silenced them and the struggle they have had to be heard. Children, now formally recognised as a minority rights group through the provision of their own UN Convention, share many experiences of oppression with such minorities. Earlier I have indicated that one such feature has been that their own subjectivities have been denied; a second is that there has been a paucity of research on the *experiences* of those whose voices have been, as a result of this denial, silent. 'The views which permeate social science from the perspectives of the silenced are *etic views*: the views of those with power and access to control the naming process, even while being outsiders to marginal lives' (Lincoln 1993, p.30). The nature of this silence and an examination of the processes which create it are developed further in this and the following chapter. The structure, practices and research which liberate the voice of the child within the political process – 'power', as I have used it in this book – relate to the ability to get other people to accept your definition of reality. It is also is about controlling the naming process. The relationship between voice, the identifying of individual experience and power is important to understand.

> Power exercised in silence, is even less likely to know restraint; for silence whilst sometimes eloquent, can seldom challenge power. Language, accompanying power, enables the powerless to challenge power. Without language, and especially without language recognised by the powerful, those who would challenge or resist power are quite disabled. (Minow 1987, p.1904)

In the case of children, *their* language, whatever its forms, about *their* worlds is rarely recognised by the powerful. The changes arising from the UN Convention on the Rights of the Child have been subtle and the revolution it brought about has been muted. The fact that the Convention legitimised the recognition of the child's experiences, via the child's own voice and by listening to children, has major implications in relation to the work and responsibilities of psychologists.

The implications of equal opportunity policies, the rethinking of the full inclusive implications of a democratic society, the challenges emerging within critical and radical psychology for the discipline to get involved with the meaning of the child's immediate experiences have become important in recent years. The pressure for the discipline to develop a more political edge (Reicher and Parker 1993) and the slow ending of conceptions of children as 'property' rather than as persons in their own right have all led inescapably to an examination of where children as autonomous individuals fit in these 'opportunities' and the decision-making process. As with other minority rights groups there has been confusion about what the child's voice means with an eagerness to act as advocates for children, interpreting them to 'us' – the adult world. Accessing their worlds in authentic ways has called for ingenuity and skill.

In 1998, Scottish children set up Article 12 which is a network of young people, aged 12 to 18, that promotes the UN Convention on the Rights of the Child. Local and national groups have undertaken a range of initiatives to inform others about children's rights. They have created a website for young people and developed information resources. Campaign work was also undertaken by them suxrveying 100 young Scottish people seeking views on communities, crime and curfews to challenge the developing interest in local curfews by politicians and the police (Article 12 1998).

In an international context, the variety of ways in which children's views and voices have been important in the development process is reported by Johnson *et al.* (1998) and by Hart (1997) who examines the theory and practice of involving young citizens in community development and environmental care. The British Council has supported activities to hear the voice of children in matters which concern them. In Nigeria and Vietnam, for instance, it has worked with health professionals, and women's and children's groups, to develop programmes based on the 'Child-to-Child' concept of health education (Young 1996). This encourages children to take an active and responsible role in the health of themselves and their families. The child's voice is also facilitated by work the British Council has undertaken with street children in the Philippines in supporting a drama project, 'The Lost Child Trilogy'. These are but a few examples of the ways in which various agencies have been working on voicing.

UNITED NATIONS SPECIAL SESSION

The United Nations General Assembly's Special Session on Children, eventually convened in May 2002, was the first global discussion in over a decade devoted solely to children, who now make up 40 per cent of the world's population. At a time when children's rights were receiving so much attention globally by world leaders, reporting in the UK seemed largely preoccupied with issues of controlling children. The UN was stating that 'by speaking directly to children we can discover what they believe to be the issues affecting their lives'. Meanwhile the responsibilities of UK parents to coerce their children to go to school and problems of control in the classroom were receiving a regular airing in the UK media. It was ironic to find radio, TV and the press giving the Special Session little if any attention, revealing by its preoccupations how little progress had been made on children's rights in the popular consciousness. One could be forgiven for thinking that children were still regarded here as 'the new dangerous classes' (Ingleby 1985). We all heard that Pauline Amos had been sent to prison for 60 days for failing to ensure that her children attended school. Now what is intriguing about this, in the context of a particular point in history when in New York the UN were allegedly 'Taking Children Seriously', is that so little attention was given to what was so very aversive about school. What were the views of the Amos children and other children who truanted, or the growing number who misbehave and are excluded from school? William Blake spoke about education as 'The Great Sin' as it stopped children 'seeing angels standing in the corn' (Wilkinson 1974). What do the children do who do not go to school – what from *their point of view* is their new culture of schoollessness and what do they perceive to be wrong with the education they are currently offered? What a pity that the UK media did not seize the moment to capture the climate of the global stocktaking on the United Nations Convention on the Rights of the Child. To look backwards and reiterate old resistances and abiding worries about threats to parental control that arise in any talk of children's rights seemed to miss an opportunity to raise consciousness. This could have been a time when children's lives, their culture and their concerns and aspirations received long-overdue full attention in a medium uniquely placed to present young voices so that they are heard. It is sadly, although not necessarily on this scale of collective blindness, a familiar story. Children remain the 'slow news' identified by Pilger in Chapter 3.

Two major emphases in the Convention were developments from earlier instruments such as the Declaration of the Rights of the Child adopted by the League of Nations in 1924. This represented a culmination of the work of Eglantine Jebb, founder of Save the Children, who had been an early campaigner following her involvement in trying to protect, in whatever way she could, the young victims and child refugees of World War I. Concern about children's rights is not entirely new though it has only recently started to capture more generally the public imagination and engage sociologists, lawyers and belatedly a few psychologists. The early Declaration of the Rights of the Child, which was later revised and adopted by the United Nations in 1979, stressed the needs to protect and provide for children with the emphasis very much on their material needs. The image of the child contained in such declarations was not that of the citizen but that of the dependent weak member of society that had to be protected and provided for. It is still acknowledged that child welfare needs to be protected but now it is children themselves who are pressing for a collective concern.

A world fit for us

The message delivered from the Children's Forum to the Special Session by child delegates Gabriela Azurduy Arrieta, 13, from Bolivia and Audrey Cheynut,17, from Monaco demanded a 'World Fit for Us'. They identified who they they represented, namely the world's children, making clear that those were: victims of exploitation and abuse; street children; children of war; victims and orphans of HIV/AIDS; children denied good quality education and health care; and victims of political, economic, cultural, religious and environmental discrimination. 'We are children whose voices are not being heard: it is time we are taken into account. We want a world fit for children, because a world fit for children is a world fit for everyone' (UN Children's Statement 2002). The children presented their view on how children could be protected from all the suffering they had identified. Clear indications were given as to how this could be achieved. Children were not seen just as dependent on the implementation of their recommendations by adults. The ways in which the active participation of children could be achieved were outlined. New relationships with adult providers involving a powerful reciprocity were seen as critical. They go on:

> We pledge an equal partnership in this fight for children's rights. And while we promise to support the actions you take on behalf of children, we also ask for your commitment and support in the actions we are taking, because children of the world are misunderstood... We are not the source of problems; we are the resources that are needed to solve them. We are not expenses; we are investments. We are not just young people; we are the people and citizens of this world. Until others accept their responsibility to us, we will fight for our rights. We have the will, the knowledge, the sensitivity and the dedication. We promise that as adults we will defend children's rights with the same passion that we have now as children. We promise to treat each other with dignity and respect. We promise to be open and sensitive to our differences. We are the children of the world, and despite our different backgrounds, we share a common reality. We are united by our struggle to make the world a better place for all. You call us the future, but we are also the present. (UN Children's Statement 2002)

The presence of these children at the Special Session on Children was augmented by illustrative material in a publication, *Taking Children Seriously*, in which children from around the world talked about their lives (Save the Children 2001). One child living in India wrote about how she worked to support her family; a child in Uganda reports on how, having lost both her parents to the AIDS epidemic in Uganda and Liberia, she still wants to learn about the good things in this world; a child forced from his home by war in Afghanistan tells of how he now works to support other young asylum-seekers in the UK. The fact that the authentic – to the extent that transcribed and translated interviews are truly 'authentic' – voices of young children are being presented to the world in this way marks a growing recognition that the voice and the direct experience of children themselves are vital to taking them seriously. Developing policies on the basis of the lives children actually live and the realities as perceived by them marks an acknowledgement, more than ten years after the Convention was ratified, that this simply has to happen and marks a subtle change in the relationships between the adult 'provider' and the child.

Changing relationships

The search for the authentic voice of the child in the stocktaking on the Convention raises general questions about how children are now viewed and what this might indicate about society's changing values and power relationships. In the very early days, referring to the Convention, Richard Reid, Director of Public Affairs for UNICEF (Reid 1994, p.28) said:

> The law on children's rights has three parts: provision (food, medical care, education etc.), protection (from child labour, adult abuse, under the law etc.) and participation by children. Few governments have any philosophic problem with the first two. It's the third part that worries them.

It is arguably one of the most important features of the UN Convention that in addition to the traditional abiding concerns with protection of and provision for children the child's right to participate is included, embodied particularly in Articles 12 and 13. Article 12 makes clear that the child has the right to express his/her view and have that view taken into account in any matter or procedure affecting him/her. Article 13 goes on to outline the child's right to express his/her views, obtain information and access information regardless of frontiers. This apparently endowed the child with a new status in the international arena, which the UN has been at pains to recognise in the recent Special Session in 2002. The practitioner community has been presented with new challenges. The UN Convention has been a landmark as a legislative instrument that put children's participation firmly on the agenda – an agenda on which, following the UN International Year of the Child in 1979, children had begun to appear more prominently. The question remains as to whether the policy makers' rhetoric then has matched realities in children's lives 23 years later. Whether the children's aspirations at the beginning of this new century to work together to reduce the suffering of children will have real outcomes remains to be seen. Gordon Brown, Chancellor of the Exchequer, and as such the most senior financial spokesperson for the government of the UK, in calling for an 'Investment Pact for Children' at the Special Session concluded by saying, 'Whether we can help the world's children should be the true litmus test of globalisation' (Brown 2002). It is hoped that the 'help' he has in mind is of a reciprocal relationship rather than patronage.

The Convention provided a benchmark statement on the need for a change of priorities in relationships, professional and otherwise, with children. Important to note is that it was not the child who has to change but the relationship. Children were no longer seen as standing in the wings waiting to become agents in their own lives and be taken seriously by the rest of the world. Waiting and watching is not what they are actually doing; they are learning from the treatment meted out to them – learning whether or not their voice counts and by implication what their own worth is. They are often learning to endure rather than participate. By examining various paradigms of action with children in the decade that has followed ratification of the Convention, we can perhaps learn something about how to treat the generation of tomorrow as citizens of today.

EARTH SUMMITS

Great efforts were made to ensure that children participated meaningfully in the latest UN Special Session in New York. Questions remain about the way that 'children's participation' is orchestrated at such major gatherings. Are they brought on just to show that children can think and adults care? In the great machinery of global organisations one wonders whether they have any real influence. It is a fact, however, that no longer can such meetings take place without some representation by children. This is progress of a kind. One issue in which children have an undoubted vested interest is in the matter of the global environment – an environment that is often regarded as 'our' legacy to them. The participation of children in the meetings of the World Summit on Sustainable Development also provides something of a barometer on how relationships and attitudes have changed in the ten years since the Rio experience.

Rio rhetoric

At about the same time as many of the activities relating to the drafting of the UN Convention on the Rights of the Child, pressure was mounting in quite another quarter for the involvement of children in world and in local affairs. In 1972, 70 governments met in Stockholm for a conference which created the United Nations Environment Programme (UNEP). The main task of this programme was to put pressure on governments to take more care of the environment. Environmental education was also encouraged through collaboration that was set up with UNESCO (United Nations Educational, Scientific and Cultural Organisation). In 1989 it was decided to hold a Conference on Environment and Development in Rio de Janeiro, Brazil. Kristen Eskeland (1996) describes children's involvement at that Earth Summit. In March 1992, before the meeting of the Earth Summit in June, young people converged on San José, Costa Rica, to prepare for the Earth Summit. A total of 300 young people were there from 97 countries 75 per cent from developing countries, 50 per cent female and 10 per cent indigenous – an exact replica of the world's population. Out of this week emerged the Youth Statement to Rio which dealt powerfully with issues from poverty to pollution. Official youth speakers were promised an hour. From the report in *Rescue Mission Planet Earth* (Children of the World 1994) the experience of being 'heard' was described as follows.

> Young people are half the world's population, so one hour in 14 days seemed fair. When they arrived, they were told they only had ten minutes. Two minutes in the TV cameras were turned off; reporters watching in the pressroom couldn't hear. When the youth tried to tell the eager press what they'd said, UN police arrested them for holding an 'illegal' press conference. So what everyone remembers is images of kids being hauled off by police, nothing of the statement. It said things like 'all Third World debt should be cancelled because rich countries had earned more than enough out of the period of colonialism'. A bit radical but that's the way youth should be. No diplomatic games.
>
> Children were also snubbed. A group called Voice of the Children had organised hearings all round the world. It was the Prime Minister of Norway's idea and she promised to bring six world leaders to hear their statement. None came. She did not even turn up herself...(Children of the World 1994, p.80)

Severn Suzuki did, however, speak and she tried to speak for children who had no voice at Rio 'and she was great; she got [a] standing ovation! But the voiceless children did not ask her to speak: the Director of

UNICEF did. In truth, she represented herself' (Children of the World 1994, p.80). In listening to children the issue of representation is important. Are the children chosen as spokespersons for a group of peers or have they been chosen by adults on account of their acceptability/articulateness? Following the Rio Summit, for a further two years governments, non-governmental organisations and experts worked on a document that 179 states could agree to. Agenda 21 was the result.[1] While this is not a legally binding instrument the fact that so many governments agreed to it is important. One significant feature of Agenda 21 is that, like the Convention on the Rights of the Child, it embodies the right to be heard, as follows:

> Each country should include children's concerns in all relevant policies for environment and development and support their involvement in the United Nations. (Agenda 21, Chapter 25)

On the matter of children's involvement relative to Agenda 21, the Executive Director of the United Nations Executive Programme, Elizabeth Dowdeswell, despite the disastrous experiences in Rio was very positive:

> I have absolutely no doubt that children are leaders where environmental matters are concerned. They have the power to educate their parents as decision-makers and change what's happening at an individual level. (Children of the World 1994, p.82)

From the children's experiences at Rio they can only be 'leaders' if they are given the opportunity for voicing their concerns and if they are indeed listened to. Her optimism was borne out. Over 10,000 children in 200 groups in 75 countries around the world (members of the Children's Agenda 21 Task Force) put in thousands of hours' work, co-ordinated by an international team of 28 child editors, to produce a children's edition of Agenda 21 (*Rescue Mission Planet Earth*, Children of the World 1994). This powerful document is commonly regarded as the best and clearest overview of the rather tortuous and complicated Agenda itself. It is lively, fresh and identifies the issues intelligently. Moreover it makes clear that whatever statements are issued in relation to visionary manifestos they have to be realised in practice. Another message comes across in this impressive piece of work that counters the ill-thought-out criticism that children want rights without responsibilities. The many young authors of this crucial guide to Agenda 21 have demonstrated that they do care about their planet, they care about what we are doing to it and what the legacy for them will be, and they care about what *their* responsibilities are.

The work of Voice of the Children International has continued the work of ensuring that children have a voice on the global, national and local scene and demonstrates the way in which adults acting as allies can provide appropriate structures to facilitate and support children's self-advocacy (Eskeland 1996). Following the success of *Rescue Mission Planet Earth – A Children's Edition of Agenda 21* (Children of the World 1994), which has now been translated into 18 different languages, Peace Child International have now produced *Get Up, Stand Up – A Children's Book of Human Rights* (Peace Child International, 1998) in time for the fiftieth anniversary of the Declaration of Human Rights on 10 December 1998. Peace Child International is an educational charity working with young people in over 100 countries to produce music and books on global issues. In August 2002, roughly a decade after the meeting in Rio, the World Summit on Sustainable Development (WSSD) was held in Johannesburg.

Johannesburg jamboree

Over the last few years children's involvement in environmental issues has been growing apace. Roger Hart has produced many examples of projects and activities which have involved young citizens in community development and environmental care (Hart 1997). He says that these days we need:

> ...fewer trite examples of children speaking about or singing about how they are the future or how they alone best understand global environmental problems and more models that genuinely recognise the untapped competencies of children to play a significant role in community-based sustainable development, particularly when collaborating with adults. (Hart 1997, p.16)

He also points out that while the development of the various electronic media is enabling children to have an increasingly sophisticated knowledge of earth and global environmental issues, this contrasts sharply with their own direct geographical mobility and ability to explore at first-hand the natural world around them. In industrialised countries they are becoming increasingly constricted by their parents' fears. It is his belief that grounding children's education on the environment in actual practical immediate experiences, however, teaches them far more than simply environmental concerns. It introduces them in a very real way to democratic thinking and the nature of power itself in that it can lead them on to asking questions about inequities in the use of environmental resources. It can also act as a vehicle for integrative activities. In Cyprus, for instance, the British Council and Peace Child International have worked with Greek and Turkish children to produce a book about environmental issues.

Other works have been slowly emerging, charting children's and young people's involvement not just in environmental and community issues but in the development process itself. A notable contribution to this literature was made by the publication of papers from an international workshop on children's participation held jointly by the Institute of Development Studies, the (London University) Institute of Education and Save the Children UK in September, 1997 (Johnson *et al.* 1998). This is an important collection, once again, because it illustrates how powerful children's participation can be. Many of the contributors to this workshop stressed their view that the reason that children's voices have until recently been crowded out by the clamour of adult voices has been a matter of power.

Preparations for the World Summit were able to take advantage of the huge growth and development of the Internet in the last ten years with organisations such as the World Wildlife Fund setting up an interactive website for children to use in preparation for Johannesburg. The Summit again involved preparatory meetings. An International Children's Conference of the UN took place in Victoria, BC, Canada, three months before the meeting in Johannesburg. Four hundred children from over 80 countries attended that conference. They felt that they had plenty to say but 'the number one thing that all delegates were concerned about is that most leaders don't listen' (Children's Speech 2002). They sent representatives from the conference in Canada with a presentation to make to the world leaders. Three children from different continents made the presentation: Mingyu Liao from China, Justin Friesen from Canada and Analiz Vergara from Ecuador:

We were just babies when you met 10 years ago in Rio. What we are about to say is basically the same thing you heard then, and many times since. This is because children are close to the ground and to the environment and suffer more from problems in the world. The children of the world are disappointed because too many adults are too interested in money and wealth to take serious notice of problems that affect our future. (Children's Speech 2002)

They went on to outline what the International Children's Conference in Canada had come up with, including a set of things that 'Governments of the world must', which included 'spend more money in helping the poor people and children around the world, rather than on attending too many meetings'. A second list of things outlined what 'People of the World must'. These can be read on the Web (Children's Speech, 2 September 2002). They concluded by saying, 'What we now have is "us" versus them. This needs to become "us" and them, young people and adults, rich and poor people and rich and poor countries'.

It seems that just as in New York the children had been making clear that bringing about change was a joint endeavour, the children here were stressing the same approach, although the edge was taken off this when, in closing, they repositioned themselves. 'Thanks for having us here and for recognising the importance of children. Don't walk off and forget about the challenges. We finally challenge the leaders of the world to accomplish them.' This changed the emphasis. They were not there by right and the ultimate responsibility for getting things done lay with adults. It will be important to look behind the scenes and identify to what extent the young people's presentation had been modified by adult views of appropriate courtesies and positioning.

A strident presentation by Pelin Ayan from Turkey, who made the Major Youth Statement on Youth Participation, Education and Employment, was less deferential and conciliatory. She stressed:

We, as youth, embrace our role as key partners in sustainable development – today and in the future. [...]Youth participation does not mean 'youth washing'. Youth participation requires governments to take into account a youth perspective, even when these are contrary to government policy. [...] We congratulate the governments here, in agreeing upon the final Article of the draft plan of implementation, which

supports local and national youth councils and their equivalent. However, it is essential that authorities at all levels ex-
tend this support to technical and financial support. [...]

Intergenerational justice is at the core of sustainable
development. With what you are currently negotiating here at
WSSD, we ask you, leaders of the world: Do you sincerely
believe that you have here negotiated – as the slogan goes –
'Some, for all, forever'?

Remember we are not only the leaders of tomorrow, but
the partners of today... And that it is *us* you are negotiating!
(Pelin Ayan 2002)

It is clear that children and young people are positioning themselves as
partners in decision making in world affairs. They are trying to ensure
that their realities are recognised as part of the negotiations about the
future of the planet and the children on it.

Many of the draft commitments of the World Summit came out of
the four pillars of action from the first ever UN Special Session on
Children a few months earlier (May 2002): promoting healthy lives;
providing quality education; protecting children from abuse, exploitation and violence; combating HIV/AIDS. Carol Bellamy, Executive Director of the United Nations Children's Fund, in her statement to the
World Summit outlined the improvements to children's lives that had
been achieved since Rio while stressing there was still much to be done.
She claimed, 'Children have the greatest stake in the preservation of the
environment because their survival and development depends on it'
(Bellamy 2002b).

PARTICIPATION

Children's participation may pose threats to established power relationships between adults and children. It will be desirable to follow up, now
the excitement has died down, with the children involved in various
ways in the Special Session and the World Summit how they felt they
had been treated and to what extent their own views were really presented. A period of cool, distanced reflection may be necessary as part of
a holistic evaluation by them of the role they played or were given. The
various ethical dilemmas which face adults in involving children in the
decision-making process and in various projects are identified and discussed in the collection of papers presented at the workshop on

children's participation at the London Institute of Education (Johnson *et al.* 1998).

One of the principles thought to be most important was transparency. This is illustrated by the example of confidentiality. It is stressed that it should be negotiated at the very start of the participatory activity so as to make it clear to all the participants what stance and practices on this issue are to be adopted. The project objectives and the legal and socio-political context of it will all influence the level of confidentiality that is possible and desirable. Clarity in terms of the adults' responsibilities to the children and in terms of the dissemination of information from the project to the wider world must also be achieved at the outset. Issues relating to the project such as informed consent should continue to be renegotiated throughout the project. Revisiting the reasons for embarking on the project, so that expectations as regards outcomes and achievements remain realistic and do not escalate too high, is essential. Other issues to be acknowledged in any project in which children are participating are the differences between children. This acknowledges that they do not form a homogeneous group. There are individual differences around age, disability, gender, ethnicity, religion, etc. Ethical issues, informed consent and access might affect each of these groups in different ways. The benefits of a project involving children's participation have to be seen in terms of its long-term positive and negative impact on children's lives.

> In altering the fundamental power relationships between adults and children, the long-term risks to the latter must be understood and evaluated. It is also important to recognise that change is not always immediately beneficial and a longer time-frame than is often allowed for in projects may be needed to evaluate longer term consequences. (Johnson 1998 p.61)

Participation is a fundamental issue in children's rights, as is acknowledging children as powerful agents in their own lives and citizens in their community. Participation without influence is mere window-dressing. An issue which is commonly raised in relation to participation, notably engaging lawyers involved in various affairs concerning children, has been that of competence. The global dimension of this concern was given emphasis by the World Platform for Action voted on at the close of the UN's Fourth World Conference on

Women in Beijing in 1995. On the issue of children's rights it was agreed 'that children have the right to privacy when receiving health information and services but their rights must be balanced against the parent's rights and duties. Whose rights will dominate will vary according to the child's maturity'. What is not made clear is who will be the judge of the child's maturity. There is always lurking in the background the fear that giving rights to children could let things career out of control and adult/parental rights might be infringed. Maturity and competence have been used as excuses for not treating the child as a responsible person and reinforce abiding myths about the nature of childhood.

CHILDREN'S POLITICAL RIGHTS

Does agency and self-determination extending to political rights only appertain to adulthood? Such rights ensure that children are able, if they so wish, to participate at various levels in the promotion, formulation and enactment of policies. Geraldine Van Bueren, who represented Amnesty International at the United Nations during the drafting of the Convention on the Rights of the Child and other subsequent UN instruments, comments on the situation after the introduction of the Convention. She talks of a 'quiet revolution' that had taken place, 'first in formulating and then establishing children's rights firmly on both the diplomatic and international legal agenda' (Van Bueren 1996, p.27). She describes this revolution in the early days after the ratification of the Convention. At first sight it appears that children under international law do not possess political rights. If the highest form of political expression is seen as the right to elect a government through the ballot box, international law is admittedly not very helpful as far as children are concerned.

In Article 25 of another major human rights treaty, the International Covenant on Civil and Political Rights 1966, which entered into force in March 1976, every citizen is guaranteed the right to vote. There is nothing to prevent a State Party from defining children above a certain age as citizens. Article 27 of the 1987 Constitution of Nicaragua does just that by giving children above the age of 16 the right to vote. This pioneering example has been followed by Brazil. International law, however, does not guarantee to children such a right. A petition to any of the international or regional human rights tribunals, from a child of a State

Party which does not enfranchise children, alleging a breach of his/her right to freedom of political expression would fail (Van Bueren 1996).

It is worth remembering that the definition of political rights does not limit itself to the ballot box and standing for election. It concerns an input to policy promotion, adoption and implementation at all levels. Van Bueren (1996) describes an initiative taken by the President of Venezuela. Once a week a car left the presidential residence to go to a poorer section of the capital. The car picks up a 12-year-old boy and takes him back to the President. He is one of the President's advisers on the environment and reports on the changes in the quality of the environment in his neighbourhood. This may be dismissed as tokenism but Venezuela is challenging, in a very immediate way, the assumption that young children do not have anything to say of political significance. In fact on local issues that also concern children the former Norwegian Child Ombudsman found that children sometimes have a superior knowledge of local conditions and service provision (Flekkoy 1991).

The United States Supreme Court has also recognised that children have and are entitled to exercise their political rights. In the case of *Tinker* v *Des Moines School District*, the Supreme Court upheld the right of school students to wear black armbands in school to protest against the Vietnam war. The Court held that school students cannot be punished for expressing their views: ...even if they are political views, unless the school authorities have reason to believe that such expression will:

> substantially interfere with the work of the school or impinge upon the rights of other students. Although this was a case decided under American national law the relevant provisions of the Constitution of the United States are similar to international legal provisions and hence this landmark decision has implications for children outside of America. (Van Bueren 1996, p.29)

Children's agency and self-determination does not necessarily relate just to formal political activities. Their political rights include an important international legal right to freedom of association and assembly. Article 15 of the Convention on the Rights of the Child provides that, 'States Parties recognise the right of the child to freedom of association and freedom of peaceful assembly'. In Chapter 6 the importance Miljeteig attaches to democratic rights for child workers, of which this is one, has been discussed (Miljeteig 2000).

Participation in group activity, which freedom of association allows, is important for children and other vulnerable members of society because it increases the power of individuals, enabling them to speak with a collective voice. In Brazil, from 1989 onwards, the street children succeeded in attracting both national and global media attention. There they marched through the streets of the capital, protesting at the lack of government action and even government complicity in the murders of street children. The placards they carried, including the ones which said, 'We don't want to be a social problem', were far more eloquent than any adult statement. Hence the right to freedom of assembly is particularly relevant for children because children do not generally have access to the mass media. Access to the media increasingly now means that issues become forced on to the political agenda.

> These are the kinds of political issues from the raising of specific problems to be placed on the political agenda, to the meeting with politicians, that children do and are capable of doing successfully. To ignore the political rights of the child is not in the best interests of children. Not to acknowledge the exercise by children of their political rights is to deny the bravery and the pain of child political prisoners be they Turkish, Palestinian or Kurdish schoolchildren. (Van Bueren 1996, p.31)

The importance of the UN Convention on the Rights of the Child has not simply been symbolic. It has also acted as a catalyst for reforms in the area of children's rights in many countries, not necessarily just the wealthy ones. The Organisation of African Unity became the first regional organisation to adopt its own treaty on the rights of children in Africa. A number of states including Uganda, Tanzania and Zimbabwe established law reform committees reviewing national legislation to bring their national laws up to the required international standards. Mozambique adopted its own Declaration of the Rights of the Mozambican Child and Sri Lanka developed a national five-year plan for Sri Lankan children with specific targets for child development. Following the UN Special Session in 2002 many pledges for further action and reform have been made by countries throughout the world.

In the years before the Special Session, the Committee on the Rights of the Child, an independent body entrusted with monitoring the Convention, worked hard to maintain its visibility. States were called on to report, on a regular basis, on how they had implemented each of the Articles in the Convention. They were questioned in public on their reports which were published. National accountability was important, as seen in the public reception of the UK's first submitted report which attracted a considerable amount of adverse criticism about its accuracy and omissions (HMSO 1994c). The Committee also facilitated the provision of technical advice and assistance to states who have difficulties in implementing specific provisions in the Convention. Despite the urgings of Amnesty International, a weakness in the Convention is that it did not enshrine a right of individual petition. The intention had been that each of the Government reports would be made 'widely available' and so be used to stimulate national debates on the rights of children. The Committee did not have the jurisdiction to respond to individual children's complaints. A number of children have taken their cases to Strasbourg to the European Commission and Court of Human Rights.

Important issues are raised by Articles 12 and 13 in the Convention about the ways in which the child can exercise these rights to influence events. Article 13 augments the rights of Article 12 to express a view by providing rights to obtain and access information regardless of frontiers. Being heard is one thing; having one's views acted upon or acting on one's views is often quite another. The UN Convention has been a landmark as a legislative instrument but the question remains as to whether this is just a 'hurrah' idea or whether the policy makers' rhetoric can change the political realities in children's lives.

SCHOOLING AND POWER

Schooling in democracy

One would think that the obvious places to learn about how to participate and to influence policies would be in school. The Convention on the Rights of the Child established a clear imperative to ensure that children are prepared in their education to fully participate in free democratic societies and that they should be recognised players in decisions that are relevant to their lives. Gerrison Lansdown, formerly Director of the Children's Rights Office in the UK, gives five reasons why the participation of children is so important (Lansdown 1999).

- Respecting children's voices is a vital element in protecting human rights as a whole. Here she emphasises the importance of proper structures for ensuring that they are heard.

- Engaging children and young people will lead to better-informed decision making. In this she emphasises that it is no longer good enough for adults to decide what is in the best interests of the child. Adults do not necessarily know.

- Children acquire skills and competencies from participation. They develop the vital skills of negotiation, conflict resolution, and learning that they have rights to be listened to and respected, and likewise that they have some responsibilities towards others.

- Commitment to democracy relies on a belief that democracy works. She cites evidence that a substantial proportion of young people are growing up with a belief that political institutions have no relevance for them. If adults care about the future of democracy, they must encourage young people to care about it too.

- Children have the right to be listened to.

Lansdown concludes her review of the situation in the UK towards the end of the twentieth century by saying:

> At present, too many young people feel alienated and dis-affected with the political world inhabited by adults. And a minority of young people express that alienation through opting out of school and mainstream society. Changing experience requires us to make a commitment to changing our institutions and our attitudes towards all children and young people. It will take time, it does involve the commitment of resources – democracy is not the most efficient way of making decisions. But it can be done and we owe it to our children to make the investment. (Lansdown 1999, p.10)

This view of the shortcomings of the educational system as we currently know it in the UK is further reinforced empirically by the work of Rhys Griffith. On the basis of a five-year fieldwork study undertaken in all the secondary schools of one local education authority, 97 in all, he questions the rhetoric and reality of empowerment as an aim of the educational process. Pupils were interviewed about existing methods of teaching citizenship. He concluded on the basis of this and classroom observation of the National Curriculum as typically presented to pupils that its 'content-laden syllabi and concomitant dependence on a didactic transmission of knowledge is not effective in developing attributes of citizenship that the literature suggests will be appropriate to the next century' (Griffith 1998, p.9). He goes on to examine how citizenship is ignored or even suppressed in schools. He defines the characteristics of the ideal global citizen as 'critically reflective, morally autonomous and socially active'. These characteristics in his view are typical of an educated person. He concludes that the current emphasis of the curriculum is on a perception of the child as a passive vessel for accumulating knowledge, which encourages conformity rather than the agency, determination and active interrogation of the culture which he considers as essential to the global citizen of the twenty-first century. He argues that it is a nonsense to talk of education *for* citizenship if the young person is not being educated *as* a citizen in a fully democratic way.

> Educational citizenship inverts the traditional notion of a liberal education: that the process (the way in which pupils learn) serves its product (subject-based knowledge). In educational citizenship a subject curriculum has no intrinsic value – simply seeming to know something is not being educated as a citizen. Educational citizenship is dynamic; based upon a tenet that no knowledge is neutral, devoid of cultural meaning, it requires pupils to exercise their critical faculties to question and, perhaps, to change attitudes and behaviour. Thus it might be said that educational citizenship regards the process of learning as its product, the experience as the outcome. The philosophy of educational citizenship abuts closely to Meighan's (1995, p.12) definition of the aims of what he calls 'The Democratic View of Education': '…essentially to produce people with the confidence and skills to manage their own lifelong learning within a democratic culture'. (Griffith 1998, p.49)

He sees the way forward as lying in the transformation of power relationships between teacher and pupil, adult and child (Griffith 1996, 1998). Roger Hart's ladder of the steps in child participation, which was initially based on community participation work, points out false

participation where children are manipulated or used as tokens or deco-
ration in adult decision making. In his view the ideal situation is evidenced when activities are initiated by children but the decisions they
make are shared with adults (Hart 1992, 1997). Children who have
been educated as democratic citizens are more likely to demonstrate
their initiative in this sort of way. He echoes Griffith's point of view.

> But schools are rarely democratic institutions, and many
> other settings suffer from similar constraints in their func-
> tioning. Facilitators and teachers adopting the principles out-
> lined in this book should defend themselves in democratic
> terms but should be aware that by adopting the principles of
> participatory democracy they are, in effect engaging in 'radi-
> cal democracy' and should be prepared for conflict with some
> over their orientation. (Hart 1997, p.25)

Hart goes on to provide an example of how children who attended what
was commonly thought to be a happy, culturally integrated school were
involved in a community-based environmental research project. It became clear, as data was collected by the pupils, that there was a real issue
of racial discrimination in the community – yet the school had simply
ignored cultural tensions in the surrounding community, just pretend-
ing they did not exist. Moreover they had no plan how to deal with the
consequences of such findings by the children, so the research was simply stopped. The radical democracy he talks about and which I advocate
throughout this book is never tension-free.

It is the fear of encountering political and cultural conflict, suggests
Hart, that makes many teachers withdraw from community participatory activities and rely on textbooks within the safety of the
unthreatening classroom. He goes on to say that the answer to such anxieties is that 'civic education must involve exposing children to different
perspectives and values in their own communities. This is at the very
core meaning of democracy' (Hart 1997, p.26). In a sense this 'exposure' is contained within the duties of Article 42 of the Convention. Article 42 provides that States Parties are under a duty to make the
provisions and principles of the Convention widely known by active
means to both adults and children. The 'active means' involves teachers
in examining their position in the power hierarchy and ruthlessly considering whose interests this serves.

Subversion of old powers in Japan

The power of the teacher over pupils in Japan has until recently been legendary, as has the obedience, self-discipline and diligence of the Japanese student. Violent reaction against the enforced discipline has begun to be evidenced in attacks on teachers and peers. Female pupils, however, have been using the opportunities offered by mobile phones to exercise personal power and agency in acting in ways that have echoes of ancient Japanese culture. Mobile phones have frequently been bought for the young pupils by parents anxious that the co-ordination of school, evening classes and cramming classes is smooth and contact is maintained with the home. The girls have used these phones to liberate themselves from parental and institutional control and as a new source of income. They register with agencies who will put through Japanese businessmen to their number. For such a businessman it is regarded as a mark of status and youthfulness to have a 'joshi kousei' (a girl high-school student). These girls in their sailor-suit school uniforms make him think he is still young – it tickles his ego to have such a friend. These men are not paedophiles as such and the encounters are not always sexual, although there are indeed hotels specifically for this purpose where they can book in by the hour to rooms with Mickey Mouse or various other themes. Sometimes the men simply want to talk to the girls and have them as companions (Hirayama 1999). There are strange resonances with the vanishing world of the geisha. Geishas were not prostitutes but literally 'arts people'. Their accomplishments might include singing, dancing or playing a musical instrument but, above all, they were accomplished in conversation, soothing with extreme skill and patience the worries of the highly paid businessmen who could afford their attentions, with extreme skill and patience (Downer 2000). Strangely the mobile phone has provided a contemporary take on this ancient tradition. A generation of social theorists has seen patterns in the re-creation of ancient patterns, like Giddens (1979) who describes 'rule governed creativity' and Bourdieu (1977) who discusses what Feierman refers to as 'regulated improvisations' (Feierman 1990, p.4). I have also discussed in Chapter 5 the ways modern practices are subtly informed by ancient myths. 'Connecting people rather than locations, the mobile phone alters people's expectations about what is possible and desirable and changes the parameters of their social lives. It affects their perceptions of themselves, their boundaries and capacities...' (Plant 2002). In

Japan the teenage generation has become known as *oya yubi sedai* (the thumb tribe) on account of the dexterity with which they transmit text on their cellphones (Plant 2002).The mobile phone revolution has had a particularly big effect on the agency and self-determination of the young. Following a commission to study the sociological impact of mobile-phone usage throughout several regions of the world, Sadie Plant concluded: 'Teenagers have become the conduits through which mobile phones have found their way into wider society. For the young throughout the world the sense of freedom of movement and privacy afforded by the mobile are highly valued' (Plant 2002). The mobile phone has given children the chance in some areas of their lives to be fully in charge.

Schooling in politics in South Africa

In South Africa throughout its turbulent recent history the voice and actions of children have played a special part. No work on children and power could fail to include these young heroes. Many children, refusing to endure passively what was happening to them, became significant players in a movement that was to change them and their country for ever. Sometimes they were manoeuvred by chance circumstances into these roles and, incarcerated in solitary confinement, had to learn for themselves what it was to be a freedom fighter. Some, by other young people or more mature prisoners, were taught the importance of resistance and political action. It is not for nothing that Robben Island was dubbed the most important 'university' in South Africa during the many years of resistance. For many of the young, political involvement began either at school or at demonstrations. A turning point came when on 16 June 1976 the police fired on thousands of children who were peacefully protesting against the enforcement of Afrikaans as the language of instruction and 500 people were killed. This was in many minds the language of the oppressor and a signifier for their resentment against the Bantu education system. This system was seen as 'designed to ensure that the African people of South Africa were not educated beyond their perceived place in an Apartheid regime.' (Thomas 1990, p.438). The protests spread countrywide and although the children won that particular battle there were many young casualties. Thomas saw it as a new phase in resistance with the emergence of politicised and politically active youth. 'Schoolchildren now became leaders in seeking an effective means of changing the structure in which they were trapped' (Thomas 1990, p.438). A number of factors including the activities of these children led to an increasing period of unrest and violence, in order to quash resistance to apartheid, during the following nine years. 'During this time, the liberation movements also increased their armed attacks. So as the 1980s progressed, political violence became an increasingly common feature of the lives of young black people in particular' (Dawes 1994, p.177). By July 1985 this resulted in a partial state of emergency. Following this the usual detentions without trial increased enormously. Far more than previously significant numbers of young people were detained, rising to an estimated 4000 countrywide by November 1986 (Thomas 1990, p.439).

Reynolds explored the social means of support that these children could draw upon in surviving the consequences of their political involvement (Reynolds 1995). She reports on a study of the young people's experiences during the years of repression. The story she told of those years is about the process of transformation in which young people gave the process of change its momentum. They had neither initiated nor directed it yet some of them helped to 'shoulder the revolution' (Reynolds 1995, p.221). Reynolds points out that it is not possible collectively to describe their experiences as typical because 'the creative force that makes the character of this kind of revolution decries the appellation of typical' (Reynolds 1995, p.221). There were a number of studies of their peers, comrades or fellow prisoners – for example, by Ractliffe (1990) and Winslow (1991) – that gave some insight into their range of experience. These were powerful children in that they in their various ways refused to accept some other people's versions of reality and they paid a high price for stubbornly adhering to their own. In an example of the re-creation of culture and the endurance of cultural norms, which I discuss in Chapter 5, Reynolds points out the central role young people had in patterning discourse and innovating in the repetition of inherited patterns within the strange context of political change in South Africa (Reynolds 1995, p.222). Young people drew upon the 'incorporated past' (Bourdieu 1990, p.178) in their participation in the creation of a culture. They also struggled, in Reynolds' view, for 'legitimate representation, expressed in their stand against symbolic domination' (Reynolds 1995, p.222).

She points out that whereas one would have expected that it would be the adults that shaped the discourse of resistance, they had been worn down and silenced by their long-term oppression and the fragmentation of communities and families. It, therefore, fell to young people to take on the stand against the symbols of domination and in so doing their identities were shaped. The year 1976 was:

> a symbolic divide [...] it cuts the umbilical cord separating the young people from childhood, and it marks their entry into the maelstrom of adult politics. Part of what interests me is what the young brought from the first half of their lives into the next half: what moral stance and values, what conscious-ness of right and wrong, and how these were fertilised by nurturant care. (Reynolds 1995, p.223)

Her explorations of these issues had been published earlier (Reynolds 1991a), and her moral questions resonate with those in Chapter 6.

None of the young people had been asked to become politically ac-tive by parents or other adults. Some became active with peers at school or university. They tried to protect their families from the consequences of their own actions. Reynolds suggests that adults imbued children with sets of attitudes and morals, embedded in which were views of po-litical disinheritance that, to some extent, the young adopted as descrip-tions of reality. This she sees as part of the transformation of knowledge across generations, out of which communities carve identities – a pro-cess which does not exclude innovation. The generation that reached adolescence in 1976 adopted an activist position in the face of what it read as passive endurance or even adult complicity of state. The black consciousness movement led by Steve Biko prepared the ground for youths' opposition. Students in recounting their life stories traced conti-nuity in political consciousness and even action across generations (Reynolds 1995, pp.224–30). While these are fascinating accounts of courage within families and communities the point for us here in this book on rights and power is how the young people survived the harsh penalties of involvement in the political struggles.

> It seems to me, no mean task to sustain rebellion before the power of a ruthless state over an extended period of time and to emerge, not unscathed but well enough, confident enough to become a university student or to resume an education at whatever level possible. (Reynolds 1995, p.227)

Reynolds goes on to examine what the sources of such endurance were, and although she finds precise analysis almost impossible, she does identify five layers in the support system upon which the students drew (Reynolds 1991b). They included: the ingredients of each one's individuality; the family; the peer group; political comrades; and prisoner solidarity.

In terms of the nature and development of powerful identities these young people have a particular place in history. In psychological terms they combined amazing characteristics of individual endurance and powerful personal identities in their commitment to the fight for human rights and democracy. What have been the long-term consequences for them and the country? Harber (2000b) tells us, however, that today South Africa is still a violent society, illustrating this belief by stating that 52 people were murdered each day in 1995, (which is a murder rate of 80 times more than Britain), making the country the most violent country in the world outside a war zone (Weekly Telegraph, 20 April 1996). He sees, among the factors contributing to this state of affairs, violent oppression by the apartheid state precipitating violent resistance to it. He notes that schools have inevitably been affected by violence and paints a horrifying picture, drawn from press reports, on incidents in schools.

Griggs, surveying schools in Durban, found that in nine out of ten incidents gang-related violence was a major problem (Griggs 1997).The Independent Project Trust's review of urban schools in South Africa (Independent Project Trust 1999) described a 'culture of violence' in South African schools. They felt that this systematic cycle of violence had its origins in the years of resistance to apartheid when institutionalised violence became a way of life in homes, schools and communities. In those days this was seen as a way of bringing about change, and social status was conferred by carrying a gun. A survey they conducted with students found that 84 per cent reported that they had lost one or more of their schoolmates in the violence and 87 per cent said that they had been directly and personally affected by the violence (Nzimande and Thusi 1998). The surrounding violence has affected schools with gangs coming into school buildings but the schools themselves have also, in Griggs's view, helped to reproduce violence. Traditionally they are highly authoritarian with great emphasis on obedience, conformity and passivity (Christie 1991). Corporal

CHILDREN'S RIGHTS AND POWER

punishment was widely used even after it was made illegal and is still supported by many parents and students (Morrell 1999). The South African Human Rights Commission found that racism was still so rife in schools that school playgrounds were battlefields between white and black pupils (Valley and Dalamba 1999). An alarmingly high incidence of sexual harassment and sexual violence was revealed in a study by the government's Gender and Equity Task Team (Wolpe, Quinlan and Matinez 1997).

Harber reports on the workings of an educational policy which now exists to promote human rights, democratic values and practices, and peaceful conflict resolution (Griggs 1997). Part of this involves student representation on the governing body of the school and work with school staff on the development of democratic forms of education. The evaluation of one of the pilot projects (Harber 2000a) suggests that it has been successful in reducing crime and violence and in particular the fear of crime and violence. Harber feels that there is still some way to go to ensure that in school policy, management and practice these issues are understood and internalised as part of the process of democratising a school.

CHILDREN IN CHARGE

Children across the world are now seeing themselves as partners in the challenge to improve conditions in the world for everyone. They are re-positioning themselves, not as powerless and dependent but as partners in a new relationship with adults involving reciprocal responsibilities. For some children this has been an effortless rethinking of their views of reality. Others who have had their resilience and endurance tested to the full have acted out their responsibilities to change the world, sometimes having to act very much alone and unsupported. Increasingly in many countries young people are beginning to find that the education system does not recognise them as the citizens that they are. Increasingly young people are revolting against educational systems that are out of touch with their realities and the lives they lead and many are voting with their feet or, in the face of singularly undemocratic institutions, are respond-ing with violence and disrespect. The response has been to increase control of the young rather than transform the institutions. In France, for example, recent legislation has been passed that will result in legal proceedings against young people who are rude and abusive which might even result in a jail sentence. There are many instances in the developed world of the struggles of young people for ascendancy when faced with archaic educational institutions.

It is ironic that the violence that was part of a struggle for recognition of human rights and democracy in South Africa should have left a legacy such that schools themselves now have to be taught how to teach about and practise democracy in the interests of reducing violence. The democratisation of South Africa partly brought about by the agency and activism of a whole generation of young activists removed that agency for later generations of youth. There is a considerable difference between doing it 'for real' – that is, participating, risking even your life in the struggle for change as an activist – and the safe eloquence, however strident, of participating in the 'theatre' of the conference or as an 'actor' on the world 'stage'.

Children at large throughout the world seem no longer to be prepared to be left out of decision making, of service provision, of political processes. The Earth Warriors have come down from their protest tantrums in the trees, have come of age and become Earth Champions, responsible citizens of the world.

Endnote

1.   The complete text of Agenda 21 in all six UN languages is available from the UN Information Centre, 21st Floor, Millbank Tower, Millbank, London, SW1P 4QH. Agenda 21 (and many other Rio documents including the plain language edition of Agenda 21: *Agenda for Change*) are available from Centre for Our Common Future, 52, rue de Paquis, 1201, GENEVA , Switzerland.

CHAPTER EIGHT

Young Citizens in Action

> In the final analysis, power is the right to have your definition
> of reality prevail over other people's definitions of reality.
> (Rowe 1989, p.16)

The ways in which children's activities have influenced the adult world, which we examined in the previous chapter, demonstrate that children's participation around the world could take a variety of forms. There follows a set of examples in which I have been directly involved. They range from a relatively local example of the work of a Young People's Council to a Children's Parliament in India and the Albany Free School. These examples of participation help us understand that real education is not a management technique but rather a socially embedded power sharing. Whether power is shared by a process of bestowing or transformed into a truly reciprocal relationship is evaluated after the examples. Where power is not shared at all, participation may be destructive, as was seen in Chapter 6 on child soldiers and child workers.

DEMOCRACY IN DEVON?

The county of Devon is an administrative region in the UK. It is the third largest shire county in England with a population of just over a million (in 1998). Young people were disproportionately represented (in 1998) in the county's unemployment statistics and were significantly marginalised in service provision. Eligibility for election to the County Council is 21 years of age, so that even if young people were politically aware and active, they believed there were not enough of them elected as members of the County Council to make any significant impact. As a result, the Devon Youth Council was formed. It is an institution of local government, which ensures that national legislation is followed, and which manages a decentralised budget in response to perceived local needs. The Youth Council works in a similar way to the County Council in terms of its democratic function. It is there to influence the distribution of resources, representing the 'purchaser' rather than the 'provider'.

The Youth Council, in 1998, had a membership of about 150 – 40 to 50 of that membership being made up of individual members, and the remainder being affiliates, ranging from small youth clubs to the Devon Guides. It answered a need in that the Devon Youth Service, social services, Devon and Cornwall Constabulary, etc., were all anxious to work with and be advised by a representative body of young people. The initial setting up of this Council was at a relatively low level of participation. An informal group of young people was consulted and an idea took shape. The idea itself, however, originated with and was facilitated by adults. It rapidly moved to full participation of young people initiating shared decisions with adults and directing activities of their own – work which gathered momentum and consolidated as a force to be reckoned with. A measure of the success of the Council was that its members were much in demand as informants up and down the country. This has been seen as a triumph because of the way they had overcome the traditional cynicism of young people, involving their peers effectively in the political processes of traditional agencies within their local authority. Importantly, members have been transformed in their belief in the system of local government, and they have transformed that system itself. It provides an excellent demonstration of the way young people can influence their own communities and their peers to take charge of aspects of their life.

The emergence of the Devon Youth Council (DYC) as an independent organisation had its roots in the Devon Year for Youth (1992) and the Youth Awareness Day. Young people, aged 13 to 19 years, were invited to attend to find out how their local authority worked. They began to appreciate the anomaly that the local authority was very significant to their lives yet it seemed very remote from their lives. The proposal for a Junior County Council put forward by a group of youth workers was enthusiastically received. March 1993 saw the official press launch of the constituted Devon Youth Council. It had drawn up a long list of things that the Council would address, including bullying and youth crime – two areas in which they were to do substantial work.

Through direct consultation, the Devon Youth Council identified a degree of rejection of the traditional political system by young people in favour of issue-based 'pressure group' politics. It seemed that as the percentage of young people in the population decreased, so did their sense of value within political processes. At an individual level, young people did not seem to trust politicians and revealed a cynicism about traditional three-party politics. Where young people were notably involved and committed was in pressure-group politics as, for example, Greenpeace, the veal trade protests, etc., in which they felt they could join with belief and conviction. The Devon Youth Council has responded to this situation by influencing the decision making of the local authority, while acting in a similar way to a pressure group in order to win support among young people.

In September 1993, a co-ordinator post was established. The way in which this post was set up emphasised its value and status within the local authority. In those days, the co-ordinator was provided with a car and a mobile phone – important, as part of the job was to involve rural as well as urban youth. The salary of the co-ordinator, the running costs and a budget for conferences and publications were provided. Small grants were also given for specific projects and for preparing bids, such as a successful one to the Department of Health (Drugs Grant Programme) for £20,000, for a 'Young People at Risk' project.

In establishing young people's participation in this realistic and effective way, the support and resourcing by the key decision-makers in the county was sensitive, insightful and crucial. Youth Councillors' own perceived needs for training were responded to by sending them on courses on how to chair meetings, IT training, etc. They were therefore given power, resources and, most importantly, trust. While adults created the space for this organisation to develop, young people capitalised upon this. It became their own by the work *they* put into analysing young people's resistances and activating them to become involved in their community as powerful agents for change. Their aim was to establish a fully inclusive, representative group of active young people, which thoroughly embodied equal opportunities and was able to deliver specialist services to and about young people. The process initially involved the highest degree of control and direction over its own activities by the Devon Youth Council and this certainly paid off in what was achieved (John and Townsend 1997).

Some sectors of the community were surprisingly opposed to the idea. Such opposition acted as a catalyst to raise the consciousness of young people about their democratic rights. The Council's dual role in being accountable to and representative of young people created some tensions, dilemmas and internal debates, some of which have been growth points; others proved to be weaknesses.

The Council from its establishment had considerable impact within Devon and, as one of the first councils of its kind, on the national and international scene. It gave advice to a variety of other organisations within the UK and inputs to international conferences and associations. The Youth Council undertook a number of activities and brought out a publication pack of advice and information. The work was important in ensuring that other organisations in the county took young people seriously and treated them with respect. The Youth Council, for example, animated and motivated a number of organisations to work with them around a matter of common concern, particularly to young people and future generations. The Youth Council sponsored, organised and wrote the submission to Rural Challenge in 1996 for the economic regeneration of the county. The Youth Council was held in high esteem for the highly professional way in which it worked in preparation for this bid.

A member of the Youth Council chaired the County Council Working Party for the implementation, in Devon, of the UN Convention on the Rights of the Child. This was seen as vital work, as the Convention provides a clear indication of young people's rights and a useful starting point for work with decision makers in Devon. At their invitation I worked with them as their adviser for a number of years. The Council had been increasing its level and diversity of influence, its membership and links with the national and international movement. Further work was undertaken in imaginative new partnerships with the local authority. The Youth Council's 'The Next Generation' project defined young people's Agenda 21 for Devon in the context of environment, citizenship and international responsibility. It also produced some excellent information booklets and has mounted some effective campaigns (Bite the Ballot, Kick Bullying. Homelessness, A Guide to Making Student Councils More Effective, Partners Against Crime, etc.).

It seemed the work had come full circle, with the Youth Council, at one time, setting up an Adult Advisory Panel! The Youth Council initially worked hard to fully involve Devon's young people themselves, in exploiting the opportunities for participation and in claiming their rights to a full partnership in the lives of their communities into the next millennium (John and Townsend 1997).

New European funding opportunities available to Youth Councils provided an added stimulus to growth, and the Youth Council became known more widely. The Council had played a significant part nationally, being represented at the first national Youth Councils Conferences from 1996 onwards, hosting an International Conference on 'The Participation of Young People' in 1996, and, in 1998, chairing the National Youth Conference. It became involved internationally in the International Next Generation Conference and the European Youth Parliament, and in the setting up and first meeting of the United Kingdom Youth Parliament in 2001.

As Devon was one of the first local authorities to encourage the participation of young people following the ratification of the United Nations Convention on the Rights of the Child, it has been exciting to see how far its influence and activities have spread. Particularly gratifying has been the way the Local Government Association, in conjunction with the National Youth Agency, produced *Hear by Right; Setting Standards for the Active Involvement of Young People in Democracy* (Wade, Lawton and Stevenson 2001), as the first phase of Better Government With Young People, and held conferences to disseminate the message. These standards aimed to promote the active involvement of young people in local democracy and local decision-making. Local councils were urged to look seriously at how they involved and engaged children and young people in local democratic processes and to improve this. Case studies and illustrations were provided to put across the message. Self-assessment exercises were provided as part of the implementation of these standards and the self-diagnosis divided into three levels: 'emerging', 'established' and 'advanced'. The standards were designed to help councils secure long-term and sustainable active involvement of young people in local democracy and to encourage continual improvement in these activities.

Paradoxically, just as much of their local work began to really take off at a national and international level, the DYC was faltering and failing to fulfil its early promise. It seemed that it had been difficult to keep up the local momentum and consciousness-raising and handle increasing demands upon it for national consultancy and attendance at regional, national and international conferences. By early 2001, the

effectiveness of the DYC had reduced at county and local level; it met ir-
regularly and only had half the number of youth councillors out of a full
complement of 24, of which only four were active. There had been no
election of councillors for over two years. At a stage in the early 1990s
when young people's participation was very new, the work of the DYC
had provided a model of how to proceed and had, with its activities and
interventions, raised the consciousness of many County Councillors
about young people's views. I remember, with wry amusement, the faces
that greeted the request that every major decision by the County Council should be accompanied by a child-impact statement. The response to
the DYC emphasis in the early days that transport policy was also a
young people's issue, 'You have school buses, don't you?', remains in my
memory as a marker of how much progress it eventually made. Now that
this sort of participation has been established on the national agenda, it
is instructive to examine why the DYC got into difficulties.

Helpfully, in 2001, Devon County Council undertook internal review of the DYC and of 'the opportunity for young people in Devon to
be represented and to represent themselves' (Devon County Council Internal Review). The review was presented to the Executive Committee
of Devon County Council and, importantly, to the DYC itself. While acknowledging that the achievements of the DYC had been considerable,
several problems were identified, including representation, staffing,
workloads, priorities, constitution and line management. The roots of
many of these problems were seen as a restrictive constitution and weak
foundations at local level.

On the issue of representation it was pointed out that the election of
youth councillors was by affiliated organisations, yet there did not seem
to be any record of affiliations of either organisations or individuals.
There was also an ill-defined relationship between the DYC and Local
Youth Forums; only three of a possible 26 of the latter had ever been affiliated to the DYC, seeing it as rather middle class, representing only a
narrow constituency. Only a third of school councils were affiliated. The
DYC newsletter, Buzz, while very exciting, was found not to be widely
read, least of all by adults. There were effective links with the Devon
Voluntary Youth Services Council. In sum it was felt that too few young
people in Devon knew about the existence of the DYC or its function or
workings. The DYC was seen as being more effective in sending out information than seeking it. Representation is always an issue in activities

involving the participation of the young and is particularly challenging in a large county, much of which is rural, making it difficult for a central organisation to feel relevant in every locality. In addition, travel, transport, distance and costs were disincentives for young people becoming councillors. Moreover as the DYC became more famous and further demands put upon it, stretching its staffing resources, work with local groups became less of a priority and led to a great weakness in the organisation.

The direction of the DYC had become over-dependent on the personality and style of the co-ordinator. While leadership, energy and commitment had been important in getting such a movement off the ground, it was felt necessary to ensure that the function of the co-ordinator should be more important than the character of the co-ordinator. There were many demands on the time of the co-ordinator and the few youth councillors, and a need for a setting of priorities, clearer line management and induction. One of the problems with any young people's organisations is turnover, continuity and succession. The short-term, one-year contract of the co-ordinator did not help. This was further compounded by the late appointment procedure; it restricts the number of applicants, as most students planning a gap year have fixed this by Easter but the interviews for the co-ordinator rarely take place before July for a September start. The induction procedure is casual, which further reduces the effectiveness of a person on such a short-term contract.

There had been frequent changes to the DYC constitution, no less than five in the previous five years, and a significant number of county councillors and officers were not familiar with the constitution which has led to confusion about the degree to which it is part of the County Council structure or an independent organisation representing the views of young people. The DYC had written a number of reports on the structure and workings of the DYC, but they were rarely acted upon.

Fortunately at the time this long hard look at the council was taking place, the Local Government Association was launching its 'hear by right' proposals, to encourage councils to look seriously at how they currently involve and engage children in local democratic processes. These standards will be reviewed in 2003 to assess their practical impact and benefits. This process will actively involve young people as well as local authorities. The standards cover seven areas: shared values;

strategy; structure; systems; members and officers; skills and knowledge; and leadership style.

> There is no guarantee that once a council has reached an 'advanced' level that it will stay there. Particularly as the cohort of young people changes year on year, councils will need to ensure that they are actively taking action to ensure they maintain their 'advanced' status. This underlines the importance of building the capacity of more young people to regenerate their active involvement. (Wade *et al.* 2001, p.25)

The Devon Youth Council, supported by the County Council, is now addressing the 'growing pains' it has experienced while regenerating commitment and participation among its peers. The new proposal places the DYC as part of a new structure for the consultation with, and representation and empowerment of, young people in Devon. One of the advantages of this structure would be to tie young people into the organisation and monitoring of the new Connexions service. The Connexions service is a major government initiative designed to give all young people above the age of 14 years enhanced guidance and counselling. The DYC has recently renamed itself the Devon Youth Network to reflect more realistically how it now operates. The progress of this organisation since the ratification of the United Nations Convention on the Rights of the Child provides a case study illustrating some of the challenges of fully involving young people in a democratic way in local decision-making.

INSPIRATION IN INDIA

The Children's Parliament – Bal Sansad – in rural Rajasthan, India, had been of considerable interest to me as an example of young people's ability to influence their communities, particularly in relation to my involvement at that time with the DYC. I had read about it in an article in the *Independent* (*Independent Magazine* 1996). It formed part of a system of rural sustainability that had some quite innovative features, and in which democratic practices were fostered and encouraged. To consider the parliament without appreciating the whole system of which it is a part is to underestimate its significance.

Rajasthan (the land of 'Drought and Colour') is a semi-arid state in North West India, one of the country's poorest regions, with a population of 45 million people. It is divided into 58 blocks with 37,890 villages. Illiteracy is a problem, with the indications being that around 45 per cent of males and 80 per cent of females are illiterate. Schooling is also a problem, as children are needed to contribute to the family economy by working, largely looking after cattle and on the family farms. More than half the children of school age (6 to 14) do not attend schools and the majority of these non-attendees are girls. Most people survive on subsistence farming and manual labour. Sanjit (Bunker) Roy is the founder Director of the Social Work and Research Centre (SWRC), or the Barefoot College as it later came to be known. He started work in the early 1970s with a two-year ground-water survey of 110 villages; the early work on water set the scene for later developments. Initially the emphasis had been on drilling wells and irrigation schemes in this drought-stricken area. The focus changed dramatically when it was decided to focus on the rural poor and address 'the politics of water'. The mission of the SWRC became the empowerment of local villagers in the interests of rural sustainability. The centre started officially in 1972 in the village of Tilonia, about two hours' drive West from Jaipur, when, for one rupee a month, it leased an abandoned tuberculosis sanatorium from the government. Bunker Roy's vision was to break away from the Indian social-work tradition, which had an urban, middle-class and academic orientation. He hoped to attract young urban professionals to come and work in a development process alongside villagers fully integrating with the local situation. The research was to be action based, providing effective practices and lasting partnerships of mutual support with the deprived. S. Srinivasan, Deputy Director of SWRC, describes the philosophy as meaning 'that urban-educated professionals had to go through a deschooling process. Whatever they had learnt in their university education was in direct conflict with what was happening in the field' (Srinivasan 1998). At first, economic and technical services to the villages were prioritised. The siting of wells close to where the poor lived and the training of locals as pump maintenance engineers broke the village dependence on urban mechanics. Further independence and efficiency was achieved by providing solar panels and training in their maintenance, saving the time-consuming daily collection of kerosene. Villagers were trained as paramedics to service their own villages.

A system of training the trainers was set up in the college, where lo-cal villagers trained other villagers in the skills needed to support these technological breakthroughs. In all of this work, anyone regardless of caste, class or gender was eligible for any staff position. For many of the staff who came from villages, living and eating together in the college was a new experience. In the villages, caste hierarchies were still very rigid. For many it was the beginning of a whole new world. My guide to the night schools talked to me with great enthusiasm about how he had been an 'untouchable' in his village but now he was a fully-fledged member of the staff at the Barefoot College, as was his wife. All the col-lege programmes emphasised collective decision-making skills and in-deed practised them.

The establishment of the night schools – and eventually the Children's Parliament, which grew organically out of the schools – was a natural development of the general principles. A typical working day for many children in this area begins shortly after dawn with household chores to be done, water and wood to be collected, before setting off for work in the fields looking after cattle or doing agricultural tasks – a long day which finishes around dusk. These children cannot attend school as family survival depends on the labours of every member and, if anyone can be spared, it will be the boys who are sent to school. The Barefoot College realised this and, with the villagers, collectively thought about how they could educate these children while still respecting their family responsibilities. They founded the night schools, which matched the needs of these children in the villages around Tilonia. The formal educa-tion system and the traditional curriculum were seen as having an urban bias, oriented to meet the needs of the middle class. The language of in-struction was also distanced from that used in the daily life of rural chil-dren. The schools were rarely within a reasonable daily walking distance for young children. As a result many rural children were unable to participate fully in the educational process. The Barefoot College emphasised learning from doing rather than formal classroom teaching. 'The importance of education lies not in paper qualifications or exams but in achieving the skills that guarantee the sustainable development of rural communities' (O'Brien 1996, p.13). The traditional teacher–pupil relationship was restructured and rethought into a relationship in which everyone teaches and learns. It was to be a joint learning experience. Lo-cal communities are a source for teachers, who have generally completed their eighth grade, then trained intensively at the Barefoot College for two years; in the summer vacation they take a two-week further-training course to strengthen their classroom skills. 'The most important point during the training is to instil a spirit of voluntarism in the teachers' (O'Brien 1996, p.17). With the increasing involvement of these village teachers in the educational process, serious rethinking of approaches was undertaken and it came to be thought that night schools could play an important part in providing a structure around which development could take place: '…the importance of the night school as a nucleus of awareness building began to emerge' (Roy 1982, p.12). As these ideas started to take shape the Barefoot College asked the night-school teachers, day-care teachers, midwives and village education committees what rural communities needed to sustain themselves. Information and the educational process emerged first on virtually every list. It was thought that communities could be self-reliant if they had access to information, particularly government programmes and legal literacy. The community felt that they did need learning opportunities, which would develop their literacy and numeracy skills, partly for reasons to do with rural sustainability and also to protect them from being exploited by the literate. They felt that the learning process should enable the beneficiaries to serve their communities rather than seek individual gain and prosperity. A relevant education was needed that did not alienate children from their surroundings.

In the night schools, children are taught in the evenings, after the day's work. Their teachers come from the same village; this is highly important both for the relevance of what they teach and their ongoing involvement and dialogues with parents. They cover classes one to eight. Children learn about things that are useful in their daily lives with a strong emphasis on environmental education. As the children get older, vocational training forms another part of the curriculum. There are now over 150 night schools with nearly 3000 children. Two out of three pupils are girls so the night schools are particularly important for girls' lives and education (Naylor 2001a).

Where possible, the night schools use formal school buildings; otherwise they operate in teachers' houses or outbuildings. The one I visited took place in a disused stable. They are supervised by the education staff of the Barefoot College and have a curriculum specifically adapted to rural surroundings with innovations in teacher–student relations, teaching methods, the use of local people as resources and on the education of girls. The atmosphere is informal. I was impressed on my visit to one night school that as the teacher and I approached the stable we could hear the children singing. There they were, packed tightly into the space, children of all ages, tiny ones of about five, some teenagers, a young girl with her baby and some of the villagers. Even after a very hard day in the fields they were there, cheerfully and calmly singing while they waited for the teacher and his strange visitor to arrive.

It is from these night schools, introduced in 1993, that the idea of the Children's Parliament emerged. Innovations in education, they felt, should serve to make children feel equal and responsible society members regardless of caste, gender or economic situation. The idea of the parliament was to open up children's minds to possibilities. The children all contribute to their family incomes, yet their opinions and contributions had not previously been sought or acknowledged. Moreover in a community where the caste system disappears but slowly, many of their views had been structured within the outlook of their own caste. The Barefoot College was anxious that through the educational process they should have exposure to other points of view and the opportunity to debate these. The Children's Parliament has been developed so that children can learn how a democracy functions, the importance of the vote, standing up for their rights and not letting themselves be exploited because they are poor.

Let us look for a moment at how the Children's Parliament works. This parliament is the first of its kind anywhere. There have been children's parliaments in Slovenia and Germany, for instance, for quite some time and now from 2001 in the UK, but those parliaments are largely in the form of role-play and debating fora and have little power. The Bal Sansad is different in that, through it, children exercise real power by getting adults and decision makers to accept their view of reality. There are now 23 organisations in 14 states running night schools and at least 10 of them have started their own children's parliaments. The Barefoot College's way of facilitating children's influence over things important to their lives has been copied outside India. The Parliament has developed from the 60-odd night schools established in the district of Ajmer.

Children from each of the night schools – about 2500 children (aged 6 to 14 years) – are engaged in elections through which they elect a Member of Parliament. The experiment was initially launched as a way of teaching the children about politics and the electoral process and has now been copied in various ways across India. The young members of the parliament are voted into office at the night schools in an entirely proper and serious election with clear rules. To be eligible to stand for election, candidates have to be able to read and write and, for election as a Cabinet Minister, have to have reached Level 3 or above (John 1997, 2000; O'Brien 1996). There are 17 seats in the Parliament. The Parliament teaches all children about the political process and the value of democracy. Candidates represent two parties: Ujala (meaning 'light') and Guaval (meaning 'shepherd'). The elected members meet every two months. The adults function as civil servants servicing the Parliament, which has Members aged between 11 and 14. There is a Prime Minister, a Speaker and Ministers for Finance, Health, Agriculture and Animal Husbandry, Home Affairs, Environment, Children and Women's Affairs, Energy, Water, Industry and Education. The meetings are vigorous and lively with members asked to report on each of their activities, one of which is to recruit children to enrol in the night schools. The duties of elected representatives are clearly defined (John 1997, 2000; O'Brien 1996). They can make decisions about the running of their schools and dismiss teachers who neglect their duties. The children also discuss and take an active part in matters concerning their village, such as the provision of services and utilities. Monitoring the night schools is important. Each Minister is expected to visit at least two night schools a month and report on the quality of the teaching, attendance levels, the availability and suitability of the equipment and whether the records are being properly kept. They also provide feedback on pupils' views. The MPs have the power to govern all the schools in this district and to fire teachers who, on the basis of detailed investigation following a complaint, are not felt to be doing their job. They also provide pressure for further improvements in the village. Six years ago the Speaker of the Parliament, Devkaran Guijar, who was 11 at the time, turned to the Barefoot College and asked for a pump for his village, Solgaon, where there was a shortage of drinking water. The response was that the village would first have to raise 20,000 rupees (£300). Single-handedly, Devkaran managed to raise double that amount from the villagers in a short period and, thanks to his efforts, the villagers had tap water directly to their homes (Naylor 2001b). Involvement in the Parliament has bred a sense of responsibility and power in children to bring about change. The

Parliament also organises children's festivals, which are cultural and entertaining and provide a light relief from their hard everyday farm work. In February 1999 there was a National Children's Fair (Bal Mela) lasting five days. More than 1500 children from eight states of the country participated. 'It was a spectacle, an event of such a magnitude which gave children from all parts of the country a few days when they can be themselves – far removed from playing grown ups at such a tender age' (Srinivasan 1999). Children through this Parliament are fully involved in every aspect of their lives.

The Barefoot College believes that today is on loan to us from the children who will be the citizens of tomorrow. Thus it is entirely appropriate that they should be the guardians and the monitors of the services that they will inherit. They have their own magazine to keep the children of the desert informed about local politics and their rights. The Barefoot College puppet show travelling from village to village undertakes further consciousness-raising about issues such as respecting the environment, being wary of moneylenders, women's and children's rights and the value of good teachers!

The Parliament, in some ways, represents the reverse thrust of socialisation; parents, relatives and older villagers learn much about democratic practices from the children and the reasons for these and their importance. The remarkable thing about the Parliament is that children do indeed have considerable power in a society that is regarded as very traditional and patriarchal. Hence, it must be seen as a considerable achievement that so much power has been relinquished to the children. The question arises as to whether power has really been transformed or whether the Barefoot College has, in a top-down way, 'bestowed' certain aspects of power on the child MPs. The staff of the Barefoot College have every confidence in the children's abilities to take their own decisions – a confidence which had been continually vindicated over the 20 years or so that they have been developing this work. Initially there was some resistance based upon fears that it might result in a 'lack of respect' from the children. This was an important concern as respect is a key feature binding people together in the hierarchy of Indian society – a hierarchy which was being challenged on all fronts not just by the children but also by all the interlocking activities of the Barefoot College. There was also considerable unease in the early days about educating girls. In a system where children are usually married off when they are but a few years old and then, in the case of the girls, go to live in their father-in-law's house when they are about 15, there could be great resistance from the girl's new family to the girl's continuing education and her involvement in the political process. The Barefoot College is there to support the young people through this process.

As the term of the third Children's Parliament came to a close in 1999, the children as well as the SWRC were reviewing the Children's Parliament. They took stock of experiences since 1993, when the night schools were first introduced. The child Members of Parliament, on their own initiative, had expressed the need to know more about geo-political situations and to broaden their world-view. The Barefoot College responded with a series of workshops. Another concern that was expressed spontaneously by the existing MPs was absenteeism among members of the Cabinet. Problems had arisen about the regularity of attendance at Cabinet meetings. These concerns had led them to elect a new party leader, Devki, who was later elected as Prime Minister, replacing the earlier one who had not been present for four sessions in the past. The irregularity of child MPs' attendance was mainly due either to economic pressures or the fact that some girls had had to join their husband in their in-laws' village. This difficulty had been compounded in that all the four Prime Ministers until 1999 had been girls. Interestingly Devki, now aged 13, who was elected in 2001 as Prime Minister, reported that most of her peers were now betrothed or married, but since her election, her relationship with her father had changed. He was proud of her, treated her with respect and contrary to tradition had delayed choosing a husband for her (Evans 2002). The term of the third Children's Parliament ended in December 1999. In August of that year a caretaker government took over as many of the MPs who had been found to be irregular attendees were replaced by other nominated MPs, which was a collective decision taken by the Children's Parliament and supported by SWRC. During the first quarter of 2000, elections to the fourth Children's Parliament were due to take place after a review had been undertaken. About that time S. Srinivasan wrote:

> It is with a great amount of satisfaction and a sense of accomplishment we feel that the Children's Parliament has been sustained by us for more than 7 years. On the children's part, they seem to have a genuine urge to continue having the

space, mindspace and freedom of choice enjoyed at the Children's Parliament later on in their lives – maybe it is time for us to change the attitudes of their parents and in-laws to facilitate this. The task is all the more awesome since 80 per cent of the MP's have all been girls since 1993. In a male-dominated rural society this attitudinal change is a pre-cursor to social, economic and cultural change – but, of course, political change too. We feel that Children of the World shall unite someday to break these shackles, until such time when they grow up and provide the same mindspace to their children. (Srinivasan 1999)

One might well ask whether the development of the Parliament will ultimately mean that the children will wish to leave their villages. It seems not, as they say that their ambitions are the fields, goats and their homes. The whole system appears to have strengthened a feeling of belonging and ownership. The Children's Parliament has been a very useful means of impressing upon the children the values of responsibility and makes clear to them that power comes with responsibility, as they become actively involved in running their schools. One wonders whether in time, for girls, more widespread changes in relationships within the family will come about. The Barefoot College say that ultimately what they have been hoping to develop in the children of Tilonia are three things – resourcefulness, resilience and fearlessness.

I have indeed been lucky to have experienced, at first-hand, a democratic system of rural sustainability developed by the Barefoot College that has honoured and resourced children. The Children's Parliament is the beginning of a system of power sharing between adults and children. Both the innovations, of the Bal Sansad and the DYC, which have been operating for about the same length of time and aimed to empower young people, ran into difficulties in keeping up the momentum and commitment. The role of adults in these power relationships needs further examination, which I will undertake at the end of this chapter.

ALCHEMY AT ALBANY

Resourcefulness, resilience and fearlessness characterised both children and staff at the Free School in Albany, which it was my good fortune to visit shortly after leaving Rajasthan. My good fortune was that, in changing cultures and geographical locations so rapidly, it sharpened comparisons, counterpoint and understanding. It was also surprising to find halfway across the world that the resonances were stunning. The connectedness was of communities, which prioritised educating the human spirit rather than the mechanics of the institutionalised educational process. These were children facing different challenges to the Indian children's responsibilities as members of their family economy. Many of the Albany children were alienated, disenfranchised and damaged by 'education', families and the community. In Albany, relationships with the community were immediate and tangible, while at Barefoot College, it was larger and more distributed in the outlying village night schools spread over more than 3000 kilometres. Only for rare special occasions like Children's Festival could the whole community get together as one celebrating 'family' having fun together – fun as an oasis in hard-working lives. The Free School was similarly 'an oasis', although it is strange to refer to it as such given the cacophony of sound and activity that greeted me when first I stepped through the door – yet it is a place where children are resourced and their great 'thirsts' assuaged. Both initiatives had been works of visionaries who grasped the wider context of learning and made the impossible happen. In Tilonia it was Bunker Roy; in Albany it was the intuitive understanding of what was needed and the sheer educational and financial flair of Mary Leue which made things begin to stir and happen. Eventually the whole community could take it forward and let it grow into the joint enterprise it is today – 'joint' since the generations of children who have attended the school have been an essential part of shaping it too. Like the night school, it provides relevant learning opportunities and experiences which have grown organically and relate to the realities of the children's daily lives. The community at the Free School provides for children – many of whom have little in the form of social capital–models of what it is to be a caring, committed, human being in the present, in the community and, in the case of many encounters there, 'in your face'! Both in Rajasthan and in Albany the children know they are valued, cared about and are important members of their communities.

The particular alchemy that makes up the Albany Free School is difficult to capture as it has, certainly for all the depth of thinking that goes into it, a magical air. Fortunately Chris Mercogliano, the present Co-director, has written its story, titled, appropriately enough, *Making It Up As We Go Along* (1998). He sets the school within the context of various alternatives to conventional schooling. Fundamental subjects like aggression, sexuality, race/class and spirituality are addressed, topics described as 'four primary colours of human experience that are all too often relegated to the rusty side spurs of our national thinking about children' (Mercogliano 1998, p.xxiii). Ivan Illich, commenting on this tale, said:

> In touchingly plain language, Chris Mercogliano tells about 25 years of unfolding trust; how kids learn without anyone making sure; how a free school has become a pretext for a community; and how adults who care are able, by shedding their roles, to open unexpected spaces for friendship and new growth. More convincing than any book I have had the privilege to read, this one proves that learning by children ought, once and for all, to be institutionally disembedded. (Illich 1998)

In terms of the theme of my book, power, this Albany community is about power sharing, about withholding judgement while other views of reality are explored. It is also about holding children through the crises of their own terrible, uncontrollable power so that they learn gradually, in a context in which they are safe and valued, to handle it for themselves. It is about being in the present. Affectionate portraits of individual children are given to provide insights into the challenges the Free School has faced:

> She arrived at our door unannounced, three years' worth of rompin', stompin' hell's-on-fire. Since the Free School is an energetic place to begin with ('How do you people stand the noise?'), and since Mumasatou was obviously a tightly strung, high-energy kid, we knew from the outset we were about to have our mettle thoroughly tested. (Mercogliano 1998, p.21)

How did this inspirational place begin and why did I choose to go there? I decided to go there quite simply because I felt, just as I had felt about going to Rajasthan, here was a place where children were taken seriously. The actual encounter was far from 'serious' – filled with fun, high jinks, noise, rough and tumble, yelling, with purposeful activity alongside – but through it all ran a level of shared understanding I had not experienced before in an educational establishment in the industrialised world. Mary Leue started a school with four students in her home in 1969, largely to cater for the needs of one of her sons who was becoming increasingly miserable in one of Albany's better public (state) schools. While this was a response to an immediate situation, it was within a history and climate of a rich diversity of radical and alternative approaches to education, in which Mary was particularly well-versed and networked. Indeed by then, A.S. Neill's Summerhill had been in existence for over 40 years. Mary, running the gauntlet of many aspects of repressive 'officialdom', responding with typical determination and persistence, briefly moved her small but growing brood to a former church and in 1971 they relocated to a 100-year-old building, which is the present home of the Free School. The children called it the 'Free School', reflecting that it was to be free of race and class prejudice, free of consumerism and dependence on material goods for personal happiness, free of beliefs in the necessity of war as a means of solving problems, free of educational cant and mindless adherence to method. Tuition is not free but charged on a sliding scale on which everyone pays; even welfare families pay, albeit a minimum.

After the first year, Mary took stock of the future of this school. She was already knowledgeable about radical thinking in education and had some original ideas of her own, independent thinker that she is. Nevertheless, she took it upon herself to visit other free schools, notably Jonathan Kozol's Community School in Cambridge, Massachusetts, and Orson Bean's Fifteenth Street School in New York City. She struck up a correspondence with A.S. Neill, asking him what he thought of the idea of creating a school with similar freedoms as Summerhill for the inner-city poor. Neill, based on his experiences with relatively privileged young people, viewed such a generalisation of the approach an entirely risky venture and replied, 'I would think myself daft to try' (Mercogliano 1998, p.5). Inspired madness has characterised the Free School ever since! Mary also connected with her own roots and the home schooling she received at one stage in her own education. She brought disparate strands together in the way the school would operate. Formative influences on Mary's approach were Prince Kropotkin and Reich, particularly his theories relating to the healthy psychosocial development of children. The viewing by staff of Alan Leitman's films about successful educational alternatives added a further dimension. This rich brew nourished the early growth of the school. Gradually teachers and children came – teachers from all sorts of backgrounds who were seeking the freedom to be themselves in a school where method, practice, classroom technique and learning theory were relinquished in favour of what 'works'. The essential basis here was respect for the children, teachers and helpers.

The new school premises were in the centre of several blocks of run-down, rather dilapidated but elegant houses. Mary bought these buildings cheaply, as housing for staff at the school, who could be provided with rent-free accommodation in exchange for renovation work on the houses and services to the school. Besides teaching, the staff contributed carpentry, electrical and plumbing skills and helped with the cooking. There have been various weekend work parties, almost like Amish barn raisings, where tasks are accomplished collectively either on the fabric of the buildings or on developing outside spaces for collective use of various kinds. In some senses one feels that the concrete building work has provided a metaphor for the way the community has grown.

In the early years of exploring what policies, if any, to adopt, there emerged from the animated discussions a view – only those actually present in the building could determine the school's day-to-day operating policy, thus restricting the power of any commentators not immediately involved in implementation. The next innovation arose from thinking through how to empower the children to be self-governing in working out their differences in as non-violent a way as possible. From these discussions came the 'Council meeting' idea which survives to this day. Anyone in the school, teacher or pupil, who wants to resolve a dispute or wants to change school policy, can call a Council meeting at any time. This has allowed for organic growth and continual updating and support for rules in the school.

The school Council meetings provide a regular important forum for exchanging points of view. Everybody's reality counts, which is what makes these meetings so exceptional in transforming the usual power relations between adult and child. Each point of view is taken seriously and assessed collectively. Evidence is dealt with and everyone tries patiently to get at the truth. It takes place immediately after the 'offence' has occurred – which, for these young children, many with a short attention span, is important. The Council acts as a brake on escalating high spirits, bad feeling and unacceptable behaviour – a brake which is not arbitrarily applied from above by adults but which the children are party to. It follows Neill's dictum 'Freedom not licence' (Mercogliano

1998, p.6). I was there when a child, with all the urgency of a messenger from the front line of the Trojan Wars, came flying through the hurly-burly of activities calling urgently 'Council meeting. Council meeting' and everything stopped instantly and unquestioningly. The whole school gathered to hear what the trouble was. On this occasion it was straightforward enough – someone had broken the rule that there was to be no noise in the quiet room. A child, selected by the meeting to act as chairperson, conducted the meeting following formal rules of order. A discussion took place, the matter resolved and the rational basis for the rule explained and explored. The school then got back to business as quickly as it had stopped. Shortly before my visit, the Council meeting had elaborated into a full-scale mock trial lasting over three weeks (it was at the time of the O.J. Simpson trial). It related to a case of petty theft and the failure of the culprit to own up. The suspected culprit offered to 'play' the villain in the mock trial and interestingly even went so far as to execute the punishment prescribed by the 'judge'. Many weeks later, the culprit confessed. This was a long-drawn-out process but an object lesson in the nature of justice. Moreover, it gave the child himself time to reflect and take direct responsibility for his actions. Parents and teachers alike said that the children could talk of nothing else while 'The Trial' was going on. Mercogliano says of the Council meetings:

> When the focus was an interpersonal rift, meetings tended to take on a therapeutic rather than a governmental tone. They then became an empathetic space where emotions could flow freely and where the thread of the problem could be followed back to its source. (Mercogliano 1998, p.7)

The Council meeting system is a key to the democratic practices, forming the central core of the school, where staff, pupils, parents and helpers alike are equal stakeholders, bear mutual responsibility and have reciprocal rights, which makes for complete interdependence. The children really govern themselves within this framework. Aiming at a policy of complete internal autonomy was easier said than done. Avoiding competition, compulsory learning and social-class-based status rewards is difficult. Many parents wanted the Free School:

> to look and function like the local public school, which virtually guaranteed their children would remain trapped in the cycle of poverty. Their expectations were largely governed by

the class system that had only betrayed them generation after generation, one based on upward mobility as a key measure of success. They wanted their kids to have desks, textbooks, mandatory classes, competition; grades and lots of home-work. The absence of these trappings of a 'real' school be-came fertile ground for the fear that here their kids would 'fall behind', lose their competitive edge vis-à-vis the rest of soci-ety. (Mercogliano 1998, p.9)

Enlisting the help of lower-class white, black and Hispanic parents was quite a challenge, which was made no easier by the shabby sec-ond/third-hand furnishings, books and equipment of the school and the generally high-spirited atmosphere of the place with little in the way of conventional order, structure or routine. Local folklore character-ised this as a place with total freedom where children played all day and were even allowed to curse. It was difficult to convince these parents that this was indeed a school. Views about approaches to discipline and the control of aggression also revealed class differences. Middle-class par-ents were happy with a laissez-faire approach to discipline but not to ag-gression, while the working-class parents wanted a strict code of conduct enforced by punishments. As regards aggression, Mary, influ-enced by Reichian thinking on suppressed emotion and the develop-ment of armouring, was far less ready to compromise. Whatever the middle-class parents thought, Mary was insistent that the Free School should serve as a safe space where the expression of emotion would be encouraged. The school adopted techniques to enable children to 'rage it out' (Mercogliano 1998, p.11). Occasionally, a child who is ready to explode is held front-to-front on the lap of a willing and sympathetic teacher, who allows the child to safely struggle, kick and scream until his/her rage is spent, followed by the tears of pain and grief that often seemed to be trapped beneath the anger. Physical fighting, for the same reasons, was not outlawed in the school. What happened was that if two children started to fight in order to sort out a dispute, providing that the fight was fair and they were not inflicting any significant tissue damage on each other, nobody intervened. There would be an adult watching to ensure safety and to help the fighters reach a sense of completion and reconciliation. The depth of human caring that lay behind managing the children's emotional expression in these ways was impressive.

The practices fed a local belief that the school taught fighting. A number of parents stuck to it for a while and then, as their anxieties got the better of them, put their children back in the public or parochial schools from which they had come. Some of the early doubters were swayed by the atmosphere of the school where relationships were such that people, children and adults alike were cared about and cared for. The quality of human relationships in the school was rare in other educational establishments so some parents stayed with it for long enough to see profound changes in their children. On my visit, a young pupil, a one-time hoodlum and tearaway, took my hand on one of the school's local outings, asking me with all courtesy and graciousness, 'Would you like to see my River Hudson?', and he showed it to me with all the pride of a citizen of Albany. He had received from others respect, caring and consideration and saw how they valued the community and environment in which they lived. The work of the Free School is subtle, pervasive and, I would surmise, lasting. Many of these children had not been valued and responded to like the cognisant people that they are until, often as a last resort, they came to the school. There they are part of a community working towards shared understandings and shared respect, where everybody's point of view matters. In this setting, children are able to exercise their right under Article 12 of the UN Convention on the Rights of the Child to 'express a view and have that view taken into account in any matter that concerns them' (Article 12, UNCRC). Albany goes a long way beyond; their view is not just acknowledged but actually shapes decisions. Children's feelings and views are paramount and, importantly, they are encouraged to disclose these feelings, to be expressive and outspoken about their views. Truthfulness and spontaneity is encouraged in the interests of them being able to function autonomously in the present as people with intrinsic worth.

Being involved in a school of this kind is demanding and risky, and so takes its toll on staff and helpers. Tolerance of the acting out, the chaos, the riotous noise, while the children find their own way to structure, certainty and personhood, requires a certain surefootedness from the teacher. Just as the Barefoot College acted to resource and replenish the night-school teachers in Rajasthan, so the staff at the Free School actively support each other in achieving this calm acceptance of the child's behavioural progress. All live very close to one another with a lot of interaction between the houses, informative exchanges on the stoops

(front porches) of an evening and thoughtful discussions over garden-
ing, house renovation, 'barn raisings', barbecues or whatever brings
them together. This is not a 'job' that begins and ends at the school door;
it is a way of life. In fact, in the early days some of the staff took
part-time jobs elsewhere so that they could afford to work for free at the
school. Every Wednesday, a more formal meeting is held where issues
can be brought up and thoroughly examined. At these meetings, staff
are open with each other, work compassionately towards conflict resolution and decide whether or not they need specialist guidance or further study to take their individual and collective growth further. The
school is seen as a focus for the growth of adults and children alike. The
adults have fortified themselves and each other through going on
courses, inviting speakers to come to their gatherings and engaging in
various psychotherapeutic activities together. They have been meeting
weekly since 1974. The staff resourced each other's spiritual and personal growth and professional effectiveness; they also developed very
practical means of help. Synergy between the school and the community
was further enhanced by setting up the Family Life Centre for birthing,
prenatal and postnatal care and training in parenting. A bookstore and
wholefood outlet were among other initiatives.

A home-loan system was set up to assist low-income Free School
families to purchase homes. A revolving home-loan scheme was established, followed by teaching families inexpensive ways of refurbishing
and restoring these run-down properties, drawing on the skills the
teachers had developed in the early days of rehabilitating their own
homes. Of course, throughout all of these activities, children were
present, witnessing and learning from the ways in which adults worked
together and cared for each other. By 1980, the Free School community
was fairly well established and attention (not surprisingly, given the core
values of the school) turned to spiritual needs. This spiritual dimension
deepened the relationships in the wider community and added to its
stability and permanence.

Further links between the school and the community were forged by
the introduction of a system of apprenticeships. Children could opt to
spend some time as an apprentice to a variety of professionals and
craftspeople in the community. They could, for example, work with the
boat-builders in the workshop next door to the school. Some of the
pupils had chosen to do an apprenticeship in the Family Life Centre

with the midwives there. Thus, they learnt about how their community operated and the community, in turn, learnt a lot about them. They have at times, undertaken high-profile activities in their city by, for example, lobbying their Assemblyman, Capital District Legislators and a Senator's aide to save the New York State Theatre Institute from a massive funding cut. These encounters taught them, among other things, that not everyone takes children as seriously as the Free School and its community. Over the years, this community and the school acquired other resources to call upon and enjoy in country vacations, daylong and weeklong trips and a weekend workshop programme. They set about making a wilderness education centre, a teaching lodge and a wildlife sanctuary.

The school and the community have come a long way, developing organically all the time. The heart of the school's concept of education is based upon the principles of love, emotional honesty, peer-level leadership and co-operation. It has demonstrated what can be done if children are respected, cared for and taken seriously by everyone around them. This is a fine example of relationships between adults and children in which traditional models of adult–child relationships have been radically transformed and power is shared.

POWER IN PRACTICE

Of the three examples of young people being respected as persons, as citizens – in the Devon Youth Council, in a Children's Parliament in India, in a daring school in North America – the common thread has been that for children to be powerful, adult–child relationships have to change substantially from their usual form and that context and timing are critical. The power involved was the preparedness of everyone to see the world from everybody's point of view. One can question whether such preparedness had limits. Using Roger Hart's well-known 'Ladder of children's participation' (Hart 1992, 1997) it seems that the activities described were initially adult-initiated, sharing decisions with children. In the setting of the DYC and the Bal Sansad, adults created a role for children and made arrangements for them to operate in a fairly self-determined way. These roles were fully embraced and exploited by the children. The DYC made good use of the opportunities and was in the vanguard of a movement for children's participation in local government in the UK and Europe. The Bal Sansad went from strength to strength, attracted considerable international attention and was a joint winner of the World's Children's Prize for the Rights of the Child in 2001 (Childrensworld 2001).

Difficulties arose for both in the extent to which children were able to keep up the momentum of participating. Looking at these difficulties is instructive for future planning of activities involving young people's participation. With many minority rights groups, once a role has been created for them, they are able to take things forward from there; however, in the case of young people, the limited amount of power that has been bestowed on them can make it difficult for them to keep up the momentum of their work. The DYC was at the forefront of a movement for children's participation in local government. The national and international stage was seductive and, as the DYC became famous, an audience outside their own constituency was courted, but they had neither the staff nor the funds to keep up with grass-roots consultation and feedback. In a child advocacy movement, this is particularly difficult as the constituents are constantly changing yet need to be involved, consulted and informed. This is a larger burden than in other minority rights groups who can rely on a certain degree of continuity and consolidation. In children's groups there is a built-in obsolescence, so work has to be put into ensuring succession. For any minority rights group representation is always a problem. When the throughput of membership is fairly rapid, the problem is particularly acute. The DYC had conducted its own reviews and made its own recommendations, which included suggestions as to how its problems could be addressed. They were never acted upon. It is interesting, in speculating how flimsy the 'empowerment' of the young Council actually was, to note the Local Government Association's response to international pressures for young people's participation. It produced the standards, in conjunction with the National Youth Agency, and guidelines rather than the young activist groups, who had only been consulted. The DYC have become specialist advisers rather than joint parties in the decision-making process. This contrasts with the way it had started off. The Devon Youth Council can be said to have been part of the inspiration of the Local Government Association's 'hear by right' campaign. The sad bit about this is that the adult managers and administrators have very largely taken over and are now, yet again, in control of 'the game' as bestower of rights. There has been a shift of role. Power had not been divested and transformed; rather, for a short time, some invested power had been shared.

In Rajasthan and in Devon a common difficulty has been attendance at meetings, which meant that activity dropped off. Devon is a largely rural county with limited public transport in the evenings. Initially the DYC co-ordinator was provided with a car and mobile phone, but the young councillors still had to get themselves to meetings. The Bal Sansad is made up of MPs from village night schools scattered over a huge area. For both groups transport is an issue and frequently is dependent on adult support, organisation and funding. To fully transform power relationships between adults and children, this sort of dependence has to be addressed. Transport is indeed a children's issue! In Rajasthan there were further constraints on continuing involvement, which related to the lives of young girls within the culture. While the responsibilities of the Prime Minister had sufficiently impressed her father to delay her marriage, other young girls had had to conform to cultural expectations and drop out as they moved to live in their husband's family household. The adults supporting the Bal Sansad have been trying to work with the adults in the community to bring about some changes here but it requires a huge cultural shift and a big commitment to the effectiveness of the Parliament.

The DYC learnt about local government by being involved and having some responsibilities to raise consciousness and *advise* the invested power of the decision makers. In India, the children were given substantial responsibilities to *make* the decisions and *implement* them. In the latter case power appeared to have been divested. Nevertheless, one could argue that in both cases real power was invested in the adults and only *bestowed* on the children in differing degrees of generosity, the Indian children being allowed to do the most. While both of these examples signify a great step forward in acknowledging the competence of children, the long-term implications of such activities needed to be anticipated and provided for.

In both Devon and Rajasthan, structures were created for the participation of young people. In Albany, the effort was to de-institutionalise children's participation and try to work towards a transformation of power relationships between adults and children such that children played an equal part in it. Transforming power relationships in a substantial way was attempted in the development of the school Council jointly with the children as a system of regulating behaviour and sharing understandings. In this, power became 'divested' power and was shared.

PART V

Eternal Children?

CHAPTER NINE

Moving On

WHAT IT MEANS TO BE YOUNG

> All through my childhood and my young days, my life had a
> distinct meaning: its goal and its motive was to reach the adult
> age. At twenty, living does not mean getting ready to be forty.
> Yet for my people and for me, my duty as a child and an
> adolescent consisted of forming the woman I was to be
> tomorrow. (Simone de Beauvoir 1959, p.108)

© The Estate of Simone de Beauvoir.

Freedom, individuality and good times

I suggested in Chapter 1 that communities are undergoing social breakdown. Several aspects of such fragmentation are relevant to children and
their power. One relates to the nature of modernity, another focuses on
the nature of relationships and a third aspect concerns fear. Michael
Ignatieff suggests that some social anxieties are:

> ...an inseparable part of the very experience of being mod-
> ern. One of these concerns the possibility of belonging...
> Modernity and belonging just do not go together: the incom-
> patibility is not simply a matter of the brutal temporariness of
> the modern social order. It is also about how the modern
> individual is put together, whether the modern self *wants* to
> belong in the ways that were available in the face-to-face inti-
> macies of traditional and village life. Modernity's core value is
> freedom – especially freedom to fashion one's identity, and
> one's life as one wills, since the very sense of dignity and
> self-worth are tied into this idea of personal freedom. We tend
> to rank feelings of belonging to community, nation and
> family much lower in our conception than in pre-industrial
> and pre-modern society. (Ignatieff 1997, pp.85–86)

Can one feel a sense of comfort and belonging in societies which change as rapidly as modern ones? Have we been swept along to become amorphous global citizens rather than nurtured national subjects? Social anxieties can, it seems, be most easily projected onto the role of the young. Birdisha Bandyopadhyay, writing about this, said, 'The adult's depression of the last 10 years or so has resulted in a general sense of youthful nihilism. We have a need to discover new territory, to create our own moral and social order' (Bandyopadhyay 1997, p.193). The adult response to such creators of their own moral and social order is to seek for control. Dr Jonathan Miller complaining about 'feral children' now invading his part of smart North London (*Evening Standard*, 14 May 2002) has worrying resonance with attitudes to street children in Brazil and Mozambique. Prime Minister Blair's response to the escalating teenage pregnancy rate, the highest in Europe, was to embark on a moral crusade and to demonise single teenage mothers with the blame for the public costs of social welfare. Havel (1986) had long since pointed out that moral crusades usually start after people have already been demoralised. Thus the young, feeling hopeless in the face of their situation and their bleak future, become targets for a moral campaign – that is, for control rather than understanding, as witches rather than as people responding to desperate circumstances.

> ...we do not kid ourselves – the future looks bad. Issues such as the decriminalisation of cannabis, the Criminal Justice Act, personal identification and tagging, laws on immigration, general civil rights and changes in the gay age of consent are attractive to us because they give us a chance to make some noise defending the three governing principles of being young: freedom, individuality and good times. (Bandyopadhyay 1997, p.193)

These are the things that most strike terror in the adult breast: freedom, individuality and good times – but are the times really so good? In 1995, Demos (an independent think-tank committed to radical thinking on the long-term problems facing the UK and other advanced industrial societies) reported on their study of the lifestyle and values of the generation of young people born in the UK in the 1960s and 1970s. This generation, they claimed, had inherited unprecedented freedoms. They have been able to choose their own lifestyle, relationships and careers to a degree that would have been inconceivable in the past. A host of new problems beset these new freedoms: relationship breakdown, an insecure labour market, growing intergenerational conflict, and a profound disconnection from politics.

> Our map of British values also shows how values are fragmenting, as younger age groups move towards more 'modern' values such as autonomy and authenticity. Our survey evidence describes the swing away from tradition and authority and rising tolerance… We show how men's values are becoming more feminine and how women are becoming more masculine, attached to risk, hedonism and living on the edge. In particular women in the youngest age groups are taking far more pleasure in violence – more than young men… We expect female violence to become a major issue in the years ahead. (Wilkinson and Mulgan 1995, p.11)

A disengagement of the young from traditional politics (which they noted is not just a feature of the UK) has served to reinforce the complacency of the older groups. While similar trends of disconnection were apparent in other countries (e.g. Germany, France, Australia, America, Canada), these other countries have responded rather more seriously. Political disconnection also led to a broad social disconnection. Wilkinson and Mulgan found that:

> almost half of under 25 year olds register as profoundly disconnected from the system, and a growing number of 'underdogs' are now prepared to bite back – we call them the underwolves.
>
> Elsewhere – especially in the US – we can see the beginnings of intergenerational conflict over policies and resources. The divide is symbolised by towns which have gleaming new hospitals, run-down schools and impoverished single mothers. Some of the same causes are present in the UK, as this generation faces the prospect of having to pay for old people without the confidence that their own pensions and care needs will be financed. (Wilkinson and Mulgan 1995, p.18)

Wilkinson and Mulgan go on to argue that what is needed for 'freedom's children' is a new set of frameworks to define life in work, relationships and politics. 'New freedoms have brought far richer opportunities, especially for women. No one wants to give these away. But the hard task now is to define a sustainable framework for freedoms, a better balance between choice and commitment' (p.19).

Such new frameworks that have emerged since that time bear all the shortcomings of those that preceded them, in that young people have not been involved in developing them. They capture the imagination of the administrator rather than the adult-in-waiting. They are imposed from above rather than jointly developed with young people themselves. Since that survey, today's children still face a bewildering world where freedom can mean anomie, poverty and non-recognition rather than fun and good times. The intergenerational tension relates to the distribution of wealth between the generations. It seems now that the independence of the elderly is bought at the price of the increasing dependence of adolescents. It seems that they will now be a generation who, if they find work, will have to work on into their seventies since retirement pensions for many of them are a remote and unrealistic possibility.

The route that has for many provided a ray of hope in a bleak present is also now becoming increasingly difficult and privileged – namely, education. My father eventually escaped misfortune and an impoverished childhood working down the mines in the Depression by embracing education. The chance of young people using education as the escape from poverty and disadvantage is now being seriously compromised both by the nature and the costs of education in the United Kingdom. I have already discussed elsewhere the feudal nature of schooling in this country with its scant regard for democracy in practice and young people in the making. Now further and higher education is slipping increasingly beyond the reach of many of our young people.

To this has been added a further dimension, which is the polarisation of the group of young people themselves. Since 1997 a programme of research looking at young people's transitions into adulthood has suggested that these transitions have changed in recent years (Jones 2002). At a time when a major policy thrust in the UK is allegedly to combat social exclusion, this work reveals that this will be extremely difficult to address. Adolescence, an artificially-created, cold waiting-room to life, appears now to have to endure more waiting, on the basis of an outdated policy assumption that young people are, or can remain, dependent on their parents. Parents, it is assumed, will accept extended responsibility for their children. It also appears that financial disincentives prevent poorer prospective students from applying to universities in the first place.

> The increasing delay in achieving economic independence, coupled with Government policies which assume that parents will accept additional responsibilities and extend their financial support to their adult children, has redoubled the importance of positive family relationships to young people's life chances... Formal education cannot always overcome the effects of early family disadvantage. (Rowntree 2002, p.2)

This is especially troubling when compared with prevailing values and trends in other parts of the world, a broad canvas interpreted by Will Hutton. He suggests that in the United States there is the emergence of an aristocracy of the wealthy professions (medicine, law, finance, etc.). The cost there of going to university has exploded over the last 25 years. States have cut their support for college students by 32 per cent since 1979. The result of this has been 'a calamitous drop in the chances of a poor student acquiring a university or college degree' (Hutton 2002, p.155). The consequences are important in terms of power measured by influence.

> Despite America's public attachment to the idea of a meritocracy, the wealthy – just as Warren Beatty argues – ensure that their children get privileged access to the best schools, the best universities and the most influential networks. They can pay the fees. The Bush, Gore and Kennedy families are only three of the most famous political examples of how wealth begets more wealth and influence. (Hutton 2002, p.157)

Dynastic access to power and influence on this scale is troubling and is used by Hutton to contrast education in Europe and North America. Most of these elite members also defend the myth of extremist free-market economics. Hutton points out that the British approach to the social contract and the public realm lies much nearer to Europe than to the US. Nevertheless in the UK there seems increasingly to be an elite among young people who can call on the necessary support of families over an increasingly long period of time.

Understanding the 'underwolves'

I have made much in the early part of this book about promoting resilience in children. The review of the Rowntree-funded research concludes:

> Inequalities persist among young people and in some respects they have deepened. However, the polarisation described here hides a more complex and disturbing picture. In the social hierarchy of young people, between the 'socially included' and the 'socially excluded' there is a large (and largely invisible) group trying to survive on scarce resources, including their own resilience. (Rowntree 2002, p.7)

This is followed by the suggestion that although there is work being undertaken to ameliorate the situation of the most socially included, the group that just 'get by' are drastically under-supported. The possibilities of them developing resilience, let alone indomitability, are seriously compromised. Grotberg identifies three factors in resilience or strengthening the human spirit: 'I have'; 'I am'; 'I can' (Grotberg 1995).

I have

When we look at what the 'underwolves' have, we find that they have often very little in terms not just of finance but also social capital. They may have a peer group to call upon in a life of bunking down on sofas and floors but rarely supportive and interested adults. The UK's Child Poverty Action Group publication *Not to be Ignored*, which examined the relationship between young people, poverty and health in the United Kingdom (Dennehy *et al.* 1997, pp.1–2), based its title on a poem written in 1994 by Penny Wildgoose, a young person living in UK, which concludes:

After all

Isn't it just about
The worst thing
For a young mind

To be ignored[1]

There is not much about freedom, individuality and good times as the defining qualities of youth in this poem. Indeed, according to Prime

Minister Blair's moral manifesto, these young people should be 'at home', under curfew – neither seen nor heard. Recognition is a vital part of being seen and treated as a full member of society. To be ignored is not only to be rendered powerless in the affairs of society but may have other long-term messages which travel inwards to feelings of hopelessness, doubts about self-worth and despair about identity and personhood. There are a number of points of relevance here to the consideration of the development of power in children's lives which have been taken up throughout the book. One relates to the tendency to trace back to earlier childhood problems in the here and now. I have stressed how important it is to engage with the present, not with what has gone before or is likely to come after.

I am

Not having a job or, indeed, a future makes huge inroads into any sense of personal identity and self-esteem. Identity has often been seen as one of the major tasks of adolescent transition from child to adult. With increasing dependence on parental support the young person is nevertheless adrift. The sad fact is that no-one knows more about adolescents and their identity than those who wish to exploit them. One advertising and marketing annual conference 'We're Talking Teens; Reaching a "Knowing Market"' in 1996 was unashamedly described as an essential conference for anyone interested in the latest trends and techniques for reaching young consumers.[2] It included sessions on 'Reaching the Millennium Consumer'. This further adds to the exclusion of a whole category of young people living on the edge. They are not ignored; their identity is skilfully and mercilessly exploited.

I can

There has been a small but much publicised shift in society's thinking in the world about involving the young in contributing to the new moral order. This has been marked, for instance, by a concern about the needs to *teach* citizenship. In the United Kingdom the Crick Report (QCA 1998) on education for citizenship failed to emphasise the urgent need for political change, the need to *create* democratic schools and the need to respect the contribution of children and young people (Lansdown 1999). With all that has been discussed earlier in this book it seems clear that their resilience may well be under-resourced in that they end up as demotivated, undereducated and underskilled. Maybe these days they simply, *can't*.

CHILDREN OF THE WORLD
Seen from above
Cloning globally

Global generalities about children are not helpful. Children and young people are often written about as if they form a homogeneous group. Many of the examples illustrating my arguments confound such a view. Children respond to challenges in their lives by calling on resources which are shaped by the immediate circumstances, values and belief systems of their culture and the point in its history. The technological revolution has made some images and values accessible across the globe, which play their part in influencing thinking and desire in comparable ways in vastly contrasting contexts. As part of a global village there is sadly an increasing conformity of all sorts of signals and signifiers across the world.

In post-civil-war Maputo, amid the dire poverty, hunger, upheaval and despair, I saw the ubiquitous big red and yellow 'M' sign among the decaying and destroyed relics of the once-stylish capital city. There were also, in unbearable counterpoint, fleet upon fleet of new UN-liveried vehicles gleaming in a parking lot alongside a heaving mass of flimsy encampments of thousands upon thousands of rural families who had fled to the towns to find food and work. Two realities were poised each side of a gulf in understanding. Some things know no frontiers, and are indifferent to difference.

One of the ways that globalisation has affected children is in the way the international donor aid in some subtle ways moulds the people they are to become. They are viewed as people that are not the product of their own regional cultures and specific languages but formed by what some pan-world donors think they ought to be. Policies too are frequently based on assumptions and world-views which are out of step and sympathy with local conditions.

Policy development

In a global economy, resource allocation indicates the importance that is given to children worldwide. Children now make up 40 per cent of the total population of the world yet this is not reflected in the ways that money is allocated to services associated with their welfare or advancement. One suspects that a dossier on Third World debt about the activities of the International Monetary Fund, the World Bank, G8, the EU and large international corporations, in terms of the child impact of their policies, would make depressing reading. Lip service to children as 'the future' fails to be met with practical financial activities that could make such a future a significant one. To do so would challenge present distributions of wealth that are still concentrated on the comfort and wellbeing of a disproportionately small number of adults.

Debt bondage is now a feature of the developed world. Young people who are not rich have had to take out loans to further their education, and now have their working life blighted by the repayment of that loan and their old age spent working in the absence of an adequate pension. It is almost as if policy makers feel that as children are growing up they will 'grow out of it', not realising that the shadow of a poor childhood will darken their adult life in a variety of ways I have mentioned. Even within one country children do not form a homogeneous group. These gates are beginning to shut out the deserving poor, narrowing the range of 'uppers' who are in control and pushing them further up the hierarchy and increasing their distance from the young. Money as power speaks only to the rich and knowledge as power can only be accessed by the relatively well-to-do. Putting vocational, further and higher education beyond the reach of many young people in the developed world will have damaging consequences. Global monetary policies are throttling the voice of the young. Relative affluence has made their natural campaigning allies complacent and blind and deaf to what needs to be done. The young need to endure it and not be seen. Some are responding with physical violence and rebellion, the only power left to them.

International donor aid

When the global community does face up to the needs of the developing world they often still exert the power of imposing their realities on their beneficiaries. Some organisations, such as the Barefoot College in Rajasthan, are wise to this. It is a difficult situation in that many countries are desperate for financial help yet this does not come without consequences. Mikael Palme describing the situation in Mozambique illustrates this powerfully.

> Tendencies are that the national elite – if this sociologically
> vague term can be accepted – orients itself primarily in rela-
> tion to the international society and its organisations. It is not
> only that this is where the benefits can be obtained, for exam-
> ple salaries compared to the ones of expatriates, it is also im-
> portant that this is the only visible landscape. (Palme 1997,
> p.215)

He goes on to explain that it is unlikely that such 'elites', who will deal
with educational issues, will favour the kind of investments that are
needed for real *national* capacity building and competence. Such competence would involve profound understanding of the particularities of regional cultures and national languages as well as a concern and respect
for lowly primary-school teachers and their problems. Palme doubts
whether such criteria would ever govern the selection of such elites. He
goes on:

> Do not the acculturation effects that are so obvious and visi-
> ble in the national education system – the basic experience of
> becoming different by and through education and the en-
> trance into modern, 'civilised' society [...] – in conjunction
> with the additional effects of having to adapt to a world of the
> donor-ruled elite, favour other basic qualities such as forget-
> ting or suppressing one's cultural origin and opening oneself
> to the language, the values and the ways of thinking and be-
> ing of the really dominating culture – that of management,
> statistics, English, planning – thus making oneself the African
> copy of the organisational culture of the dominating donor
> agencies that these agencies so much need in order to manage
> education in Africa? (Palme 1997, p.215)

The tensions between the status and credibility of academic qualifications and the drive for vocational relevance can be illustrated in many
other projects, for instance the World Bank-funded Basic Education
Project in Kenya (Peacock 1996, p.85). Fortunately the tendency of international donor aid to reproduce, particularly in education, outcomes
modelled on their own imperial views of realities are being challenged
and beginning to change. Save the Children (SCF), through its many
branches throughout the world, the Bernard van Leer Foundation and
UNICEF are working really hard to get close to children's realities and

evaluate service provision in ways sensitive to cultural and local perspectives.

Seen from 'abroad'

Process or categories?

The participation of children in the UN Special Session in New York and in the Earth Summit in Johannesburg reminded us that we live in a global economy and that children might have common aspirations. While there are important commonalities – for instance, everyone wants children to have clean water, a nutritious diet, appropriate health care and relief from poverty – these may be commonalities of basic survival needs. Some needs are non-negotiable. Children's aspirations, how they interpret their world to themselves and the meaning they make of it are culturally shaped and contextually constrained. I have stressed that to get to grips with these differences it is important to be attuned to children's experiences.

The Euro-American domination of the literature in child development has led to a false idea that children develop in much the same way around the world. It has been part of an intellectual imperialism that a view of children suggesting universal stages in child development is presented that takes little regard for difference. Often an implicit view of the child as a bounded individual immune from various interactive social and cultural forces, prevails. The recent emergence of a socio-cultural study of development and the coming together of the work of scholars in development studies, psychology, sociology, economics, statistics, law, geography and anthropology, are making a fairly concerted interdisciplinary attack on such blinkered thinking. The field is opening up for new and invigorating study of the heterogeneous group of children, their various development, understandings and meaning-making activities.

Can we really talk about 'universals' in childhood and child development? Are there common elements in the socialisation and experiences of the child? It is clear that generalising about children from what I have written about child warriors, Japanese schoolgirls, children in the night schools in India, the Earth Champions at Johannesburg and the child victims of ritual abuse, getting on with their breakfast as if nothing at all had happened the night before, would not be useful. Is there any comparison? Do models help, other than to tidily archive realities we cannot even start to comprehend? If we turn away from comparing lives, can we find any comparability in process? Here again we find that there has been a normative naivety about the world in which children develop. Social scientists who have worked in countries where there has been political unrest, warfare and extreme adversity have questioned the usefulness of theories about the socialisation of the child which assume 'normal' conditions and have not examined what happens when the moral order is in chaos. Ideas and theories about the socialisation of the child growing up in such circumstances still need to be undertaken. Maybe then it will be found necessary to be culture-and circumstance-specific.

Two approaches to dealing with the problems of cultural specificity and building a useful universal reference framework are to be found in the work of Super and Harkness (1986, quoted in Woodhead 2000), which developed from their research in rural Kenya, and the response-to-challenge model of Hendry and Kloep (2002) outlined in Chapter 6. Super and Harkness provide a categorisation approach, suggesting we can examine children's environments by looking at three features in particular which contribute to a child's developmental 'niche'. These are: the physical and social setting; the culturally regulated customs and child-rearing practices; and the dominant beliefs or 'ethno theories' about childhood. It enables us to begin to appreciate and focus in on particular childhoods and specific children in local settings.

The lifespan model provides another approach. I have suggested it takes further thinking about endurance and response to stress by boldly proposing a holistic theoretical model. It suggests that there are individual differences in potential resources, with development occurring each time life's challenges are met successfully and further resources are added. The resource pool is seen as being capable of being filled or drained, a state of dynamic security being reached when the 'pool' is relatively full. Hendry and Kloep feel it has usefulness in 'studying development cross-culturally. Which challenges stimulate development varies across cultures and over time. Yet the mechanisms of development are the same, irrespective of time and place' (2002, p.37). It is not clear in using such a model how challenges and responses can be identified ahead of time or whether it relies mainly on post hoc interpretation. In such interpretation the danger of ethnocentrism is ever present. The shift towards trying to identify common processes rather than common characteristics holds possibilities but these still have to be demonstrated in the field.

I have suggested other approaches. One is to use the factors identified across 14 countries in the International Resilience Project for further cross-cultural comparison (Grotberg 1995). I have also suggested that a further look at factors in the development of 'endurance' might be a productive line to follow.

ALTERNATIVE REALITIES, POWER AND RIGHTS

For many years Euro-American conceptions of the child and child development have dominated thinking about children worldwide. Such conceptions have also influenced how policy, provision and assessment have been framed both nationally and internationally. I have noted elsewhere that the UN Convention on the Rights of the Child is implicitly based on a particular view of children – a restricted view of what they are like and what should be done. This is changing as children themselves contribute information about their highly differentiated life worlds and their own aspirations.

The child I have sketched is one who endures one world – a world of constraints, structures and often hardship – and lives another world – a world of risk, excitement, imagination and creativity. I have, however, fallen into yet another trap. Not this time of a conception of the Northern indoor child so much as a child in whom the development of autonomy, individuality and independence is a central goal. This is ethnocentric in that individuality is not necessarily what is encouraged in some other societies as, for example, in traditional agrarian societies or in conservative Japan. In such societies, to the extent that it is possible to generalise, interdependence, co-operation, obedience and conformity are stressed, with tensions arising when, as part of 'modernisation', views emphasising individualism as a goal of socialisation develop as part of social change. Views of individuality or interdependence as distinct goals in socialisation lead us on to thinking further about freedom and rights.

Robert Chambers, the arch-practitioner and advocate of participatory approaches, believes that the benefits and the avoidance of suffering provided by participatory approaches in rural development are vast (Chambers 1997). Crucial in this is understanding other people's realities and making sure that they count. Emphasising that the 'global child' is a myth and urging a more differentiated view is the approach I have used in stressing how important it is to tap children's own experiences in order to have some insight into their realities. The definition of power throughout relates to the ability to have one's own definitions of reality prevail over other people's views of reality. Taking an 'invested power' approach, then, it is vitally important not only that a child's realities are sought and understood but that they 'prevail' and count. An alternative view of power, namely divested power, involves and values everybody's realities – a view of reality which is negotiated and takes account of differing realities. This is important as regards the relationship between freedom and belonging, which opened this chapter, as apparent polarities. These mirror the differences between freedom and rights, which contribute to notions of civil society.

Civil society can be seen as accommodating a plurality of freedoms, or 'realities', which serve as a check on the domination of a single view, authoritarianism. Freedom can be seen at the personal level as individual liberty. Indeed part of the child's liberation is facilitating the voicing of his/her individual concerns, the expression of his/her own hopes and aspirations. In stressing how important it is to understand that children across the world can not be lumped together as an undifferentiated group, then, one is partly stressing the individuality of their experience and thinking and that this is important in recognising their personal power.

Rights are an aspect of freedom where a plurality of interests come into play, when other people's realities and freedoms have to be accommodated and negotiated. Having stressed how important it is to recognise that children, child development and children's lives are substantially different in various cultures, belief systems and settings, it seems odd then to talk of common rights. This is in no way strange. Other minority groups are made up of vastly different individuals. Take, for instance, disabled people as a minority rights group. This group is worldwide, made up of people with quite different disabilities and life experiences. The difficulties arise when able-bodied people start to interpret what they want. Similarly children as a minority rights group are made up of children with very different backgrounds, experiences and resources, yet they can be seen as a group in that they share in common experiences of oppression, being at the weak end of an invested power relationship in which adult realities dominate. In sum, freedom is

about individuality whereas rights are about a particular form of belonging to a group with similar oppression and aspirations. This is why
rights cannot be given or bestowed; they arise from common experiences. In codifying common rights, children's participation in establishing with other children their shared views is essential.

One major difference children as a minority rights group have compared with other minority rights groups is the issue of built-in obsolescence and succession. Whereas other such groups can build on work
they do together and consolidate, children have the double responsibility of exercising their own rights and also training younger children in
politics so that they can take over as some children age and leave the
constituency.

The reason that the idea of children's rights frightens so many
adults, who mutter 'What about responsibilities?' is based on a false
view of the sort of power children are after. It is assumed that they seek a
form of power which involves unlicensed freedom. This is not the case.
Children are not out to grab some of the action of invested power. What
is involved in the exercise of children's rights is working towards changing the relationship between adults and children so that, through participation and voicing, each person works towards understanding and
respecting each other's realities and points of view. On the basis of this
shared understanding, plans and policies can be developed. The power
involved is divested power in which all parties have a voice, influence
and potential benefit.

ETERNAL CHILDREN

I suggested early on that in seeking new paradigms of research that were
themselves empowering, approaches to voice and voicing were important. Elbaz (1990) suggests that a concern with voice is implicit in the
work of all those committed to empowerment (in his case of teachers)
and that where the notion of 'voice' is used 'the term is always used
against the background of previous silence, and it is a political usage as
well as an epistemological one' (p.7). Voice and voicing has a political
dimension, indicating that life-history work is not limited to documenting the experience and thinking of individuals. It can also throw into
sharp focus a range of structural constraints that shape the construction
of any life. My concerns about children's power and a general process of
empowerment towards indomitability has made me reflect on life story

as life history, the distinction being that the story is one we tell about our life but the history draws on a wider range of evidence. This wider range is provided by this book in which my own story is embedded as life history.

Returning to school after the long solitary powerlessness in hospital which begat this book, my withdrawn demeanour was interpreted as that of a quiet reflective child, living in the parallel universe I just described. It was known that my brother, only 14 months my senior, was brilliantly clever. No-one guessed I was silent because I could not read the hieroglyphs on the board nor did I know how to navigate the playground networks of the peer group. I later became one of the few professors of education in this country with 'special needs': difficulties in reading, punctuation an unknown land (which I hope my copy-editor will have hidden from you). That is but the past. In the present I now move on using the strategies to respond to challenge and stress developed in childhood (looking at the hospital ceiling in a solitary state) and honed in academia in another sort of solitary state (under subtle devaluing and disempowerment) to face the same challenges that children and adults face life long. Who am I; what do I have as my resources; what can I do; what are my competencies? The resilience of 'I have, I am, I can' will carry me through to endure with fortitude and ingenuity the seventh age of my life as I move on and out of the institutional world.

> We do not receive wisdom. We must discover it for ourselves after experiences which no-one else can have for us and from which no-one else can spare us. (Proust 1918)

Endnote

1.   Penny Wildgoose's poem is reproduced with permission from Child Poverty Action Group.

2.   Conferences organised by TCC Events; Advertising and Marketing Series 30 and 31, Tuesday 25 June 1996.

References

Abramson, B. (1996) 'The Invisibility of Children and Adolescents. The Need to Monitor our Rhetoric and our Attitudes.' In E. Verhellen (ed) *Monitoring Children's Rights*. The Hague: Martinus Nijhoff Publishers.

Adamson, P. (1996) 'Beyond Basics.' In P. Adamson (ed) *The Progress of Nations 43*. New York: UNICEF.

Agenda 21 (1994) The complete text of Agenda 21 is available in all six UN languages from the UN Information Centre, 21st Floor Milbank Tower, Milbank, London SW1P 4QH or from Centre for Our Common Future, 52, rue de Paquis, 1201, Geneva, Switzerland.

Alderson, P. (1995) *Listening to Children. Children's Ethics and Social Research*. Barkingside: Barnardos.

Alderson, P. (2000) *Young Children's Rights: Exploring Beliefs, Attitudes, Principles and Practice*. London: Jessica Kingsley Publishers.

Alston, P. (1994) 'Reconciliation of Culture and Human Rights.' In J. Eekelaar and R. Dingwall (eds) *The Best Interests of the Child. Special Issue of the International Journal of Law and the Family, 8*. Oxford: Oxford University Press.

Amnesty International (1992) *The Extrajudicial Execution of Suspected Rebels and Collaborators*. London: International Secretariat of Amnesty International, Index AFR 51/02/92.

Amnesty International (1995) *Childhood Stolen. Grave Human Rights Violations Against Children*. London: Amnesty International British Section.

Aries, P. (1979) *Centuries of Childhood*. (Translation London: Jonathan Cape Ltd.) Harmondsworth: Penguin.

Arita, M. and Yamaoka, S. (1992) Title translates as 'The "Over-worthy Child" Syndrome.' *Asahi Journal* 20 March, 11–16.

Arnstein, S.R. (1969) 'The Ladder of Citizen Participation.' *The American Institute of Planners Journal 35*, 216-224

Article 12 (1988) An Organisation Run by Children and Young People for Children and Young People Under the Age of 18. London: Article 12.

Baltes, P.B. and Goulet, L.R. (1970) 'Status and Issues of a Life-span Developmental Psychology.' In L.R. Goulet and P.B. Baltes (eds) *Life-span Developmental Psychology: Research and Therapy*. New York: Academic Press.

Baltes, P.B., Reese, H.W. and Lipsitt, L.P. (1980) 'Life-span developmental psychology.' *Annual Review of Psychology 31*, 65–110.

Bandyopadhyay, B. (1997) 'Young and Anxious.' In S. Dunant and R. Porter (eds) *The Age of Anxiety*. London: Virago.

Bank of Scotland (2000) *Omnibus Survey Results for the Scottish Market – Wave 4 (1999–2000)*. Edinburgh, Bank of Scotland.

271

Barnett, L. (1999) 'Children and War.' *Medicine, Conflict and Survival 15*, 315–327.

Bateson, P. and Martin, P. (1999) *Design for a Life. How Behaviour Develops*. London: Jonathon Cape.

Bayer, B.M. and Shotter, J. (eds) (1998) *Reconstructing the Psychological Subject. Bodies Practices and Technologies*. London: Sage.

Befrienders International (2001) *Reaching Young Europe*. Brentford Community Partnership Programme: GlaxoSmithKline.

Bellamy, C. (1998) *The State of the World's Children 1998*. UNICEF. Oxford: Oxford University Press.

Bellamy, C. (1999) *The State of the World's Children 1999. Education*. UNICEF. New York: United Nations Children's Fund.

Bellamy, C. (2000) *The State of the World's Children 2000. Poverty*. UNICEF. New York: United Nations Children's Fund.

Bellamy, C. (2002a) *The State of the World's Children 2002. Leadership*. UNICEF. New York: United Nations Children's Fund.

Bellamy, C. (2002b) www.unicef.org/exspeeches/02esp17-wssd.htm.

Ben-Arieh, A. and Wintersberger, H. (eds) (1997) 'Monitoring and Measuring the State of Children – Beyond Survival.' *European Centre, Eurosocial Report 62*. Vienna: European Centre.

Blagborough, J. (1998) 'Collecting Information from Child Domestic Workers; Some Ethical Issues.' In B. Pettit (ed) *Children and Work in the UK. Reassessing the issues*. London: Child Poverty Action Group.

BMRB International (2000) quoted in Bank of Scotland (2000) *Omnibus Survey Results for the Scottish Market – Wave 4 (1999–2000)*. Edinburgh: Bank of Scotland.

Boal, A. (1974) *Theater of the Oppressed*. New York: Urizen.

Boal, A. (1992) *Games for Actors and Non-actors*. London: Routledge.

Bourdieu, P. (1977) *Outline of a Theory in Practice*. Translated by R. Nice. Cambridge: Cambridge University Press.

Bourdieu, P. (1990) *In Other Words: Essays towards a Reflexive Sociology*. Translated by M. Adamson. Cambridge: Polity Press.

Bourdillon, M. (2001) 'Child Labour and Tea in Zimbabwe.' Paper presented at *Children in their Places* International Conference. London: Brunel University 21–23 June.

Boyden, J. (1990) 'Childhood and Policy Makers: A Comparative Perspective on the Globalisation of Childhood.' In A. James and A. Prout (eds) *Constructing and Deconstructing Childhood: Contemporary Issues in the Sociological Study of Childhood*. London: Falmer Press.

Boyden, J. (2001) '"A Residual Fear of Children": Childhood Transformations and Theoretical Challenges in the Context of Political Violence.' Paper presented at the *International Conference on 'Children in their Places*, Brunel University.

Boyden, J. and Myers, W. (1995) *Exploring Alternative Approaches to Combating Child Labour. Case Studies from Developing Countries*. Florence: UNICEF.

Bradley, B. (1989) *Visions of Infancy. Critical Introduction to Child Psychology*. Cambridge: Polity Press.

Bradley, B. (1998) 'Two Ways to Talk about Change. "The Child" of the Sublime versus Radical Psychology.' In B.M. Bayer and J. Shotter (eds) *Reconstructing the Psychological Subject. Bodies Practices and Technologies*. London: Sage.

Brain R. (1970) 'Child Witches.' In M. Douglas (ed) *Witchcraft. Confessions and Accusations*. London: Tavistock Publications.

Bread for the World Institute (1997) *What Governments Can Do; Seventh Annual Report on the State of World Hunger*. Silver Spring: Bread for the World Institute.

Brizzio de la Hoz, A. (1997) 'Children's Labour in Mexico.' In M. John (ed) *A Charge Against Society: The Child's Right to Protection*. London: Jessica Kingsley Publishers.

Brown, G. (2002) http://www.unicef.org/special_session/_activities/gordon-brown.htm.

Bruner, J. (1990) *Acts of Meaning*. Cambridge, Massachusetts: Harvard University Press.

Bruner, J. (1996) 'A Little City Miracle.' In catalogue of the exhibit *The Hundred Languages of Children*. Reggio Emilia, Italy: Reggio Children.

Butler-Sloss, E. (1988) *Report of the Inquiry into Child Abuse in Cleveland 1987*. London: HMSO.

Chambers, R. (1997) *Whose Reality Counts? Putting the First Last*. London: Intermediate Technology Publications.

Chavarria, E.M.Z. (1992) 'The Rights of Children in Democratic Societies.' In M.D. Fortuyn and M. de Langen (eds) *Towards the Human Rights of Children Lectures given at the Second International Conference on Children's Ombudswork*. Amsterdam Netherlands: Children's Ombudswork Foundation and Defence for Children International.

Child Poverty Action Group (1999) 'Tackling Poverty – An Acceptable Living Standard.' In *Poverty 103*, Summer www.cpag.org.uk.

Children of the World (1994) *Rescue Mission Planet Earth – A Children's Edition of Agenda 21*. Peace Child International in association with UNICEF. London: Kingfisher Books.

Children's Speech (2002), 2 September, www.unicef.org/exspeeches/02esp19-wsdchildren.htm.

Childrensworld (2001) *The Globe*. Mariefred, Sweden: Children's World. (www.childrensworld.org).

Childwatch International (1996) *Project: Indicators for Children's Rights*. www.childwatch.uio.no/.

Christensen, P. and James, A. (eds) (2000) *Research with Children*. London: Falmer Press.

Christie, P. (1991) *The Right to Learn*. Johannesburg: SACHED/Ravan.

Clark, R. (1992) *The Fire This Time: War Crimes in the Gulf*. New York: Thunders Mouth Press.

Clark, R. (1996) *The Children are Dying*. New York Times: World View Forum.

Coles, R. (1986) *The Political Life of Children*. Boston: Atlantic Monthly Press.

Collier, P. (2000) *Economic Causes of Civil Conflict and their Implications for Policy*. Washington: The World Bank.

Curtis, M. (1995) *The Ambiguities of Power: British Foreign Policy Since 1945.* London: Zed Books.

Datamonitor (2000) Reported in D. Hutton (2000) 'The Rise of the Pocket-money Moguls.' *You (Daily Mail* weekend magazine), 26 Novemnber.

Dawes, A. (1994) 'The Emotional Impact of Political Violence.' In A. Dawes and D. Donald (eds) *Childhood and Adversity. Psychological Perspectives from South African Research.* Cape Town: David Philip.

de Beauvoir, S. (1959) *All Said and Done.* London: Penguin Books.

de Beauvoir, S. (1995) *Memories of a Dutiful Daughter.* London: Andre Deutsch.

de la Hoz, A. and Martinez Morales, M. (1997) 'Children's Labour in Mexico. Rights, Protection and Violation.' In M. John (ed) *A Charge Against Society: The Child's Right to Protection.* London: Jessica Kingsley Publishers, 64–76.

Deane, S. (1996) *Reading in the Dark.* London: Jonathon Cape Ltd.

Dennehy, A., Smith, L. and Harker, P. (1997) *Not to be Ignored; Young People, Poverty and Health.* London: Child Poverty Action Group (CPAG) Ltd.

Denzin, N.K. and Lincoln, Y.S. (eds) (1994) *Handbook of Qualitative Research.* First edition. London: Sage Publications Inc.

Denzin, N.K. and Lincoln, Y.S. (eds) (2000) *Handbook of Qualitative Research.* Second edition. London: Sage Publications Inc.

Department of Social Security (1999) *Opportunity For All: Tackling Poverty and Social Exclusion. Indicators of Success: Definitions, Data and Baseline Information.* Cm 4445. London: The Stationery Office.

Detrick, S. (1992) *The United Nations Convention on the Rights of the Child: A Guide to the Travaux Preparatoires.* Dordrecht, Boston, London: Matinus Nijhoff Publishers.

Devereux, G. (1968) *From Anxiety to Method in the Behavioural Sciences.* The Hague: Mouton.

Dia, F.F., Diagne, N.G., Gueye, A.K. and Gueye, S. (1995) *Indicateurs relatifs aux droits de l'enfant; étude de cas du Senegal.* Childwatch International/Plan International Senegal: Global Gutter Press.

Donald, J. (1993) 'The Natural Man and the Virtuous Woman: Reproducing Citizens.' In C. Jenks (ed) *Cultural Reproduction.* New York: Routledge.

Douglas, M. (1970) 'Introduction. Thirty Years after Witchcraft, Oracles and Magic.' In M. Douglas (ed) *Witchcraft. Confessions and Accusations.* London: Tavistock Publications.

Downer, L. (2000) *Geisha. The Secret History of a Vanishing World.* London: Headline Book Publishing.

Drabble, M. (2000) 'What Were You Looking At? A List of of Celebrity Critics Choose Their Books of the Year.' *Guardian.* 16 December.

DSS (2001) *Households Below Average Income 1999/2000.* London Department of Social Security.

Dunn, J. (1988) *The Beginnings of Social Understanding.* Cambridge, MA: Harvard University Press.

Dunn, J. (1995) 'Children as Psychologists: The Later Correlates of Individual Differences in Understanding of Emotions and Other Minds.' *Cognition and Emotion 9,* 132–139.

Dunn, J. (1996) 'Family Conversations and the Development of Social Understanding.' In B. Bernstein and J. Brannen (eds) *Children, Research and Social Policy*. London: Taylor Francis.

Dunn, J. and Kendrick, C. (1982) *Siblings. Love, Envy and Understanding*. London: Grant McIntyre.

Dunn, J., Slomkowski, C. and Beardsall, L. (1994) 'Sibling Relationships from the Pre-school Period through Middle Childhood and Early Adolescence.' *Developmental Psychology 24*, 376–385.

Durkheim, E. (1952) *Suicide. A Study in Sociology*. London: Routledge and Kegan Paul.

Duron Segovia, M de J. (1993) 'Sindrome de maltrado social del menor en los paises deudores de America Latina' ('Syndrome of the Social Maltreatment of Minors in the Indebted Countries of Latin America'). *Revista de la Universidad del Valle de Atemajac, Guadalarajara, 19*. Summarised in 'Structural Adjustment, Modernisation and Children'. *Bernard Van Leer Foundation Newsletter 74*, April 1994, The Hague.

Edelman, M.W. (1996) 'Foreword.' In L. Lantieri and J. Patti *Waging Peace in our Schools*. Boston: Beacon Press.

Elbaz, F. (1990) 'Knowledge and Discourse: The Evolution of Research on Teacher Thinking.' In C. Day, M. Pope and P. Denicolo (eds) *Insight into Teacher's Thinking and Practice*. Lewes: Falmer Press, 15–42.

Elder, G.H. Jr (1974) *Children of the Great Depression: Social Change in Life Experience*. Chicago, IL: University of Chicago Press.

Elder, G.H. Jr (1997) 'The Life-course as Human Development.' In W. Damon and T.M. Lerner (eds) *Handbook of Child Psychology*. Fourth edition, volume 1. New York: Wiley.

Elder, G.H. Jr (1998) 'The life-course as developmental theory.' *Child Development 69*, 1, 1–12.

Eliot, T.S. (1923) '*Ulysses*, Order and Myth.' Published in *The Dial*. Quoted in D. Kibberd (1992) 'Introduction.' In J. Joyce *Ulysses*. Harmondsworth: Penguin Books.

Ennew, J. (1986) *The Sexual Exploitation of Children*. Cambridge: Polity Press.

Ennew, J. (1995) 'Outside Childhood Street Children's Rights.' In B. Franklin (ed) *The Handbook of Children's Rights. Comparative Policy and Practice*. London: Routledge.

Ennew, J. (1996) *Indicators of Children's Rights: A Source File*. Prepared for Childwatch International January 1996 (typescript) for the Childwatch International Project on Indicators for Children's Rights. Childwatch International.

Ennew, J. (1998a) *Monitoring Children's Rights: Indicators for Children's Rights Project*, Childwatch International Research Network, Centre for Family Research, University of Cambridge, wwwchildwatch.uio.no/cwi/projects/indicators/monitoring/monitoring.html.

Ennew, J. (1998b) 'Stepping Forward: Children and Young People's Participation in the Development Process.' In V. Johnson, G. Ivan-Smith, P. Pridmore and P. Scott (eds) London: Intermediate Technology Publications.

Ennew, J. and Miljeteig, P. (1996) 'Indicators for Children's Rights: Progress Report on a Project.' *The International Journal of Children's Rights 4*, 213–236.

Eskeland, K. (1996) 'Voice of the Children; Speaking the Truth to Power.' In M. John (ed) *Children in Charge: The Child's Right to a Fair Hearing.* London: Jessica Kingsley Publishers.

EU (1999) *The Week in Europe. 22 July 1999.* London: The European Commission Representation in the UK.

EU (2000) *Violence at School and Public Policy.* Conference organised by the European Centre on Violence at School in co-operation with the European Commission's Directorate-General for Education and Culture and the French Ministry of Education. Results of actions supported by the Commission are available on http://europa.eu.int/comm/education/violence/home.html.

Evans, A. (2002) Personal communication following a visit to the Children's Parliament in July 2002.

Feierman, S. (1990) *Peasant Intellectuals: Anthropology and History in Tanzania.* Madison: University of Wisconsin Press.

Ferguson, S. (1994) 'The Comfort of Being Sad.' *Utne Reader 64,* July/August, 60–61.(1994)

Festinger, L. (1950) 'Informal Social Communication.' *Psychological Review 57,* 271–282.

Field, N. (1995) 'The Child as Labourer and Consumer.' In S. Stephens (ed) *Children and the Politics of Culture.* Princeton Studies in Culture/Power/History. Princeton: Princeton University Press.

Fischer, P. *et al.* (1991) 'Brand Logo Recognition by Children Aged 3 to 6 Years.' *Journal of the American Medical Association 266,* 22, 3145–3148.

Fiske, J. (1993) *Power Plays, Power Works.* New York: Verso.

Flekkoy, M.G. (1991) *A Voice for Children; Speaking Out as Their Ombudsman.* Commissioned by UNICEF. London: Jessica Kingsley Publishers.

Food and Agriculture Organisation (FAO) (1995) *Evaluation of the Food and Nutrition Situation in Iraq.* Rome: United Nations.

Freire, P. (1970) *Pedagogy of the Oppressed.* Harmondsworth: Penguin.

Fukuyama, F. (1992) *The End of History and the Last Man.* London: Hamish Hamilton Ltd.

Fukuyama, F. (2002) *Our Posthuman Future. Consequences of the Biotechnology Revolution.* London: Profile Books Ltd.

Fyfe, A. (1989) *Child Labour.* Cambridge: Polity Press.

Gabriel, Y. and Lang, T. (1995) *The Unmanageable Consumer: Contemporary Consumption and its Fragmentations.* London: Sage.

Galston, W. (1991) 'Home Alone: What our Policy Makers Should Know about our Children.' *New Republic* 2 December.

George, S. (2001) *Taking Children Seriously.* Produced by the *Guardian* in association with Save the Children in preparation for the UN Special Session on Children. London: Guardian Newspapers.

Gergen, K.J. (1985) 'The Social Constructionist Movement in Modern Psychology.' *American Psychologist 40,* 266–275.

Giddens, A. (1979) *Central Problems in Social Theory: Action, Structure, and Contradictions in Social Analysis.* Berkeley and Los Angeles: University of California Press.

Giddens, A. (1990) *The Consequences of Modernity*. Cambridge: Polity Press.

Giddens, A. (1991) *Modernity and Self-identity. Self and Society in the Late Modern Age*. Cambridge: Polity Press.

Giddens, A. (1992) *The Transformation of Intimacy. Sexuality, Love and Eroticism in Modern Societies*. Cambridge: Polity Press.

Gilligan, C. (1994) 'Getting Civilised.' *Fordham Law Review 63*, 17–31.

Ginsberg, H.P. and Opper, S. (1988) *Piaget's Theory of Intellectual Development*. Engelwood Cliffs, NJ: Prentice Hall.

Giroux, H. (1994) *Disturbing Pleasures: Learning Popular Culture*. London: Routledge.

Giroux, H.A. (1997) 'Are Disney Movies Good for your Kids?' In S.R. Steinberg and J.L. Kinchloe (eds) *Kinderculture. The Corporate Construction of Childhood*. Boulder Colorado: Westview Press.

Goffman, E. (1979) *Gender Advertisements*. London, Macmillan.

Gosse, E. (1980) *Father and Son*. London: Penguin.

Gregg, P., Harkness, S. and Machin, S. (1998) *Poor Kids: Trends in Child Poverty 1968–96*. Mimeo available on request from the Centre for Economic Performance, London School of Economics.

Griffith, R. (1996) 'New Powers for Old: Transforming Power Relationships.' In M. John (ed) *Children in Our Charge: The Child's Right to Resources*. London: Jessica Kingsley Publishers, 192–201.

Griffith, R. (1998) *Educational Citizenship and Independent Learning*. London: Jessica Kingsley Publishers.

Griggs, R. (1997) *Children at Risk: The Security Situation in Durban Schools*. Durban: Independent Projects Trust.

Grotberg, E. (1995) *A Guide to Promoting Resilience in Children; Strengthening the Human Spirit. Early Childhood Development: Practice and Reflections. Number 8*. The Hague: Bernard Van Leer Foundation.

Hammarberg, T. (1993) 'The Rights of the Child and the Industrialised Countries.' In K. Ekberg and P.E. Mjaavatn (eds) Children at Risk: Selected Papers. Trondheim: Norwegian Centre for Child Research.

Harber, C. (2000a) *Protecting Your School from Crime and Violence: Skills for Creating a Safe School. Evaluation of a One Year Programme*. Durban: Unpublished Report for Independent Projects Trust.

Harber, C. (2000b) 'Schools, Democracy and Violence in South Africa.' In A. Osler (ed) *Citizenship and Democracy in Schools: Diversity, Identity, Equality*. Stoke on Trent: Trentham Books, 143–150.

Harre, R. (1983) *Personal Being*. Oxford: Basil Blackwell.

Hart, R.A. (1992) *Children's Participation: From Tokenism to Citizenship. Innocenti Essays No. 4*. Florence: UNICEF International Child Development Centre, 44.

Hart, R.A. (1997) *Children's Participation; The Theory and Practice of Involving Young Citizens in Community Development and Environmental Care*. London: Earthscan Publications.

Harvey, D. (1989) *The Condition of Postmodernity*. Oxford: Blackwell.

Havel, V. (1986) 'The Power of the Powerless.' In J. Vladislav (ed) *Living in Truth*. London: Faber and Faber.

Hendry, L.B. and Kloep, M. (2002) *Lifespan Development. Resources, Challenges and Risks*. London: Thompson Learning.

Henley, W.E. (1875) 'Invictus.' In L. Untermeyer (ed) (1920) *Modern British Poetry 1885–1977*. New York: Harcourt Brace.

Henriques, J., Hollway, W., Urwin, C., Venn, C. and Walkerdine, V. (1984) *Changing the Subject. Psychology, Social Regulation and Subjectivity*. London: Methuen.

Henriques, J., Hollway, W., Urwin, C., Venn, C. and Walkerdine, V. (reissued 1998) *Changing the Subject: Psychology, Social Regulation and Subjectivity*. London: Routledge.

Herman, J.L. (1992) *Trauma and Recovery*. New York: Basic Books.

Hernandez, D.J. (1993) *America's Children: Resources for Family, Government and the Economy*. New York: Russel Sage Foundation.

Hilberman, E. (1980) 'The Wife-beater's Wife Reconsidered.' *American Journal of Psychiatry 137*, 13–41.

Hill, F. and Michelson W. (1981) 'Towards a Geography of Urban Children and Youth.' In D.T. Herbert and R.J. Johnston (eds) *Geography and the Urban Environment: Progress in Research and Applications, 4*. Chichester: John Wiley, 193–228.

Hill, M. (1996) 'Engaging with Primary-aged Children about their Health and Well-being: Methodological Considerations.' *Children and Society 10*, 129–144.

Hillman, M., Adams, J. and Whitelegg, J. (1990) *One False Move... A Study of Children's Independent Mobility*. London: Policy Studies Institute.

Hirayama, F. (1999) Personal communication during and following a visit to Japan.

HMSO (1994a) *Economic Trends. December 94*. London: HMSO.

HMSO (1994b) *Social Focus on Children*. London: Central Statistical Office.

HMSO (1994c) The UK's First Report to the UN Committee on the Rights of the Child. London: HMSO.

Hobbs, S. and McKechnie, J. (1997) *Child Employment in Britain. A Social and Psychological Analysis*. London: Stationery Office.

Hobbs, S. and McKechnie, J. (1998) 'Children and Work in the UK: The Evidence.' In B. Pettit (ed) *Children and Work in the UK. Reassessing the Issues*. London: Child Poverty Action Group.

Howard, M., Garnham, A., Fimister, H. and Viet-Wilson, J. (2001) *Poverty: The Facts*. London: Child Poverty Action Group.

Hubbard, J. (1991) *Shooting Back: A Photographic View of Life by Homeless Children*. San Francisco, CA: Chronicle Books.

Hutton, D. (2000) 'The Rise of the Pocket-money Moguls.' *You* (*Daily Mail* weekend magazine), 26 November.

Hutton, W. (1995) *The State We're In*. London: Jonathan Cape.

Hutton, W. (1999) *The Stakeholding Society. Writings on Politics and Economics*. Edited by D. Goldblatt. Cambridge: Polity Press.

Hutton, W. (2002) *The World We're In*. London: Little, Brown.

Ignatieff, M. (1997) 'There's No Place Like Home; The Politics of Belonging.' In S. Dunant and R. Porter (eds) *The Age of Anxiety*. London: Virago.

Illich, I. (1998) Quoted in C. Mercogliano *Making It Up As We Go Along. The Story of Albany Free School*. Portsmouth, NH: Heinemann.

Independent Magazine (1996) 'A Far Cry from Westminster.' 4 May.

Independent on Sunday (1991) February 10.

Independent on Saturday (1997) 'Blair Promises All Parents the Right to Smack their Children.' 8 November.

Independent Project Trust (1999) *Annual Report for the Period March 1997 – March 1998 for SMART Project*. Durban: IPT.

Ingleby, D. (1985) 'Professionals as Socializers: The "Psy" Complex.' In S. Spitzer and A.T. Scull (eds) *Research in the Law, Deviance and Social Control: A Research Annual, vol. 7*. London: JAI Press, 79–109.

International Herald Tribune (1991) Articles about the Gulf War. 23–24 February.

International Labour Organisation (1996) *Child Labour: Targeting the Intolerable*. Geneva: International Labour Office.

Jackson, D. (1995) 'Why Did the Two Boys Kill James Bulger?' *Destroying the Baby in Themselves*. Nottingham: Mushroom Publications.

James, A. (2000) 'Researching Children; The Way Ahead in Theory and Practice.' In J. Mason and M. Wilkinson (eds) *Taking Children Seriously*. Campbelltown: Childhood and Youth Policy Unit, University of Western Sydney.

James, A. and Prout, A. (eds) (1990) *Constructing and Reconstructing Childhood*. London: Falmer Press.

James, A., Jenks, C. And Prout, A. (1998) *Theorising Childhood*. Cambridge: Polity Press.

Jensen, A.M. and Saporiti, A. (1992) *Do Children Count? Children as a Social Phenomenon. A Statistical Compendium*. Eurosocial Report 36/17. Vienna: European Centre for Social Welfare Policy and Research.

John D.R. (1999) 'Consumer Socialisation of Children: A Retrospective Look at 25 years of Research.' *Journal of Consumer Research, 26*, 3.

John, M. (1986) 'Kid's Lib; The Politics of Childhood.' Unit 2 Open University. Second Level Course: *Social Issues and Social Intervention*. Milton Keynes: Open University Press.

John, M. (1993) 'Children with Special Needs as the Casualties of a Free Market Economy.' *International Journal of Children's Rights 1*, 1–22.

John, M. (ed) (1994a) *Children's Rights: International and Interdisciplinary Approaches. Special Issue Division of Educational and Child Psychology. Educational and Child Psychology, 11*, 4.

John, M. (1994b) 'The UN Convention on the Rights of the Child: Development and Implications.' In M. John (ed) *Children's Rights: International and Interdisciplinary Approaches. Special Issue Division of Educational and Child Psychology. Educational and Child Psychology 11*, 4, 7–17.

John, M. (1995) 'Children's Rights in a Free Market Culture.' In S. Stephens (ed) *Children and the Politics of Culture*. Princeton: Princeton University Press, 105–137.

John, M. (ed) (1996a) *Children in Charge: The Child's Right to a Fair Hearing.* London: Jessica Kingsley Publishers.

John, M. (ed) (1996b) *Children in Our Charge: The Child's Right to Resources.* London: Jessica Kingsley Publishers.

John, M. (1996c) 'In Whose Best Interest?' In M. John (ed) *Children in Our Charge: The Child's Right to Resources.* London: Jessica Kingsley Publishers, 1–16.

John, M. (1996d) 'Monitoring Children's Rights to Education. An Inter-agency Approach in the South-West of England.' In E. Verhellen (ed) *Monitoring Children's Rights.* Dordrecht: Kluver Law International, 49–666.

John, M. (1996e) Voicing: Research and Practice with the "Silenced".' In M. John (ed) *Children in Charge: The Child's Right to a Fair Hearing.* London: Jessica Kingsley Publishers, 1–42.

John, M. (ed) (1997a) *A Charge Against Society: The Child's Right to Protection.* London: Jessica Kingsley Publishers.

John, M. (1997b) 'Protecting Children or Reinforcing Dependency?' In M. John (ed) *A Charge Against Society: The Child's Right to Protection.* London: Jessica Kingsley Publishers.

John, M. (2000) 'The Children's Parliament in Rajasthan: A Model for Learning about Democracy.' In A. Osler (ed) *Citizenship and Democracy in Schools: Diversity, Identity, Equality.* Stoke on Trent: Trentham Books.

John, M. and Griffith, R. (1994) *The Transformation of Power.* Unpublished research paper, University of Exeter.

John, M. and Townsend, P. (1997) 'Working Towards the Participation of Children in Decision Making: A Devon Case Study.' In B. Cohen and U. Hagen (eds) *Children's Services: Shaping Up for the Millennium. Supporting Children and Families in the UK and Scandinavia.* Edinburgh: The Stationery Office.

Johnson, V. (1998) Conclusion to Part 2 'Building Blocks and Ethical Dilemmas.' In V. Johnson, E. Ivan-Smith, G. Gordon, P. Pridmore and P. Scott (eds) *Stepping Forward: Children and Young People's Participation in the Development Process.* London: Intermediate Technology Publications.

Johnson, V., Ivan-Smith, E., Gordon, G., Pridmore, P. and Scott, P. (eds) (1998) *Stepping Forward: Children and Young People's Participation in the Development Process.* London: Intermediate Technology Publications.

Joliffe, F., Patel, S., Sparks, Y. and Reardon, K. (1995) *Child Employment in Greenwich, London.* London Borough of Greenwich: Social Work and Education Service.

Jones, G. (2002) *The Youth Divide: Diverging Paths to Adulthood.* York: York Publishing Services.

Joseph Rowntree Foundation (1999) *Findings. March 1999.* York: Joseph Rowntree Foundation.

Judd, T. (2002) 'Evidence of Abuse was "Systematically Ignored".' *Independent,* Wednesday 20 February.

Kent, G. (1995) *Children in the International Political Economy.* Basingstoke: Macmillan.

Kessen, W. (1979) 'The American Child and Other Cultural Inventions.' *American Psychologist 34,* 815–20.

Kiberd, D. (1992) 'Introduction.' In J. Joyce's *Ulysses*. The Bodley Head text offset and reissued with this introduction in 1992. Harmondsworth: Penguin Books.

KIDS. http://www.wits.ac.za/birthto20.

Kincheloe, J.L. (1997) 'McDonald's, Power and Children: Ronald McDonald (aka Ray Kroc) Does It All for You.' In S.R. Steinberg and J.L. Kincheloe (eds) *Kinder-culture. The Corporate Construction of Childhood*. Boulder, Colorado: Westview Press.

Kinsey, R. (1996) 'The Time of your Life? Children's Knowledge of Crime.' In M. John (ed) *Children in Charge: The Child's Right to a Fair Hearing*. London: Jessica Kingsley Publishers.

Korczak, J. (1923) *Krol Macius Pierwszy [King Matthew I]*. *Warsaw: Interpress.*

Kroc, R. (1977) *Grinding It Out: The Making of McDonald's*. New York: St Martin's.

Kundapur Declaration (1996) Proceedings of the International Meeting of Working Children, Kundapur, India 27 November – 9 December. Reproduced in Miljeteig 2000.

Kundera, M. (1995) Interview with Ian McEwan extract reproduced in P. Reynolds 'Youth and the Politics of Culture in South Africa.' In S. Stephens (ed) *Children and the Politics of Culture*. Princeton NJ: Princeton University.

La Fontaine, J.S. (1998) *Speak of the Devil*. Cambridge: Cambridge University Press.

Lambert, A. (2002) 'Political Correctness Helped to Kill Victoria Climbie.' Wednesday Review of the *Independent*, Wednesday 20 February.

La Monde (2002) 6 August.

Lansdown, G. (1999) *Human Rights and Democracy in Schools. Preparing Young People for Citizenship Through Formal and Informal Education: Marginalised and Excluded Young People*. Unpublished paper presented to the ESRC Seminar Series on Human Rights, 18 June.

Lantieri, L. and Patti. J. (1996) *Waging Peace in our Schools*. Boston: Beacon Press.

Lasri, D. (1994) 'On the Non-existence of the Child.' Translated by Joanie and Douglas Calem. *Hadera Conference Journal 2*, 2–5.

Lavine, T.Z. (1962) 'Some Reflections on the Genetic Fallacy.' *Social Research 29*, 321–336.

Leboyer, F. (1977) *Birth Without Violence*. London: Fontana/Collins. (Original work published 1974 as *Pour Une Naissance Sans Violence*, Editions de Seuil.)

Lewis, M. and Rosenblum, L.A. (eds) (1974) *The Effect of the Infant upon its Caregiver*. New York: Wiley.

Lincoln, Y.S. (1993) 'I and Thou: Method, Voice and Roles in Research with the Silenced.' In D. Mclaughlin and W. Tierney (eds) *Naming Silenced Lives. Personal Narratives and the Process of Educational Change*. New York and London: Routledge.

Lincoln, Y.S. and Denzin, N.Z. (2000) 'The Seventh Moment: Out of the Past.' In N.K. Denzin and Y.S. Lincoln, (eds) (2000) *Handbook of Qualitative Research*. London, Sage Publications Inc, (1047–1065).

Lipsky, D. and Adams, A. (1994) *Late Bloomers*. New York: Times Books.

Lomranz, J. (1995) 'Endurance and Living: Long-term Effects of the Holocaust.' In S.E. Hobfoll and M.W. de Vries (eds) *Extreme Stress and Communities: Impact and Intervention*. Dordrecht: Kluwer.

Lukes, S. (1974) *Power*. Basingstoke: Macmillan.

Luthar, S. (1999) *Poverty and Children's Adjustment*. London: Sage.

Lyon, C.M. (2000) *Loving Smack or Lawful Assault. A Contradiction in Human Rights Law.* London: Institute for Public Policy Research.

Maberly, Glenn F. (1997) *Iodine Deficiency in Georgia: Progress Towards Elimination, Summary Report.* Atlanta: The Program Against Micronutrient Malnutrition.

Machel, G. (1996) *Impact of Armed Conflict on Children.* Report of the Expert of the Secretary General, Ms Graca Machel, submitted pursuant to General Assembly Resolution 48/157. New York: United Nations Department of Public Information, Development and Human Rights Section.

Marcus, R. (1998) 'Learning from International Experiences.' In B. Pettit (ed) *Children and Work in the UK. Reassessing the Issues.* London: Child Poverty Action Group.

Mayall, B. (1994a) *Children's Childhoods Observed and Experienced.* London: Falmer Press.

Mayall, B. (1994b) 'Children in Action at Home and School.' In B. Mayall (ed) *Children's Childhoods Observed and Experienced.* London: Falmer Press.

McCulloch, A. and Joshi, H. (1999) 'Child Development and Family Resources: An Exploration of Evidence from the Second Generation of the 1958 British Birth Cohort.' *Working Papers of the ESRC Research Centre on Micro-social Change 99–15.* Colchester: University of Essex Institute for Social and Economic Research.

McGurk, H. (ed) (1992) *Childhood and Social Development.* London: Lawrence Erlbaum.

McKendrick, J.H. (2001) 'Coming of Age: Rethinking the Role of Children in Population Studies.' *International Journal of Population Geography 7*, 461–472.

McLaren, P. and Morris, J. (1997) 'Mighty Morphin Power Rangers: The Aesthetics of Phallo-Militaristic Justice.' In S.R. Steinberg and J.L. Kincheloe (eds) *Kinder-culture. The Corporate Construction of Childhood.* Boulder, Colorado: Westview Press.

Mead, G.H. (1934) 'Mind.' In A.S. Strauss (ed) *The Social Psychology of George Herbert Mead.* Chicago: University of Chicago Press.

Medawar, P. (1957) *The Uniqueness of the Individual.* London: Methuen.

Meighan, R. (1995) *The Freethinkers' Pocket Directory to the Educational Universe.* Nottingham: Educational Heretics Press.

Mercogliano, C. (1998) *Making It Up As We Go Along. The Story of Albany Free School.* Portsmouth: NH: Heineman.

Micklewright, J. and Stewart, K. (1999) 'Is the Well-being of Children Converging in the European Union?' *Economic Journal 109*, 459, F692–714.

Miles, R. (1995) *The Children We Deserve: Love and Hate in the Making of the Family.* London: HarperCollins.

Miljeteig, P. (1999) 'Understanding Child Labour' *Childhood 6*, 1, 5–12.

Miljeteig, P. (2000) 'Children's Democratic Rights – Are We Ready for it? What Can We Learn from Young Workers Speaking Out on Their Rights?' In J. Mason and M. Wilkinson (eds) *Taking Children Seriously.* Campbelltown: Childhood and Youth Policy Unit, University of Western Sydney.

Miljeteig, P. (2001) *Creating Partnerships with Working Children and Youth*. Social Protection Unit. Discussion paper 21. Washington, DC: The World Bank. www.worldbank.org/sp.

Milk for Schools (1996) *The Hunger Within*. Stafford: Milk for Schools Campaign.

Miller, A. (1991) Interview by Alix Kirsta, *The Observer*. London. 15 September.

Miller, G.A. (1969) 'Psychology as a Means of Promoting Human Welfare.' *American Psychologist 24*, 1063–1075.

Miller, J. (2002) *Evening Standard*. London. 4 May.

Mills, H. (1996) 'Breadline Britain.' *The Observer*, 11 August.

Minow, M. (1987) 'Interpreting Rights: An Essay for Robert Cover.' *96, Yale Law Journal 8*, 1904.

Moore, S. (1993) 'Beyond Good and Evil.' *Guardian*, 26 November.

Moran, J. (1998) 'The Dynamics of Class Politics and National Economics in Globalisation: The Marginalisation of the Unacceptable.' *Capital & Class 66*, 53–84.

MORI (2000) Reported in D. Hutton (2000) 'The Rise of the Pocket-money Moguls.' *You* (*Daily Mail* weekend magazine), 26 November.

Morrell, R. (1999) 'Beating Corporal Punishment: Race, Masculinity and Educational Discipline in the Schools of Durban, South Africa.' Paper presented at the *Voices in Gender and Education Conference*, Warwick, UK, March.

Morrison, B. (1997) *As If*. London: Granta Books.

Morrow, V. and Richards, M. (1996) 'The Ethics of Social Research with Children.' *Children and Society 10*, 90–105.

Moschis, G.P. (1985) 'The Role of Family Communication in Consumer Socialisation of Children and Adolescents.' *Journal of Consumer Research 11*, (March) 898–913.

Moschis, G.P., Nelson, M. and McGrath, A. (1995) 'The Children's Birthday Party: A Study of Mothers as Socialisation Agents.' In F.R. Kardes and M. Sujan (eds) *Advances in Consumer Research, Vol. 22*. Association for Consumer Research, 622–627.

Moscovici, S. (1976) *Social Influence and Social Change*. London: Academic Press.

Mumby, D. (1989) 'Ideology and the Social Construction of Meaning: A Communication Perspective.' *Communication Quarterly 37*, 4, 291–304.

Nasman, E. (1994) 'Individualisation and Institutionalisation of Childhood in Today's Europe.' In J. Qvortrup, M. Bardy, G. Sgritta and H. Wintersberger (eds) *Childhood Matters; Social Theory Practice and Politics*. Aldershot: Avebury.

Naylor, K. (2001a) 'The Barefoot College and The Children's Parliament.' *The World Children's Prize for the Rights of the Child. The Globe. Mariefred.* Sweden: Children's World (www.childrenworld.org).

Naylor, K. (2001b) 'Devrakan, Thanks for the Water!' *The World Children's Prize for the Rights of the Child. The Globe. Mariefred.* Sweden: Children's World (www.childrensworld.org).

Nestle, M. (2002) *Food Politics. How the Food Industry Influences Nutrition and Health*. Berkeley: University of California Press.

New Statesman and Society (1996) 13th September.

Newson, J. (1977) 'An Intersubjective Approach to the Systematic Description of Mother-Infant Interaction.' In H.R. Schaffer (ed) *Studies in Mother-Infant Interaction.* London: Academic Press.

Newson, J. (1978) 'Dialogue and Development.' In A. Lock (ed) *Action, Gesture and Symbol: The Emergence of Language.* London: Academic Press.

Newson, J. and Newson, E. (1963) *Infant Care in an Urban Community.* London: George Allan and Unwin.

Newson, J. And Newson E. (1968) *Four Years Old in an Urban Community.* London: George Allen and Unwin.

Newson, J. and Newson, E. (1976) *Seven Years Old in the Home Environment.* London: George Allen and Unwin.

Nzimand, B. and Thusi, S. (1998) 'Children of the War: The Impact of Political Violence on Schooling in KwaZuluNatal.' In *Democratic Governance of Public Schooling in South Africa.* Durban: University of Natal Education Policy Unit.

O'Brien, C. (1996) *The Barefoot College... or Knowledge Demystified.* Innovations Series. 'Education for All; Making it Work.' New York: UNESCO.

Observer (1999) 'Blair's Moral Crusade.' 5 September, p.8–9.

OECD (1990a) *Employment Outlook.* July 1990. Ch.5. Paris: OECD.

OECD (1990b) *Les Familles Monoparentales.* Paris: OECD.

Opie, I. and Opie, P. (1959) *The Lore and Language of Schoolchildren.* Oxford: Clarendon Press.

Oppenheim, C. and Harker, L. (1996) *Poverty. The Facts.* London: Child Poverty Action Group.

O'Quigley, A. (2000) *Listening to Children's Views. The Findings and Recommendations of Recent Research.* York: York Publishing Services Ltd. For Joseph Rowntree Foundation.

Orme, N. (2001) *Medieval Children.* New Haven: Yale University Press.

Palinkas, L.A. (1990) 'Group Adaptation and Individual Adjustment in Antarctica. A Summary of Recent Research.' In A.A. Harrison, Y.A. Clearwater and C.P. Mckay (eds) *From Antarctica to Outer Space: Life in Isolation and Confinement.* New York: Springer Verlag, 239–251.

Palme, M. (1997) 'Teaching Hieroglyphs with Authority.' In M. John (ed) *A Charge Against Society: The Child's Right to Protection.* London: Jessica Kingsley Publishers.

Parker, I. and Spears, R. (eds) (1996) *Psychology and Society: Radical Theory and Practice.* London: Pluto Press.

Paul, W. (1994) *Laughing Screaming: Modern Hollywood Horror and Comedy.* New York: Columbia University Press.

Peace Child International (1998) *Get Up, Stand Up – A Children's Book of Human Rights.* In association with UNICEF. London: Kingfisher Books.

Peacock, A. (1996) 'Creating an Adaptable Science Curriculum for Children in Rural Africa.' In M. John (ed) *Children in Our Charge: The Child's Right to Resources.* London: Jessica Kingsley Publishers. 81–100

Pelin Ayan (2002) WSSD, 30 August, www.unicef.org/exspeeches.

Peters, K. and Richards, P. (1998a) 'Jeunes combatants parlants de la guerre et de la paix en Sierra Leone.' *Cahiers d'Etudes africaines, vv.150–152*, XXXVIII-2-4, 581–617.

Peters, K. and Richards, P. (1998b) '"Why we fight": Voices of Youth Ex-combatants in Sierra Leone.' *Africa 68*, 1, 183–210.

Petit, J.M. (1996) 'World Changes and Social Policies in Uruguay.' In M. John (ed) *Children in Our Charge: The Child's Right to Resources.* London: Jessica Kingsley Publishers.

Pettitt, B. (ed) (1998) Introduction to *Children and Work in the UK.* London: Child Poverty Action Group.

Philips, W. James T., Nelson, M., Ralph, A. and Leather, S. (1997) 'The Contribution of Nutrition to Inequalities in Health.' *British Medical Journal 314.* London: British Medical Association.

Pilger, J. (1990) 'Distant Voices of Dissent.' *Guardian,* 12 February.

Pilger, J. (1998) *Hidden Agendas.* London: Vintage.

Plant, S. (2002) 'How the Mobile Changed the World.' *Sunday Times,* 5 May.

Postman, N. (1983) *The Disappearance of Childhood.* London: W.H. Allen.

Potter, C.F. (1958) *The Great Religious Leaders.* New York: Simon Schuster.

Proust, M. (1924) *Remembrance of Things Past.* New York: Random House.

QCA (1998) *Education for Citizenship and the Teaching of Democracy in Schools.* Final Report of the Advisory Group on Citizenship (The Crick Report). London: Qualification and Curriculum Authority.

Qvortrup, J. (1990) *Childhood as a Social Phenomenon – An Introduction to a Series of National Reports. Eurosocial Reports 36/90.* Vienna: European Centre.

Qvortrup, J. (1997) 'A Voice for Children in Statistical and Social Accounting. Postscript: Six Year Later.' In A. James and A. Prout (eds) *Constructing and Reconstructing Childhood,* 2nd edition. London: Falmer Press.

Qvortrup, J., Bardy, M., Sgritta, G. And Wintersberger, H. (eds) (1994) *Childhood Matters. Social Theory, Practice and Politics.* Public Policy and Social Welfare Series. B. Marin (ed) European Centre Vienna, (volume 14). Aldershot: Avebury.

Ractliffe, T. (1990) 'Towards Re-integration: Problems for Ex-Political Prisoners.' Manuscript, University of Capetown, quoted in P. Reynolds (1995) 'Youth and Politics in South Africa.' In S. Stephens (ed) *Children and the Politics of Culture.* Princeton Studies in Culture/Power/History. Princeton: Princeton University Press.

Radda Barnen (1998) *Towards an EU Human Rights Agenda for Children.* International Save the Children Alliance-Europe. Stockholm: Radda Barnen.

Reddy, N. (1998) *Child Labour and the Value of Children's Decisions: The Child's Participation in Policy and Practice.* Paper presented at IPSCAN Congress, Auckland, New Zealand, 6–9 September.

Redhead, S. (1993) 'Rave Off: Politics and Deviance in Contemporary Youth Culture.' *Popular Cultural Studies,* 1.

Reicher, S. (1996) 'The Reactionary Practice of Radical Psychology: Revoking the Faustian Contract.' In I. Parker and R. Spears (eds) *Psychology and Society: Radical Theory and Practice.* London: Pluto Press.

Reicher, S. and Parker, I. (1993) 'Psychology, Politics, Resistance: The Birth of a New Organisation.' *Journal of Community and Applied Psychology 3*, 77–80.

Reid, R. (1994) In Children of the World (1994) *Rescue Mission Planet Earth – A Children's Edition of Agenda 21*. Peace Child International in association with UNICEF. London: Kingfisher Books.

Reuters (2002) Reuters Foundation AlertNet. Monday 9 September. www.alertnet.../relieffresources/504495.

Reynolds, P. (1991a) *Dance Civet Cat. Child Labour in the Zambezi Valley*. London: Zed Books.

Reynolds, P. (1991b) 'Youth and Trauma in South Africa: Social Means of Support.' Paper presented at the *International African Institute Conference on Healing the Social Wounds of War*, Windhoek, Namibia.

Reynolds, P. (1995) 'Youth and Politics in South Africa.' In S. Stephens (ed) *Children and the Politics of Culture*. Princeton Studies in Culture/Power/History. Princeton: Princeton University Press.

Richards, M.P.M. (1974) *The Integration of a Child into a Social World*. Cambridge: Cambridge University Press.

Richards, P. (1996) *Fighting for a Rain Forest: War, Youth and Resources in Sierra Leone*. Oxford: James Currey. (Reprinted with additional material 1998.)

Richards, P. (2002) 'Militia Conscription in Sierra Leone: recruitment of young fighters in an African War.' *Comparative Social Research 20*, 255–276.

Roberts, H., Smith, S.J. and Bryce, C. (1995) *Children at Risk: Safety as a Social Value*. Buckingham, Open University Press.

Robertson, J. (1953) *A Two-year Old Goes to Hospital*. (Film) London Child Development Research Unit. New York: New York University Film Library.

Robertson, J. and Robertson, J. (1967–1972) Film Series: Young Children in Brief Separation. London: Tavistock Institute of Human Relations.

Robinson, S. and Palus, N. (2001) 'An Awful Human Trade.' *Time*, 30 August.

Rosenbaum, M. (1993) *Children and the Environment*. London: National Children's Bureau.

Roth, S. (1992) 'Towards a Minority Convention: Its Need and Content.' In Y. Dinstein, and M. Tabory (eds) *The Protection of Minorities and Human Rights*. Dordrecht: M. Nijhoff Publishers.

Rowe, D. (1989) 'Foreword.' In J. Masson *Against Therapy*. London: Collins.

Rowe, D. (1991) *Wanting Everything*. London: HarperCollins.

Rowntree (2002) *Foundations, Analysis informing change. The Youth Divide: Diverging Paths to Adulthood*. York: Rowntree Foundation

Roy, A. (1982) *Tilonia's Night Schools – An Alternative Approach*. Tilonia: SWRC.

Rubellin-Devichi, J. (1994) 'The Best Interests Principle in French Law and Practice.' In P. Alston (ed) *The Best Interests of the Child. Reconciling Culture and Human Rights*. Oxford: Oxford University Press.

Ruxton, S. (1999) *A Children's Policy for 21st Century Europe, First Steps*. Brussels: Euronet The European Children's Network.

Safilios-Rothschild, C. (1970) *The Sociology and Social Psychology of Disability and Rehabilitation.* New York: Random House.

Sage, L. (2001) *Bad Blood.* London: Fourth Estate.

Saporiti, A. (1997) 'Statistics on Childhood.' In E. Verhellen (ed) *Understanding Children's Rights. Gent Papers on Children's Rights. No.2.* Gent: University of Gent Children's Rights Centre.

Save the Children (1998) 'Children's Perspectives on Work.' In B. Pettit (ed) *Children and Work in the UK. Reassessing the Issues.* London: Child Poverty Action Group.

Save the Children (2000) *Children, Economics and the EU – Towards Child-friendly Policies.* Brussels: Save the Children, Sweden for The International Save the Children Alliance Europe Group.

Save the Children (2001) *Taking Children Seriously.* London: Save the Children.

Schaffer, H.R. (ed) (1977) *Studies in Mother-Infant Interaction.* London: Academic Press.

Schucksmith, J. And Henry, L.B. (1998) *Health Issues and Young People: Growing Up and Speaking Out.* London: Routledge.

Scott, S. (2001) *The Politics and Experience of Ritual Abuse. Beyond Disbelief.* Buckingham: Open University Press.

Seiter, E. (1993) *Sold Separately: Parents and Children in Consumer Culture.* New Brunswick, New Jersey: Rutgers University Press.

Sereny, G. (1995) *Cries Unheard. The Story of Mary Bell.* London: Macmillan.

Sharma, M., Nepal, V.K. and Pandey, K. (2001) 'Critical Analysis of the Role and Nature of Child Advocate Organisations CCIA, NASPEC and RUGMRK in Returning Children to a Normal Way of Life.' Paper presented at *Children in their Places* International Conference, Brunel University, London 21–23 June.

Shotter, J. (1984) *Social Accountability and Selfhood.* Oxford: Basil Blackwell.

Shotter, J. (1993a) *Cultural Politics of Everyday Life.* Milton Keynes: Open University Press.

Shotter, J. (1993b) *Cultural Politics of Everyday Life: Social Constructionism, Rhetoric, and Knowing of the Third Kind.* London: Sage.

Shotter, J. (1998) 'Social Construction as Social Poetics.' In B.M. Bayer and J. Shotter (eds) *Reconstructing the Psychological Subject.* London: Sage.

Shropshire, J. and Middleton, S. (1999) *Small Expectations: Learning to be Poor?* York: York Publishing Services for the Joseph Rowntree Foundation.

Smale, D. (1987) *Taking Care.* London: Dent.

Smith, J. and Baltes, P.B. (1999) 'Life-span Perspectives on Development.' In M.H. Bornstein and M.E. Lamb (eds) *Developmental Psychology.* 4th edition. Hillsdale, NJ: Lawrence Erlbaum Associates.

Srinivasan, S. (1998, 1999 and 2002) Personal communications.

Stanley, L. (ed) (1990) *Feminist Praxis: Research, Theory and Epistemology in Feminist Sociology.* London: Routledge.

Steedman, C. (1987) *The Tidy House. Little girls' Writing.* London: Virago.

Steel, G.D. (1994) *The Structure of Environmental Relationships in Polar Regions.* Unpublished doctoral dissertation, University of British Columbia quoted in Suedfeld (1997) 'The Social Psychology of "Invictus": Conceptual and

Methodological Approaches to Indomitability.' In C. McGarthy and S.A. Haslam (eds) *The Message of Social Psychology. Perspectives on Mind in Society*. Oxford: Blackwell.

Steinberg, S.R. and Kincheloe, J.L. (eds) (1997) *Kinder-culture. The Corporate Construction of Childhood*. Boulder, Colorado: Westview Press.

Suedfeld, P. (1997) 'The Social Psychology of "Invictus": Conceptual and Methodological Approaches to Indomitability.' In C. McGarty and S.A. Haslam (eds) *The Message of Social Psychology. Perspectives on Mind in Society*. Oxford: Blackwell.

Suedfeld, P. (1980) *Restricted Environmental Stimulation: Research and Clinical Applications*. New York: Wiley.

Swift, A. (1999) *Working Children Get Organised. An Introduction to Working Children's Organisations*. London: International Save the Children Alliance.

Talom Born (1996) *Det Tvaerministerielle Borneudvalg*. Copenhagen: Danish Ministry of Social Affairs.

Theis, J. (1998) 'Participatory Research on Child Labour.' In V. Johnson, E. Ivan-Smith, G. Gordon, P. Pridmore and P. Scott (eds) *Stepping Forward. Children and Young People's Participation in the Development Process*. London: Intermediate Technology Publications Ltd.

Theis, J. and Hoang Thi Huyen (1997) *From Housework to Gold Mining – Child Labour in Rural Vietnam*. Hanoi: SCF/UK.

Therborn, G. (1995) *European Modernity and Beyond. The Trajectory of European Societies 1945–2000*. London: Sage.

Thiele, L. (1986) 'Foucault's Triple Murder and the Development of Power.' *Canadian Journal of Political Science 19*, 243–260.

Thomas, A. (1990) 'Violence and Child Detainees.' In B. McKendrick and W. Hoffman (eds) *People and Violence in South Africa*. Cape Town: Oxford University Press.

Tinker, Minors *v*. Des Moines Independent Community Schoold District (393 U.S. 503).

Tizard, B. (1990) 'Research and Policy. Is There a Link?' The Ninth Vernon-Wall Lecture. *The Psychologist*. October, 435.

Tizard, B. and Hughes, M. (1984) *Young Children Learning Talking and Thinking at Home and at School*. London: Fontana.

Tolfree, D. (1998) *Old Enough to Work, Old Enough to Have a Say*. Stockholm: Radda Barnen.

Torres, N. (1994) 'Working Children, Leading the Struggle to Obtain and Defend Their Own Rights.' In E. Verhellen and F. Spiesschaert (eds) *Children's Rights: Monitoring Issues*. Ghent: Mys and Breesch Publishers.

Trevarthen, C. (1975) 'Early Attempts at Speech.' In R. Lewin (ed) *Child Alive*. London: Temple Smith.

Trevarthen, C. (1977) 'Descriptive Analyses of Infant Communicative Behaviour.' In H. Schaffer (ed) *Studies in Mother-Infant Interaction*. London: Academic Press.

Trevarthen, C. (1979) 'Communication and Cooperation in Early Infancy.' In M. Bullowa (ed) *Before Speech: The Beginnings of Interpersonal Communication.* Cambridge: Cambridge University Press.

Trevarthen, C. (1982) 'The Primary Motives for Cooperative Understanding.' In G. Butterworth and P. Light (eds) *Social Cognition: Studies of the Development of Understanding.* Brighton: Harvester Press.

UN (2000) *Optional Protocols to the Convention on the Rights of the Child on the Involvement of Children in Armed Conflict and on the Sale of Children, Child Prostitution and Child Pornography. A/RES/54/263, 26 June.*

UN (2001a) *A World Fit for Children.* Revised Draft Outcome Document.A/AC-256/CRP.6/Rev3. Preparatory Committee for the Special session of the General Assembly on Children. New York: United Nations.

UN Children's Statement (2002) http://www.unicef.org/special session/documentation/childrens-statement.htm.

UN Convention on the Rights of the Child (1989) Available from UNICEF, 55 Lincoln's Inn Field, London WC2A 3NB.

UNICEF (1996) UNICEF Press Release, 22 November.

UNICEF (1997a) *Children at Risk in Central and Eastern Europe: Perils and Promises.* Economies in Transition Studies, Regional Monitoring Report No. 4. Florence: International Child Development Centre, UNICEF.

UNICEF (1997b) *The State of the World's Children.* New York: Oxford University Press.

UNICEF (1998) *The State of the Worlds Children 1998.* London: UNICEF.

UNICEF (2001) '*A League Table of Child Poverty in Rich Nations*' Report Card No. 1. Florence: Innocenti Research Centre.

UNICEF (2002) *State of the World's Children 2002.* London: UNICEF.

Untermeyer, L. (1920) *Modern British Poetry.* New York: Harcourt, Brace and Howe.

Urwin, C. (1984) 'Making the Evidence: Language Development as a "Normal Process".' In C. Steedman, C. Urwin and V. Walkerdine (eds) *Language, Gender and Childhood.* London: Routledge and Kegan Paul.

Valentine, G. and McKendrick, J.H. (1997) 'Children's Outdoor Play: Exploring Parental Concerns about Children's Safety and the Changing Nature of Childhood.' *Geoforum 28*, 219–235.

Valley, S. and Dalamba, Y. (1999) *Racism, Racial Integration and Desegregation in South African Public Secondary Schools.* Johannesburg: South African Human Rights Commission.

Van Bueren, G. (1996) 'The "Quiet" Revolution: Children's Rights in International Law.' In M. John (ed) *Children in Charge: The Child's Right to a Fair Hearing.* London: Jessica Kingsley Publishers, 27–37.

Verhellen, E. (1993) 'Children's Rights and Education. A Three-track Legally Binding Imperative.' *School Psychology International 14*, 3, 199–208.

Vygotsky, L.S. (1934) (translation 1962) *Thought and Language.* Cambridge MA: MIT Press.

Vygotsky, L.S. (1978) *Mind in Society: the Development of Higher Psychological Processes.* Boston: Harvard University Press.

Wade, H., Lawton, A. and Stevenson, M. (2001) *Hear by Right; Setting Standards for the Active Involvement of Young People in Democracy.* London: Local Government Association.

Walkerdine, V. (1984) 'Developmental Psychology and the Child-centred Pedagogy.' In J. Henriques, W. Hollway, C. Urwin, C. Venn and V. Walkerdine (eds) *Changing the Subject. Psychology, Social Regulation and Subjectivity.* London: Methuen.

Wall's (2000) *26th Annual Pocket Money Monitor.* Quoted in D. Hutton (2000) 'The Rise of the Pocket-money Moguls.' *You* (*Daily Mail* weekend magazine), 26 November.

Wall's (2001) *27th Annual Pocket Money Monitor.* Walton-on-Thames: Bird's Eye Wall's.

Weekly Telgraph (1996) 20 April.

White, B. (1996) 'Globalisation and the Child Labour Problem.' *Journal of International Development 8,* 6, 829–39.

White, H., Leavy, J. and Masters, A. (2002) 'Comparative Perspectives on Child Poverty: A Review of Poverty Measures.' *Young Lives, An International Study of Childhood Poverty, Working Paper No. 1.* Brighton: University of Sussex, Institute for Development Studies.

White, M. (2001a) 'Child Labour in Burkina Faso's Gold Mines; Working Too Hard.' *Taking Children Seriously London. Guardian* newspaper and Save the Children Supplement to mark the Special Session on Children (which due to events in New York in September 2001 was postponed until May 2002).

White, M. (2001b) *Taking Children Seriously.* The *Guardian* and Save the Children supplementary publication for the UN Special Session (September 2001) withheld and issued May 2002.

White, M. (2002) 'Child Labour in Burkina Faso's Gold Mines. Working too hard.' in *Taking Children Seriously.* Produced by the *Guardian* in association with Save the Children to mark the UN Special Session on Children.

Whitehead, A.N. (1932) *The Aims of Education and Other Essays.* London: Williams and Norgate. (Quotation taken from sixth impression 1966, London: Ernest Benn Ltd.)

Wilkinson, A.M. (1974) *William Blake and the Great Sin.* Inaugural Lecture delivered in the University of Exeter on 22 April 1974. Exeter: University of Exeter Publication.

Wilkinson, H. and Mulgan, G. (1995) *Freedom's Children: Work, Relationships and Politics for 18-34 year olds in Britain Today.* London: Demos.

Wilson, F. (2000) 'What the Blood Remembers.' *Guardian* 9 September.

Winslow, T.J. (1991) *Released into a Prison Without Walls: A Preliminary Inquiry into the Socio-economic Position of Ex-political Prisoners Living in the Western Cape.* Centre for Development Studies. University of the Western Cape.

Wolpe, A-M., Quinlan, O. and Martinez, L. (1997) *Gender Equity in Education: Report of the Gender Equity Task Team.* Pretoria: Department of Education and Training.

Wood, D. (1998) *How Children Learn and Think.* Oxford: Blackwell.

Woodhead, M. (1990) 'Psychology and the Cultural Construction of Children's Needs.' In A. James and A. Prout (eds) *Constructing and Reconstructing Childhood.* Basingstoke: Falmer Press.

Woodhead, M. (1996) 'In Search of the Rainbow: Pathways to Quality in Large-scale Programmes for Young Disadvantaged Children.' *Early Childhood Development: Practice and Reflections 10.* The Hague: Bernard Van Leer Foundation.

Woodhead, M. (1997) 'Postscript: "Beyond Children's Needs" to "Psychology and the Cultural Construction of Children's Needs".' In A. James and A. Prout (eds) *Constructing and Reconstructing Childhood. Contemporary Issues in the Sociological Study of Childhood.* 2nd edition. London: Falmer Press.

Woodhead, M. (1998a) *Children's Perspectives on their Working Lives. A Participatory Study in Bangladesh, Ethiopia, The Philippines, Guatemala, El Salvador and Nicaragua.* Stockholm: Radda Barnen.

Woodhead, M. (1998b) 'Child Work and Child Development in Cultural Context: A Study of Children's Perspectives in Selected Countries in Asia, Africa and Central America.' In V. Johnson *et al.* (eds) *Stepping Forward. Children and Young People's Participation in the Development Process.* London: Intermediate Technology Publications.

Woodhead, M. (1998c) *The Place for Work in Child Development.* Stockholm: Radda Barnen.

Woodhead, M. (1999a) 'Combating Child Labour. Listen to What the Children Say.' *Childhood 6,* 1, 27–49.

Woodhead, M. (1999b) 'Reconstructing Developmental Psychology.' *Children and Society 13,* 1, 3–19.

Woodhead, M. (2000) 'Towards a Global Paradigm for Research into Early Childhood.' In H. Penn (ed) *Early Childhood Services: Theory, Policy and Practice.* Buckingham: Open University Press.

Woodhead, M., Light P. and Carr, R. (1991) *Growing up in a Changing Society.* Milton Keynes: Open University Press.

Woolf, V. (1937) *The Years.* London: Hogarth Press.

Young Lives (2002) www.younglives.org.uk.

Young, B. (1990) *Children and Television Advertising.* Oxford: Oxford University Press.

Young, B. (1998) 'Book Review of Gabriel and Lang, *The Unmanageable Consumer.*' *Journal of Economic Psychology 19,* 653–656.

Young, E. (1996) 'The Child-to-Child Trust.' In M. John (ed) *Children in Charge Volume One: The Child's Right to a Fair Hearing.* London: Jessica Kingsley Publishers, 153–157.

Further Sources of Information

www.childhopeuk.org – provides information on street children

www.childnet.int – children and the internet

Www.childcarecanada.org – childcare in Canada (Childcare Resource and Research Unit)

www.childwelfare.com – gateway to information about child welfare

www.essex.ac.uk – Children and Armed Conflict Unit of Children's Legal Centre

www.child-abuse.com/childhouse/ – Children's House: meeting point for the exchange of information serving the wellbeing of children

www.child-soldiers.org – Coalition to Stop the Use of Child Soldiers

www.coe.fr – Council of Europe

www.each-for-sickchildren.org – European Association for Children in Hospital (EACH)

www.globalmarch.org – Global March Against Child Labour

www.hrw.org – Human Rights Watch

www.ilo.org – International Labour Organisation

www.ilo.org/public/english/standard/ipec – International Programme on the Elimination of Child Labour (IPEC)

www.nordicomgu.se/unesco.html – UNESCO Clearing House on Children and Violence on the Screen

www.unesco.org/education/educprog/ecf/index.htm – UNESCO's Early Childhood and Family Education Activities

www.Eurochild.gla.ac.uk – Centre for Europe's Children

www.crin.org – Children's Rights Information Network (CRIN)

www.unicef.org – UNICEF

www.worldbank.org/children – World Bank- Early Childhood Development

www.Childwatch.uio.no – Childwatch

www.defence-for-children.org – Defence for Children International

www.ecpat.net – End Child Prostitution, Child Pornography and Trafficking in Children for Sexual Purposes (ECPAT)

www.ecic.be – European Children in Crisis

www.web.net/tribunal – International Bureau for Children's Rights

www.unicef-icdc.org – International Child Development Centre, Economic and Social Policy Research Programme, Unicef, Florence

www.ipscan.org – International Society for the Prevention of Child Abuse and Neglect (IPSCAN)

www.savethechildren.net – The International Save the Children Alliance (ISCA)

Subject Index

Author Index